*The* Freudian Psychology *and*
Veblen's Social Theory

"Freud's work is the most profound analysis that history has ever known of the less human elements in human nature"—Roland Dalbiez, in *Psychoanalytical Method and the Doctrine of Freud,* Vol. II, p. 327.

"There was the disturbing genius of Thorstein Veblen—that visitor from another world, who dissected the current commonplaces which the student had unconsciously acquired, as if the most familiar of his daily thoughts were curious products wrought in him by outside forces"—Wesley C. Mitchell, in receiving an honorary degree from the University of Chicago in 1929, as quoted by Joseph Dorfman, in *Thorstein Veblen and His America,* p. 505.

# *The* Freudian Psychology *and* Veblen's Social Theory

LOUIS SCHNEIDER

*Assistant Professor of Sociology, Colgate University*

*Submitted in partial fulfillment of the requirements for the degree of Doctor of Philosophy, in the Faculty of Political Science, Columbia University*

*King's Crown Press*

MORNINGSIDE HEIGHTS · NEW YORK

*1948*

Printed in the United States of America
by Vail-Ballou Press, Inc.

KING'S CROWN PRESS

*is a division of Columbia University Press organized for the purpose of making certain scholarly material available at minimum cost. Toward that end, the publishers have adopted every reasonable economy except such as would interfere with a legible format. The work is presented substantially as submitted by the author, without the usual editorial attention of Columbia University Press.*

# *Preface*

*The writer wishes to express his gratitude and appreciation to the following persons:*

*Professor Robert K. Merton, who afforded encouragement and numerous valuable suggestions when this study was initially worked out, and stimulated its writer to better efforts;*

*Professor Robert M. MacIver, Professor Robert S. Lynd and Doctor Abram Kardiner, all of whom gave the writer a conviction of the feasibility of the study at times when he was inclined to waver on this point;*

*Professor Joseph Dorfman, who was tolerant of an effort to put Veblen to what may well have appeared to him to be strange uses.*

*None of these persons is responsible for the defects or limitations of the study, and all are in one way or another responsible for some of whatever merits it may possess.*

*Without the personal help afforded by my wife, Betty Sancier Schneider, completion would have been greatly delayed.*

The author makes grateful acknowledgment to the following publishers:

Viking Press for quotations from Aurel Kolnai, *The War Against the West;* Thorstein Veblen, *The Place of Science in Modern Civilization, The Instinct of Workmanship, Essays in Our Changing Order, Imperial Germany and the Industrial Revolution, The Theory of the Leisure Class;* George Allen & Unwin for quotations from Hermann Kantorowicz, *The Spirit of British Policy and the Myth of the Encirclement of Germany;* Sheed & Ward for quotations from Friedrich Wilhelm Foerster, *Europe and the German Question;* Alfred A. Knopf, Inc. for quotations from Sigmund Freud, *Moses and*

*Monotheism,* tr. Katherine Jones; Faber & Faber, Ltd. for quotations from J. P. Mayer, *Max Weber and German Politics;* the Institute of Social Research for quotations from the *Zeitscrift fuer Sozialforshung* and *Studies in Philosophy and Social Science;* Macmillan Co. for quotations from Sigmund Freud, *The Interpretation of Dreams,* tr. A. A. Brill; the President and Fellows of Harvard College for quotations from Elton Mayo, *The Social Problems of an Industrial Civilization;* John W. Luce & Co. for quotations from William McDougall, *Introduction to Social Psychology;* Charles Scribners' Sons for quotations from Thorstein Veblen, *The Theory of Business Enterprise;* Random House, Inc. for quotations from *An Outline of Psychoanalysis,* ed. J. S. van Teslaar; E. P. Dutton & Co., Inc. for quotations from Rohan d'O. Butler, *The Roots of National Socialism,* copyright E. P. Dutton & Co., Inc., 1942; Harcourt, Brace & Co., Inc. for quotations from Karl Mannheim, *Man and Society in an Age of Reconstruction;* Alfred Adler, *Practice and Theory of Individual Psychology;* Carl Gustav Jung, *Contributions to Analytical Psychology;* the Harvard University Graduate School of Business Administration for quotations from Elton Mayo, *The Human Problems of an Industrial Civilization; The Family* (now *Journal of Social Casework*) for quotations from Abram Kardiner, "Security, Cultural Restraints, Intra-social Dependencies and Hostilities"; *Political Science Quarterly* for quotations from an article by Henry A. Wallace; *National Academy of Sciences* for quotations from W. J. V. Osterhout's memoir of Jacques Loeb; Rinehart & Co., Inc. for quotations from C. G. Jung, *The Integration of the Personality;* Erich Fromm, *Escape From Freedom;* J. B. Lippincott for quotations from Richard M. Brickner, *Is Germany Incurable?;* Victor Gollancz, Ltd. for quotations from Francis H. Bartlett, *Sigmund Freud: A Marxian Essay;* Julius Braunthal, *Need Germany Survive?;* Hogarth Press and The Institute of Psychoanalysis for quotations from Sigmund Freud, *Col-*

*lected Papers,* Vol. II, tr. Joan Rivière, Vol. III, tr. A. & J. Strachey, Vol. IV, tr. Joan Rivière; *Beyond the Pleasure Principle; The Future of an Illusion; Group Psychology and the Analysis of the Ego;* Longmans-Green for quotations from Roland Dalbiez, *Psychoanalytical Method and the Doctrine of Freud,* tr. T. F. Lindsay.

Acknowledgment is also made for the use of the following: material from *German Philosophy and Politics,* copyright 1915, 1942 by John Dewey; courtesy of G. P. Putnam's Sons; material reprinted from *New Introductory Lectures on Psychoanalysis* by Sigmund Freud by permission of W. W. Norton & Co., Inc., copyright 1933 by Sigmund Freud; material reprinted from *The Neurotic Personality of Our Time* by Karen Horney by permission of W. W. Norton & Co., Inc., copyright 1937 by W. W. Norton & Co., Inc.; material from *A General Introduction to Psychoanalysis* by Sigmund Freud, published by Liveright Publishing Corp., New York; material from *Science & Society,* Vol. III, No. 1 (Winter, 1939), p. 78, of an article by F. H. Bartlett, "The Limitations of Freud"; material from Franz Neumann, *Behemoth,* copyright 1942, 1944 by Oxford University Press, New York; material from *The Psychology of the Unconscious* by C. G. Jung, copyright 1916, 1943, by Dr. Beatrice M. Hinkle, reprinted by permission of Dodd, Mead & Co.; material from an article by Talcott Parsons in *Psychiatry,* VIII, 79–101.

# *Contents*

## PART ONE: THE VIEWS OF HUMAN NATURE



## PART TWO: CLINICAL PSYCHOLOGY AND SOCIAL THEORY

## PART THREE: TOWARD INTEGRATION

# PART ONE

# *The Views of Human Nature*

# *1. Introduction*

THE PURPOSE of this study, as its title implies, is to examine certain connections between the Freudian psychology and Thorstein Veblen's social theory, but frames of reference are indispensable before the purpose can be more systematically stated and worked out.

Thorstein Veblen was a critic who claimed that much of economic theory was based on inadequate psychological premises. His own "institutional" contributions were given an underpinning of psychological theory notably different from that found in other economic doctrines, such as classical and marginal utility theory. Theories in social science usually do contain or involve some psychological components if not a developed psychological scheme. If these components are inadequate or actually incorrect, it is important to note this, and likewise important to remark how psychological components influence the remainder of a theoretical structure.

The reference to the remainder of a theoretical structure may be clarified. Thus, Veblen tells us that the two dominant modern institutions are the machine process and investment for a profit.[1] The machine process is to be broadly understood as the whole of modern technology, with the problems that it presents to the purposes and spirit of business enterprise. Investment for a profit is similarly to be understood in its relations to the machine process. There is presented an institutional framework not reducible to psychological terms or components. Yet at the same time as he operated with this framework, Veblen made additional psychological assumptions that he thought relevant to it. Other economic theories could recognize the same institutional framework and yet operate with different psychological assumptions. Institutional components in a theory, in the way of views or premises about social or economic structure are, in principle, distinct from psychological components. This is an unavoidable

1. *The Theory of Business Enterprise* (New York: Scribners, 1904), p. 1.

logical starting-point. Yet in any actual theory there may be considerable interplay between psychological and non-psychological components. The fact that the two are distinct does not preclude influence of either upon the other. Thus, a rigidly conceived psychology may, as in Freud's case, induce a considerable pressure upon non-psychological components. This pressure, in Freud, sometimes even operates to effect a complete reduction of non-psychological to psychological components. This is of course an extreme case. In general, we may say that the psychological and non-psychological components of a theory in social science exercise mutual selection and constraint. The precision of such a general statement does not greatly matter as long as we are careful to distinguish clearly the two kinds of components and to examine their interplay in specific theories.

If the word "psychology" is taken seriously, and social scientists are concerned with the attributes or characteristics of various psychologies, they must actually turn to these and give them close attention. One of the most highly developed conceptual schemes in the psychological field, if not the most highly developed, is represented in the work of Freud and certain of his followers. The psychoanalytical psychology also has laid claim to an illumination of at least some aspects of the social order. It has pushed this claim with some persistence, and already a body of pertinent contributions may be examined by the social scientist.

Two types of psychological theories have been mentioned. One is that of a social scientist, the other that of the psychoanalysts. How do the two psychologies compare? It has seemed that the best way to make this question concrete is to break it down in the following way: Firstly, precisely what is the psychology of the psychoanalysts, and what relation does it bear to the rest of the elements with which they deal? What light does it cast on the social order? Secondly, what is the social scientist's actual psychology and what relation does it bear to the rest of the elements with which he deals? What does Veblen's psychological theory achieve in the way of illuminating the portions of the social and economic order with which he was concerned? When these questions have been answered, we may be in a position to give a comparison of the two psychologies.

Throughout, we will address three questions to any psychology purporting to be relevant to analysis of the social order: What is the character and scientific value of the psychology itself? Is it applicable to social analysis? If so, how may the application be worked out? These questions resemble those just asked above, but we formulate them again in this way for sharpness and emphasis.

Our ultimate interest is sociological, and theories of human nature are dealt with because they may throw light on the social order. We consider the psychological theory developed by Freud and the Freudians a much more powerful tool than Veblen's. But considerable interest attaches to the manner in which a psychology is used by a social scientist. This is a major reason for the choice of Veblen. Also, after criticism, a residue of valuable social theory is found in Veblen's work, and the combination of this remnant with the Freudian psychology will be shown to be fruitful.

The psychologies of Veblen and Freud have quite diverse origins. Veblen's was developed as an instrument for criticizing economic theory. Freud's emerged from attempts to solve everyday medico-psychological problems arising in the lives of "neurotics." This very diversity of origin perhaps lends piquancy to the comparison, but a comparison of Freud and Veblen, specifically, calls for some special explanation.

Recently, some attention has been devoted in the social sciences to the relations between Freud and Marx. Freud and Marx seem far enough apart at first blush. It appears like a long way from the theory of value and surplus value or the Marxian description of the institutions of capitalism and the condition of the wage-laborer to such matters as the Oedipus complex or the supposed spontaneous envy of human male sexual equipment by the female. The Marxian theory gives the impression of being a kind of "outer drama," and the Freudian a kind of "inner drama." But if attention is then fixed on the more definitely sociological elements in the Marxian theory, an attempt may be made to integrate it with Freudian themes. One illustration of this kind of attempt is a book by Reuben Osborn,[2] who sees a lag

2. Reuben Osborn, *Freud and Marx: A Dialectical Study* (New York: Equinox Cooperative Press, 1937). The main Freudian conception which Osborn finds useful in a generally thin treatment is that of the superego. For a keen criticism of his use of this concept, see George Soule, *The Strength of Nations: A Study in Social Theory* (New York: Macmillan, 1942), ch. vii. *Cf.* also the

between the maturing of the economic conditions for the establishment of socialism and psychological preparation for it. A somewhat more modest approach is exemplified in a book by Francis Bartlett, who claims that

> the key to the relation between Freud and Marx is not to be found in the relation of the subjective to the objective, nor in the relation between society and the instinctive "desires and urges characteristic of man." It is to be sought in the relation between bourgeois society as a whole and the bourgeois family.[3]

Bartlett, however, does not succeed in demonstrating the specific value of using Marxian theory to effect an integration with Freudian theory. A liberal use of epithets such as "bourgeois" hardly serves, and one can demonstrate the "limitations of Freud" as well as Bartlett without reference to Marxian theory. No one has tried to bridge any kind of gap between the Marxian *economic* theory in its technical details with Freudian psychology, nor has any problem even been recognized in this direction. No one has assumed that the labor theory of value and the Oedipus complex can be significantly interrelated.

Another approach is exemplified in a paper by Erich Fromm,[4] whose views may be considered at somewhat greater length. Fromm states his problem rather clearly in the following:

> The sociology with which psychoanalysis appears to have the most points of contact, but to which it also presents the most antitheses, is historical materialism.
>
> Most points of contact—since they are both materialistic sciences. They proceed, not from "ideas," but from earthly life and needs. They are especially in contact in their common estimate of consciousness, which appears to them to be less a dynamic of human relationships than a reflected image of other secret forces. But here, in the question of these peculiar factors determining consciousness, there appears to be an irreconcilable opposition. Historical materialism sees in consciousness an expression of social being; psychoanalysis sees in it an expresion of the unconscious, of

---

criticisms in Francis H. Bartlett, *Sigmund Freud: A Marxian Essay* (London: Gollancz, 1938), *passim.*

3. Bartlett, *ibid.*, p. 87. *Cf.* also the same author's "The Limitations of Freud," *Science and Society* III (1939), 64–105, at 88–89.

4. "Ueber Methode und Aufgabe einer analytischen Sozialpsychologie," *Zeitschrift fuer Sozialforschung* I (1932), 28–54.

the instincts. The pressing question is raised, whether these two theses stand in contradiction to one another or, if not, in just what way they are related and finally, whether and why an employment of psychoanalytical method represents an enrichment for historical materialism.[5]

Fromm's contention that the "two theses" are not contradictory is adumbrated in a preliminary statement of the task of an analytical social psychology, which consists in "the understanding of the instinctual structure, the libidinal, to a considerable extent unconscious, position of a group, from the circumstances of its socio-economic structure." [6] The failure of previous attempts to apply psychoanalysis to sociological problems, according to Fromm, originates in an incorrect estimate of the family, an estimate that overlooks the fact that the family is the product of a determinate social and class structure, that it is only the instrument of the society and class system from which it grows. Psychoanalysts made this mistake through a preconception like that of "bourgeois" thinkers generally, namely, that bourgeois-capitalist society is the "normal" prototype for all society, and because their patients were in the first place members of this bourgeois society and family.[7] Once mistakes of this type are obviated, the way should be open to a fruitful integration of psychoanalysis and historical materialism. The manner of this integration is suggested by Fromm in the following general statement:

> The . . . application of the method of analytical individual psychology to social phenomena yields the following socio-psychological method: Socio-psychological phenomena are to be interpreted as processes of the active and passive adaptation of the instinctual apparatus to the social and economic situation. The instinctual apparatus is itself . . . biologically given, but considerably modifiable; the role of primary formative factors is to be assigned to economic conditions. The family is the essential medium through which the economic situation works out its formative influence upon the psyche. Social psychology must expound the common, socially relevant, psychological attitudes and ideologies (and especially their unconscious roots) arising from the influence of economic conditions upon libidinal strivings.[8]

Fromm further contends that the contribution that psychoanalysis can make to historical materialism consists in the extensive knowledge it provides of the "nature" of man himself as one of the condi-

5. *Ibid.*, 32–33. 6. *Ibid.*, 34. 7. *Ibid.*, 35–36. 8. *Ibid.*, 39–40.

tions operative in the general social process. It places the instinctual apparatus of man in the category of "natural condition," subject to modifications within limits. Fromm makes it clear that "instinctual apparatus" is not to be understood "in general," or in the sense of a biological "primitive form," but rather always in the sense of a definite form molded by the social process.[9]

With a good many of these contentions one can hardly disagree, although interest naturally attaches to the manner in which Fromm exemplifies and makes them concrete.[10] The contention that primary importance is to be attached to economic factors has not been given specific support or proof by Fromm. He apparently assumes its truth from the propositions of historical materialism. There is no reason for not attempting to relate psychoanalysis to historical materialism, or, for that matter, to any other sociological theory. The way Fromm has chosen may yield specific insights that might possibly not be yielded by an attempt at integration with another type of sociological theory or might only be dimly suggested by the latter.[11] But it has certainly not been shown that relating psychoanalysis to historical materialism is necessarily so much more fruitful than relating it to other sociological disciplines that the latter enterprise is not worth undertaking. At some points in Fromm's exposition the suspicion arises that if he were not seeking to give support to a particular type of vocabulary it would be clear that no special gain is to be derived from using the propositions of historical materialism.[12] On the other hand, many of his crucial statements are acceptable, even if with some qualifications. Thus, he argues that

> this much must be said: that every society has a quite specific libidinal structure as well as a definite social, political and spiritual structure. The

9. *Ibid.*, 45–46.

10. This does not imply that he has not afforded certain exemplifications. See especially his companion paper, "Die Psychoanalytische Charakterologie und ihre Bedeutung fuer die Sozialpsychologie," *Zeitschrift fuer Sozialforschung* I (1932), 253–277.

11. See "Die Psychoanalytische Charakterologie . . . ," esp. 268.

12. For example: "Psychoanalysis thus allows us to look upon the building of ideologies as a kind of 'work process,' as one of the situations of material interplay between man and nature—in which there inheres this peculiarity: that 'nature' in this case lies within, and not outside of, man." "Methode und Aufgabe . . . ," 47.

libidinal structure is the product of the influence of the socio-economic conditions upon the instinctive tendencies, and in turn it is an important determining factor for the emotional discipline within the different strata of society as well as for the quality of the "ideological superstructure." The libidinal structure of a society is the medium through which the influence of economic conditions on properly human, spiritual and psychological phenomena is consummated.[13]

One may grant that "ideological superstructure" is a peculiarly Marxian phrase. Another writer might prefer to say "socio-economic" again in the last sentence of the above, where Fromm has said simply, "economic." But substantially the same passage could have been written by other sociologically oriented psychoanalysts. The essential problem posed by Fromm may still be looked on as a general one of the relations of "sociology and psychoanalysis," on which some of the best work, certainly including some of Fromm's own, has not been done under Marxian auspices.

Logically, at least one other possibility exists. We have already stated that social theories will contain psychological components. The Marxian theory is no exception. One could pick out such psychological components as may be found in it, and compare them directly with the Freudian theory to ascertain whether any additional illumination of the social order might be achieved by a comparison or combination. One difficulty with such a procedure is that the "pickings" from the Marxian side would be rather slim. It seems pointless to take a theorist to task for not doing what he had no intention of doing unless one can, say, demonstrate that the task omitted would have accomplished something relevant to the task undertaken. Whether or not Marx, given the nature of his problems, might with profit have developed a social psychology is not our concern.[14] The fact remains that he did comparatively little in this direction except by way of throwing out hints and pregnant phrases, some of which have in fact been developed by others.[15]

13. "Methode und Aufgabe . . . ," 53.

14. By direct implication, Veblen at least makes the claim that Marxian theory would have profited from such a development. *Cf.* the papers on "The Socialist Economics of Karl Marx and His Followers," in *The Place of Science in Modern Civilization* (New York: Huebsch, 1919), pp. 409–456, esp. pp. 417–418.

15. See, *e.g.*, Karl Mannheim, *Ideology and Utopia* (New York: Harcourt,

Another difficulty comes from the fact that there is danger of remaining on an analogical level even when one has found psychological elements in Marxism and Freudianism that have a certain comparability. Take the concept of "false consciousness." Briefly, in Marx's view, this means that "distortion" of viewpoint arises from the fact of occupying certain social positions. An "ideology" develops which, objectively, is in the interest of a certain class, and thinking and perception are conditioned by that interest. Hence, for example, the ideology of the "vulgar economists," who deal "with appearances only," and confine themselves to "systematizing in a pedantic way, and proclaiming for everlasting truths, the trite ideas held by the self-complacent bourgeoisie with regard to their own world, to them the best of all possible worlds." [16] Freud operates with notions that undoubtedly bear some resemblance to the concept of "false consciousness." For him also, thinking and perception are "distorted" by "interests." But the "interests" are definite emotional forces, and are found in the psychic lives of individuals. They are not economic interests, and they do not have, in Freud, a class reference. There is a formal similarity here, but no more. One may indeed see an element of unity in the Marxian and Freudian views, and indicate that Marx and Freud were both analysts of "self-deception." [17] But this is a very general notion; its utility for purposes of a reasonably far-reaching analysis may be doubted.

A comparison of Freud and Marx, then, is open to various difficulties and dangers. It might still be a feasible enterprise, but crucial for us is precisely the relative absence of psychological components in the Marxian scheme.[18] Veblen, on the other hand, affords us a clear and

Brace, 1936). It is interesting to observe that Fromm has vigorously contended that the Marxian theory is not to be interpreted as a kind of economic psychology if fruitful relationships are to be developed between Marxian and Freudian views. The psychological elements in Marxian theory are scanty (and, the implication runs, adventitious) and, within it, economic factors are to be understood as "objective conditions" rather than as "subjective psychological motives." See "Methode und Aufgabe . . . ," 40–45.

16. Karl Marx, *Capital* (Kerr ed., 1906), vol. I, p. 93, footnote 1. *Cf.* also, *ibid.*, pp. 81–96, and *Capital*, vol. III, pp. 962–968, on the "fetishism of commodities."

17. This position is taken by Reinhold Niebuhr, *The Nature and Destiny of Man* (New York: Scribners, 1941), vol. I, ch. ii.

18. This would seem almost to contradict our general statement that theories in social science contain psychological components. Psychological components

definite opportunity to trace the manner in which a social scientist's psychology is used in relation to his general social and economic analysis. Also, Veblen is in any case quite closely related to the scheme of theory that comes from Marx.

If we retain some interest in the general problem of the relations of "sociology and psychoanalysis," the choice of Veblen is not disadvantageous. A large part of the traditional and current interest of social science is in the analysis of "institutions," and much of the interest of psychology has been and is in the understanding of "individuals." What do these two—"institution" and "individual"—have to do with one another? How are they related? So put, the problem is vast, and it may be conveniently mediated once more through an examination of some relations between Freudian and Veblenian theory. Marx was of course not neglectful of institutions. His institutionalism appears most definitely in connection with his analysis of basic factors in the structure of the capitalist order, as when he emphasizes the separation of the laborer from the means of production and the situation of the laborer as untrammeled owner of his own labor-power, and compares these institutions with those proper to serfdom and slavery.[19] But Veblen is not behind-hand in this matter. He is in fact one of the important continuators of Marx in the analysis of institutions. Whether his conception of the nature of institutions is wholly adequate is another matter, and will be considered later.

Outstanding features of the Freudian and Veblenian theories of human nature will be set out. In the case of Veblen's theory we proceed at once to examine how that theory relates to the remainder of his analysis. In the case of the Freudian theory, which is examined first, the question of its relevance to sociological problems will be deferred for later treatment except for some indispensable initial indications. Some common or converging sociological problems arising from the Freudian and Veblenian schemes of theory *in toto* will then be considered. Special emphasis will be placed on the Freudian and Veblenian perspectives on rationality and on social cohesion. The problem of social

are present in the Marxian scheme, but they are neither strongly self-conscious nor is any attempt made to get them into any kind of systematic shape.

19. See, *e.g.*, *Capital*, vol. I, ch. vi.

cohesion particularly will serve to launch us on an inquiry into the status of what we shall call a "normative component in the psyche," an indispensable perspective on which is provided by the work of Adler, Jung, and others. Finally, case studies in the integration of the Freudian type of psychology and the Veblenian type of social theory will be presented in our treatment of psychoanalysis and the leisure class and of the case of modern Germany. The entire analysis is selective rather than exhaustive, but central and important aspects of the total schemes of theory examined have been chosen.

The term "Freudian psychology," in our title, calls for comment. Considerable reference will be made to Freud himself. Although there is little doubt that his work is open to very serious criticism, he is still intimately related to the body of theory that makes up the distinctive psychology worked out by psychoanalysts. Even those who disagree with him, among the analysts, devote a good deal of energy to criticizing him, and try to show us how their formulations compare with his. Reference will be made to these critics of Freud, and to their constructive, as well as their critical, views. Although it is precisely these critics, such as Kardiner, Horney, Fromm, Sullivan, *et al.*, who have effected important changes in the original Freudian theory through their characteristic sociological perspective, the term "Freudian psychology" in our title is meant to include the outlook and work of contemporaries who have comparatively little faith in Freud's theories of instinct, who have little use for the libido theory, and who have a perspective quite different from Freud's on the role of social factors in the shaping of personality structure. We note that the doctrine of the strict determination of psychic processes, the emphasis on unconscious motivations, and the interpretation of those motivations as emotional forces—surely all fundamental in Freud—are usually retained without mitigation by these contemporaries.[20] They also repeatedly refer to themselves as Freudians. In the context of our discussion, however, we may refer to them as "neo-Freudians," or perhaps as sociologically oriented psychoanalysts. Finally, there is included some treatment of the views of Adler and Jung. Each of

20. *Cf.* Karen Horney, *New Ways in Psychoanalysis* (New York: Norton, 1939), p. 18.

these men, for his own reasons, wished to avoid being known as a Freudian. But our analysis makes it necessary to give them some attention, and their views are, in any case, importantly related to the Freudian doctrine.

# 2. *The Freudian and Neo-Freudian Views of Human Nature*

## I. A NOTE ON RATIONALITY AND RELATED TERMS

SINCE WE DEAL with theories of human nature that require frequent reference to "rationality" and closely related concepts, it is well to have some preliminary definitions of these. Rationality may be used in the sense of the adequate or efficient employment of means to attain ends. Rational behavior is, then, behavior typical forms of which consist in the action of a person closing a door in order to prevent a draft, absorbing the contents of a manual in order to pass an examination, deprecating another's ability in order to get him to put it in evidence. No question is immediately raised about the character of the ends involved. Rationality is relational in character. Given certain ends, does action undertaken ordinarily achieve them or not? The means are judged in relation to the ends posited. The failure of means to achieve ends, however, does not necessarily mean that action or behavior is irrational. The failure may be due to ignorance or error.

The failure of means to achieve ends may be said to involve irrationality only under special conditions. Irrationality has reference to the intrusion of an "alien" element, to the existence of a "distortion" in behavior. Its source may be "emotional" or "traditional." When a factor of the type that the Freudians characteristically remark—*e.g.*, reacting to a situation in adult life by means that might have been effective in childhood but are not effective now, say by a display of temper when one is proved wrong—when such a factor intrudes to "mar" a relation, we have irrational behavior whose source or basis is emotional. When, for old time's sake, let us say, in a political situation, some functionaries insist on a procedure which is at the same time revered and incompatible with the ends that the same functionaries wish to achieve, we have a traditional basis for irrationality.

There is another way of making clear the distinction between behavior that fails to achieve ends and is irrational, and behavior that fails to achieve ends but is not irrational. Adapting to our uses terms that Freud employed in *The Interpretation of Dreams,* we may distinguish manifest and latent ends. One may be overtly or manifestly trying to determine the truth of a matter, but covertly or latently attempting to prove one's self right at any cost. A group of functionaries may be manifestly attempting to attain some posited goal, but latently pursuing another incompatible one. In such cases, there is a conflict of (manifest and latent) goals or ends. From this point of view, behavior that fails to achieve ends because of "simple" ignorance or "innocent" error involves no conflict. Irrationality is not present: there is no conflict of manifest and latent goals.[1]

It is worth emphasizing the relational character of both rationality and irrationality. Thus, a display of temper when one is shown wrong might even succeed in certain situations in adult life, and it might therefore be said that it has a certain rationality, but only in a highly qualified sense. The proof of the irrationality of such behavior depends on a demonstration of its *general* incompatibility with the attainment of other goals cherished by the person. When frameworks of contact and interrelationships widen at the same time as new goals come to be desired, many old types of reactions may become irrelevant or positively detrimental from the point of view of attainment of the new goals. This statement would hold also for our political illustration. Irrationality, then, is present in view of certain goals. If the political functionaries should abandon those manifest goals that would presumably lead to desired successes, and frankly admit that their object was only to act in a traditional or ceremonial manner for its own sake, there could in a sense be no quarrel. In fact, we could hardly say any longer that the successes that would otherwise be possible were really "desired." The behavior shown might now be characterized by others as "suicidal" or "mad," but only in relation to, or in view of, goals that those others conceive to be essential (from the point of view of the functionaries themselves, if only they could recog-

1. The resemblance to Robert K. Merton's terminology will be noted, although Merton prefers to speak of manifest and latent "functions." For his usage, see Clyde Kluckhohn, *Navaho Witchcraft* (Cambridge: The Peabody Museum, 1944), pp. 45–72.

nize their own "real interests" or those of the larger groups they might represent, or from the point of view of the interests of the whole community). Persuasion and argument might or might not produce a change. Similarly, in the case of an individual, the success of a clinical psychologist in treating him would depend to a considerable extent on the growth of a conviction on the patient's part that he himself cherished goals he was not realizing, that those goals from his own point of view were more important than the latent goals he was also pursuing, and that the latent or covert goals necessarily defeated the manifest or overt or ostensible goals.

There is nothing "irrational" about tradition or emotion *as such, i.e.,* tradition or emotion when they are not assessed in the light of particular goals, or in terms of their compatibility with the requirements of specific situations. They may or may not achieve certain effects, but in themselves they are neither rational nor irrational. We prefer to characterize them as "non-rational" and accordingly use this term in two ways as our reference is either to phenomena of the type of emotion or to those of the type of tradition. In the first sense in which we use the term non-rational, behavior characterized as non-rational is more or less closely tied up with biological nature: behavior based in opaque appetites, drives, instincts, emotions. These are a part of given human (or animal) nature, and cannot be conveniently described as "ignorant" or "stupid" or "mad." They are, if anything, more aptly called "brute." The other terms simply fail to deal with their level. Any complete survey of behavior will inevitably involve the inclusion of these non-rational components.

Traditional behavior, behavior institutionally or culturally determined, may also be classified as non-rational. "Institutions," "traditions," "folkways," "mores"—these terms all have reference to a second meaning of non-rationality. The usage adopted is closely related to that of Pareto. Where Pareto uses the term "non-logical," we have used "non-rational." Pareto places the "instinctive acts" of animals in the class of non-logical actions, and this conforms closely to our term, non-rational, in its first sense. But he also clearly puts traditional human behavior into the class of non-logical action. He notes, incidentally, that both kinds of behavior, non-logical actions that have a biological background and non-logical actions that have a traditional background, may coincide with "logical ends and purposes." Thus, in discussing the instinctive action of insects, "subjectively non-logical," he says that such action "shows a marvellous objective logic." [2] That is, it accomplishes "sustaining" or "valuable" results. It "functions" to the advantage of the agent carrying it out, without having been so intended. Yet "the formation of human language is no whit less marvellous than the instinctive conduct of insects." Pareto's account, however, runs together the "non-logical" ("non-rational") and the "illogical" ("irrational"), despite a parenthetical comment that the "non-logical" is by no means the same as the "illogical." [3] The confusion manifests itself also in critical comment on Pareto.[4]

Non-rational behavior, it should be remarked, may work out in results that are, as Pareto says, "marvellous." But also, obviously, it may not. "Instincts" may "miss fire" in a sufficiently variable environment, and traditional ways of behavior, the products of unplanned growth and cumulation, may finally work out in all sorts of "stresses" for the people who have been holding to them.[5] The use of the term non-rational does not of itself imply any commitment on this point.

The two kinds of non-rational behavior cannot be equated, nor can there be an easy resolution of the one into the other. Freud's sociological work fell into the error of a failure to distinguish the two kinds of non-rationality. On the other hand, Veblen, in principle, kept apart the two kinds of phenomena denoted by the terms "instinct" and "institution."

Our terminological discussion might end at this point, but a writer on the Freudian and Veblenian theories of human nature cannot altogether evade the issue that is raised by the accusations of "anti-rational" or "anti-intellectual" currently levelled by some against

2. Vilfredo Pareto, *Mind and Society* (ed. Livingston, New York: Harcourt, Brace, 1935), vol. I, ch. ii, p. 81.

3. *Ibid.*, p. 84.

4. See, *e.g.*, in the Symposium on Pareto in *Journal of Social Philosophy* I (1935), Floyd N. House, "Pareto in the Development of Modern Sociology," 81, where the author speaks of the "general conception of the role of non-logical *or irrational* factors in the behavior of human beings in society." Our emphasis.

5. See Robert K. Merton, "The Unanticipated Consequences of Purposive Social Action," *American Sociological Review* I (1936), 894–904.

thinkers like Veblen and Freud. Typically, Veblen speaks of the "unhedonistic, unrationalistic, pecuniary traffic" in which "the tissue of business life consists."[6] Many similar phrases and pronouncements on his part could be cited. But it should be noted that the indication or claim that the rationality of (economic) behavior is relatively slight cannot be met at once with an accusation that the author of the claim is "anti-rational" or "anti-intellectual." Veblen's ostensible purpose was empirical and descriptive, and his claim needs to be met on its own grounds. To the extent that his claim proves to be valid the whole accusation becomes idle from his point of view. The issue involved is logically quite similar for the case of Freud.

Freud emphasizes emotional factors in human make-up. We have already noted that a complete survey of behavior necessarily involves the inclusion of non-rational components. The inclusion of non-rational emotional components does not therefore imply a categorical denial of rationality. But Freud is often understood to do more than simply give a certain emphasis to emotional factors in human make-up. He is by some identified with an "insurgence against reason" also represented by Bergson, Spengler, *et al.*[7] The identification seems especially serious in a world where, many claim, the tenure of "reason" in human affairs is precarious. An analyst of Nazi ideology says of Freud:

> Another aspect of the self-destruction of Liberal idealism is the glorification of urges and instincts, of complexes and natural desires which attributes overwhelming power to sensual lust and unconscious impulse. . . . Klages is not far from Freud. Nazi racialism with its false biology and fussy eugenics is very much akin to widely prevalent progressive ideas well known to us all.[8]

Professor Sorokin emphasizes a somewhat different aspect, though it is still an aspect of the same matter, when he says: "Genius becomes a species of insanity; unselfish sacrifice is explained solely in terms of an inferiority, Oedipus, Narcissus, or other complex; distinguished

6. *The Place of Science in Modern Civilization* (New York: Huebsch, 1919), p. 250.

7. See especially M. R. Cohen, *Reason and Nature* (New York: Harcourt, Brace, 1931), ch. i, and pp. 62, 64, 265.

8. Aurel Kolnai, *The War Against the West* (New York: Viking Press, 1938), p. 15.

social endeavor is motivated by the herd instincts."[9] It may at once be admitted that there is a great tendency to "psychologize" all sorts of data not properly psychological, and Freud does not emerge with a clean bill on this score.[10]

But though Freud may properly be criticized in this regard, he nevertheless has several genuine answers to the accusation that he underestimates "reason." One is stated as follows:

> It is no part of our intention to deny the nobility in human nature, nor have we ever done anything to disparage its value. On the contrary, I show you not only the evil wishes which are censored but also the censorship which suppresses them and makes them unrecognizable. We dwell upon the evil in human beings with the greater emphasis only because others deny it, thereby making the mental life of mankind not indeed better, but incomprehensible.[11]

It is the last sentence to which we would particularly give attention, for Freud here affords a medical answer to the accusation. He finds an initial skepticism of rationality in his patients indispensable in order that he may come to grips with irrational factors. His therapeutic purpose is the diminution of the sway of the latter,[12] and a necessary step is the disestablishment of the illusion that complete rationality holds sway.[13] Thus, here he might even defend himself by

9. *The Crisis of Our Age* (New York: Dutton, 1941), p. 122.

10. Some psychoanalysts realize this very well, *e.g.*, Karen Horney. We give a single bare indication. "That generosity may be a reaction-formation against greediness does not disprove the existence of generosity." *New Ways in Psychoanalysis*, p. 66.

11. *General Introduction to Psycho-Analysis* (New York: Garden City Publishing Co., 1938), p. 131. Freud's meaning in this passage could be conveyed without using his particular terms. In psychological investigation, irrational hostilities make their appearance, which, from the point of view of a patient desiring to be rid of them, may seem "evil." What Freud here presents as a conflict between "nobility" and "evil" might be restated as a conflict between ostensible and covert goals. This is something of a simplification, but will do for the immediate purpose.

12. In the curious terminology of his later years, Freud says: "Where id was, there shall ego be." See his *New Introductory Lectures on Psychoanalysis* (New York: Norton, 1933), pp. 111–112. *Cf.* also the statement: "The physician requires of him [the patient] that he shall fit these emotions into their place in the treatment and appraise them at their psychical value." *Collected Papers* (Third ed., tr. J. Rivière, London: Hogarth Press & Institute of Psychoanalysis, 1942), vol. II, p. 322.

13. "A return from the over-estimation of the property of consciousness is

saying that it is his purpose to "destroy in order to build." And he might go further in saying that among the enemies of an ultimate greater rationality in human life are the very ones who make too sweeping claims for the prevalence of "reason." If Freud and the others have uncovered previously unsuspected sources of irrationality, there is simply no point at all in calling them anti-rational for that reason.

Another answer of Freud's is one that we may simply call psychological. It is contained in some of his views on the nature of consciousness, as when he states that "for us the state of becoming conscious is a special psychic act, different from and independent of the process of becoming fixed or represented, and consciousness appears to us as a sensory organ which perceives a content proceeding from another source."[14] Again, in the same volume in which the statement just quoted appears, he asserts that consciousness is *"a sense-organ for the perception of psychic qualities."*[15] Now it is true that Freud repeatedly asserts that mental processes are *essentially unconscious.*[16] But, however this may be, it is clear that he leaves some room and function to consciousness. It may also be that this answer, formally psychological in that it asserts a certain view of consciousness, merges with the medical answer, since this view of consciousness plainly has a close relationship to psychoanalytical therapeutic technique. It is a kind of "instrumental" view of consciousness.

Finally, Freud has an answer that we might call a general philosophical one. It might on closer analysis be seen to merge with the

---

the indispensable preliminary to any genuine insight into the course of psychic events." Freud, *The Interpretation of Dreams* (tr. Brill, New York: Macmillan, 1935), p. 562.

14. *The Interpretation of Dreams,* p. 149.

15. *Ibid.,* p. 565. *Cf.* also the statement: "In psychoanalysis there is no choice for us but to declare mental processes to be in themselves unconscious, and to compare the perception of them by consciousness with the perception of the outside world through the sense-organs. . . ." *Collected Papers,* vol. IV (tr. J. Rivière, London: Hogarth Press, 1925), p. 104.

16. For example, in his *General Introduction,* p. 22, he gives as one of two essential psychoanalytical tenets "that mental processes are essentially unconscious, and that those which are conscious are merely isolated acts and parts of the whole psychic entity." For some critical cautions applying to contemporary psychoanalytical use of the terms "conscious" and "unconscious," see Robert M. MacIver, *Social Causation* (Boston: Ginn, 1942), p. 215.

other two, but that does not matter very much. It remains true that he makes statements such as this: "At first we might be inclined to think very much less of the importance of consciousness, . . . since it has proved so unworthy. But if we did so, we should be wrong. . . . Without the light shed by the quality of consciousness we should be lost in the darkness of depth-psychology." [17]

It would be idle to deny a strong "psychologizing" bent in Freud (as we have already noted), whereby he attempts to reduce to the psychological many kinds of phenomena probably not at all psychological in important respects. Nor would it be any more profitable to deny a certain romantic, quasi-anarchistic bent on his part.[18] But it is rather too simple to identify him unqualifiedly with an insurgence against "reason," in the interests of which, rather, from one point of view, he may be said to have made a considerable contribution. The accusation of "anti-rational" is no doubt just in some respects; it misses the mark altogether in others.

The accusation, "anti-rational" or "anti-intellectual," may easily overlook the distinction between irrationality and non-rationality, and this is all the more reason for being wary of it. It is not that the accusation is necessarily always unjustified. It certainly applies well to, say, Nazi ideology, but that it can be rather too facile is well seen in its careless application to Freudian thought. A theory that indicates large limitations to human rationality might indeed be called *anti-rationalistic,* just as one that puts great emphasis on rationality may be called *rationalistic*. The Freudian and Veblenian theories are aptly described as anti-rationalistic, but that does not in the case of either justify the accusation of "anti-rationality." One of the most important questions that one can ask about a thinker like Freud or Veblen is:

17. *New Introductory Lectures,* p. 99. It is true that Freud may sometimes be quoted to another effect, depending on what his interest at the time and in the context is, but the statement quoted at least is not altogether accidental, and that he asserts such a view as the above more than once may be seen in the following: "Powerful though the feelings and the self-interest may be, yet intellect is a power too. It has not, perhaps, the power that makes itself felt immediately, but one that is all the more certain in the end." *Collected Papers,* vol. II, p. 292. *Cf.* Roland Dalbiez, *Psychoanalytical Method and the Doctrine of Freud* (tr. T. F. Lindsay, London: Longmans, Green, 1941), vol. II, pp. 44–46.

18. *Cf. e.g., Civilization and Its Discontents* (tr. Rivière, New York: Cape & Smith, 1930), *passim.*

"What was he arguing *against?*" What, to use an apt phrase of Parsons', is his "polemical orientation?" Veblen was opposed to a whole range of economic theory that seemed to him to put excessive stress on human rationality, that assumed, according to him, a psychology or theory of human nature that demonstrably overemphasized the part actually played in (economic and social) affairs by deliberate "taking of thought." Much of his ostensibly non-critical work arises from this polemical orientation, as will be seen for example in his views on money. Freud's polemical orientation is rather diverse. It is sometimes easy enough to define, as in the case of his opposition to the views of some of his former disciples, well instanced in his paper of 1914 on "The History of the Psychoanalytic Movement." [19] At other times, precisely because he uncovered a new dimension in mental life, it is more difficult to define, for very few had touched upon his peculiar ground, at least as he conceived it. But a large part of his theoretical work sought to enforce the view of the importance of "the unconscious" and of the notion that "unconscious" phenomena had "meaning," *i.e.,* were not "idle," not merely by-products of, say, physiological data, not epiphenomenal. And with his emphasis on "the unconscious," stringent limitations on rationality were always at least implied. Hence our use of the negative term antirationalistic to describe the general bias of both the Freudian and Veblenian views of human nature. At the same time, this is as far as possible from claiming a point-for-point identity of the two theories.

## II. ASPECTS OF THE FREUDIAN VIEW OF HUMAN NATURE

A common-sense apprehension of mental illness might afford us some such view as this: People are in general given to a certain "foolishness" about themselves and their health, and though the mass of mankind succeeds fairly well in keeping the "foolishness" under restraint, it will take an exaggerated form among some, who will "talk themselves into" illness. (It is Freud's repeated testimony that physicians of his day took a very similar view.) There is in reality nothing seriously wrong with a mentally disturbed person. He has become

19. *Collected Papers* (second ed., tr. J. Rivière, London: Hogarth Press, 1940), vol. I, pp. 287–359.

ill in some superficial and not quite real sense through the establishment of a spurious train of thought, which should be reversible. If he "talked himself into it," then he should be able to "talk himself out of it," or someone else properly authoritative and eloquent should. A person with a character structure making for effects unhappy in his own apprehension of the matter may then be adjured to "pull himself together." This may appear to be good advice, and perhaps a temporary success can even be attained. If the success should be conjoined with some fortunate accidents (incidences of events impinging from another system than the person's own character structure), perhaps his troubles will not recur. But the advice very frequently fails to work. There are, moreover, features of the case that make for skepticism about the whole common-sense apprehension. For example, there is the curious persistence often manifested by the "absurd notions." If they are so patently absurd, why not abandon them? The street is not really peopled by cannibals, nor is all human society an association of grinning detractors. Yet the "notions" persist, even often enough with a certain sense of their "absurdity" on the part of the person holding to them. Since the afflicted person is also often an intelligent individual, we begin to suspect that we are not dealing with something that can be grasped on the intellectual level alone. The foolishness of it all may be admitted, but it does not yield to the most painstaking demonstration of just how foolish it is.

This suggests a distinction between the conception of his own difficulties held by the mentally ill person and that held by the medical psychologist. The apprehension of the former can be erroneous in important respects: it may be said that his "consciousness" is "false." He is "unaware" or incorrectly or inadequately aware. And in the Freudian theory, such "false consciousness" is intimately related to the fact that there is a totally inadequate appreciation of the considerable role of emotional factors in determining the course of mental life. Freud puts the matter thus:

In a psychic complex which has been subjected to the influence of the resisting censorship, the affects are the unyielding constituent, which alone can guide us to the correct completion. This state of affairs is revealed in the psychoneuroses even more distinctly than in dreams. Here the affect is always in the right, at least as regards its quality; its intensity may, of course, be increased by displacement of the neurotic attention. When the hysterical patient wonders that he should be so afraid of a trifle, or when the sufferer from an obsession is astounded that he should reproach himself so bitterly for a mere nothing, they are both in error, inasmuch as they regard the conceptual content . . . the trifle, the mere nothing . . . as the essential thing, and they defend themselves in vain, because they make this conceptual content the starting-point of their thought-work. Psychoanalysis, however, puts them on the right path, inasmuch as it recognizes that, on the contrary, it is the affect that is justified, and looks for the concept which pertains to it, and which had been repressed by a substitution.[20]

In this very characteristic insistence on the importance of the "affect," Freud of course squarely emphasizes emotional factors in the determination of character. It is well known to psychiatrists that obsessions may shift from one locus to another, and it may even seem to the obsessed person himself that if only he could get rid of the very peculiar tortures he suffers at a particular time, all would be well. But the obsessions may simply come to attend other activities, and persist as long as there remain underlying emotional disturbances.[21] The "trifles" of which Freud speaks may be quite variable, but not so the situation creating the "trifles." Moreover, says Freud, the sufferers strive in vain because they make the "trifle, the mere nothing" "the starting-point of their thought-work." If consciousness is thus "false," it must indeed be "false" in psychoanalytical theory, for otherwise the sufferer might be prepared for the emotional change that would mitigate his illness. Psychoanalytical therapy, in fact, consists precisely in bringing a wider and more correct awareness to the patient, that he may be able to rid himself of the genuinely significant sources of psychic discomfort or illness. In the course of the therapeutic procedure, it is constantly necessary for the patient to see the

20. *The Interpretation of Dreams,* pp. 426–427.

21. Freud's conception of the systematic, "organic" character of a "neurosis" should be remarked:

"Again, a neurosis has the character of an organism; its component manifestations are not independent of one another, they each condition and mutually support the others; a man can only suffer from one neurosis, never from several accidentally combined in his person. Suppose one had freed the patient, according to his wish, from the one unendurable symptom, he might then have discovered that a symptom which was previously negligible had increased until it in turn had become intolerable." *Collected Papers,* vol. II, p. 351.

misleading character of many of his own notions about his difficulties, to see that it is their function to mislead, and to trace whole groups of related notions to underlying psychic trends that finally become the center of his attention when he has learned enough.[22]

Symptoms and words and phrases found in "neurotic" or even in "normal" behavior and speech seemed to Freud to call for "translation" of some kind. He found "meaning" in them,[23] but not one that announced itself on the surface. In fact, attempts to work on the surface exclusively would be doomed to failure, and recall, according to him, the bootless hortatory attempts of various therapeutic procedures antedating psychoanalysis. Present-day analysts also tell us that one cannot simply argue away the "notions" of a mentally ill person, who will manifest great ingenuity in bringing forth arguments to support the view that he is liable to sudden attacks by lions in the midst of a great city, that he may acquire rare tropical diseases, etc. Before the "notions" can be adequately treated, there must be departure from the "notional" level. The latter is not self-sustaining or self-nourishing, and the Freudians seek to "translate" its terms into the terms of an emotional or dynamic level.

However, this Freudian approach has implications for the question

22. Among the most important of Freud's own writings on psychoanalytical therapy are the "papers on technique," in *Collected Papers,* vol. II, pp. 285–402. A more popular treatment is given in Part III of his *General Introduction to Psychoanalysis.* Outstanding statements are contained in Roland Dalbiez, *Psychoanalytical Method and the Doctrine of Freud,* vol. I, pp. 201–223, and vol. II, pp. 88–154 and pp. 255–279; and in Harry Stack Sullivan, "Conceptions of Modern Psychiatry," in *Psychiatry* III (1940), 1–117.

23. On the question of "meaning," we note his dictum that "a neurosis never says foolish things, any more than a dream." *Collected Papers,* vol. III (tr. A. and J. Strachey, second ed., London: Hogarth, 1943), p. 170. Again: "The arbitrary has no existence in mental life." *Ibid.,* p. 244. This implies: no meaninglessness, theoretically also no absence of determination in mental life, no "untraceability" till one gets to sheer somatic or physiological factors. We cite one more relevant statement: "Obsessional ideas, as is well known, have an appearance of being either without motive or without meaning, just as dreams do. The first problem is how to give them a sense and a status in the mental life of the individual, so as to make them comprehensible and even obvious. The problem of translating them may seem insoluble; but we must never let ourselves be misled by that illusion. The wildest and most eccentric obsessional or compulsive ideas can be cleared up if they are investigated deeply enough." *Ibid.,* p. 325. *Cf.* also, *ibid.,* pp. 357–383, and the analysis of "A Case of Paranoia," *ibid.,* pp. 387–470.

of human rationality. To make some of these clear, let us set down the following logically possible view of human nature:[24] Man knows what he is and what he wants. He makes virtually no mistakes on these grounds. His manipulation of objects and orientation toward persons are flawless. His insight into himself, into others, into the external world, works out in a comprehensive grasp that enables a faultless consummation of purposes of the significance of which he has no doubt. His foresight is very keen. . . . This picture could easily be enlarged, but it is already large enough for us to say that even great optimists might hesitate to accept it without strong qualifications. And it is characteristic of the Freudian theory that its qualifications of such a picture or view are quite strong.

"Man knows what he is and what he wants." Freud and the Freudians would agree only with serious qualifications. Freud's view is that knowledge of the self is decidedly limited and can be widened only under conditions likely to evoke pain. One of his more recurrent theories runs to the effect that an arrest or "fixation" may occur in the component instincts that finally go to make up matured sexuality; or that a "regression" may take place to a prior state of sexual development. This "regression" may be helped out by a "frustrating" environment. But in such cases libido demands expression nonetheless, and then it may express itself in a form unacceptable by the self or "ego," and thus conflict will ensue, and "neurosis." Many modern psychiatrists would be skeptical of this view of the etiology of "neurosis," and some have little use for the libido theory as Freud formulated it.[25] But in Freud's view the person is largely unaware of the forces that have produced his present state, and this is a matter of considerable agreement among the Freudians, whether one substitutes for libido "basic anxiety" (Horney) or "parataxic integrations" (Sullivan), etc.[26]

It is this unawareness, then, that must be stressed. It is of course

24. It is not implied that the view is merely logically possible. There have been enough actual approaches to it in all sorts and schools of thought about human nature.

25. See, *e.g.*, Horney, *New Ways in Psychoanalysis,* ch. iii, and Abram Kardiner, *The Individual and His Society* (New York: Columbia University Press, 1939), p. 393.

26. *Cf.* p. 40, below, for definition of the term, "parataxic."

also contended that there are important factors that make for the maintenance of this unawareness—factors of an emotional nature.[27] In his later work, Freud conceived the "anatomy of the mental personality" in terms of id, ego, and superego.[28] He summarizes the functions of the superego thus: "We have allocated to it the activities of self-observation, conscience, and the holding-up of ideals."[29] Further, he represents the child as first developing id and ego. It is only after the very earliest years that the superego, in the shape of the internalization ("introjection") of traditions, taboos, and prescriptions, comes upon the scene. This happens first when the shrewd, though much-besieged, ego sees danger by way of hostility from the father should it permit the id to indulge its libidinous impulses toward the mother. If the id were allowed free rein, dire threats and punishments might ensue, which the ego sees it is on the whole wise to avoid. Hence a compromise; and the antagonism against the father is turned into a hostility against the self through an identification with the father and an acceptance of his view of the desiderata in the child's relations to his mother.[30] In the process here described, it is, because of the child's helplessness, expedient for him to renounce certain powerful impulses in order to get indispensable gratifications from the parental side. It is even perhaps "safest" to deny the existence of the impulses, and push them from awareness or repress them.

Now there has recently been much criticism of this line of theory. Thus, the Oedipus complex is apparently not universal,[31] and the notion that it has an unequivocally sexual significance has been challenged.[32] But, aside from these and other criticisms, Freud has here indicated a mechanism, a mode of psychic functioning, which is con-

27. Note Freud's statement that "the whole of psycho-analytic theory is in fact built upon the perception of the resistance exerted by the patient when we try to make him conscious of his unconscious." *New Introductory Lectures*, p. 97.

28. *Ibid.*, ch. iii.

29. *Ibid.*, p. 94.

30. "When the Oedipus complex passes away the child must give up the intense object-cathexes which it has formed towards its parents, and to compensate for this loss of object, its identifications with its parents, which have probably long been present, become greatly intensified." *New Introductory Lectures*, p. 91.

31. Kardiner, *The Individual and His Society*, p. 246; Fromm, "Methode und Aufgabe . . . ," *ibid.*, 38.

32. Horney, *New Ways*, ch. iv.

stantly insisted on by the most divergent psychoanalysts. The individual will renounce the chance of working out important potentialities for the sake of obtaining safety, and will even force from consciousness the perception of the existence of these potentialities since such perception would be too alarming. Under appropriate conditions a highly motivated ignorance or deception of the self occurs.[33] The individual, then, is hardly in a position to know "what he is," or, for that matter, "what he wants." The wants that have been forced down are not for that reason conceived to discontinue their existence. Their dynamic power is not at all diminished. They may manifest themselves in all sorts of "odd" ways, as through the medium of dreams, in symptom-formations, in fantasies, etc.

Perception, in psychoanalytical theory, is to a very large extent emotionally conditioned. Given the proper emotional bases, then, "insight into the nature of the self" is not likely to be very thorough or effective. In Freud's view, the organism protects itself against painful or disintegrating insights through a variety of mechanisms, rationalizations, reaction-formations, etc. This is in fact one reason for his large preoccupation with dreams and fantasies, for especially in the former there takes place a process that he describes in the eloquent words of Schiller as "a withdrawal of the watchers from the gates of the intellect." [34] In dreams, in other words, the claim is in effect that one is likely to be a little more "honest" with one's self. Even here, however, in Freud's own view, there are limitations on what may be attained, for his doctrine is that there exist two systems relevant to dream-formation. In one system the "dream-wish" originates, but the other does not readily allow the wish to be represented except on condition of "forcing such modifications as are pleasing to itself upon the candidates for admission to consciousness." [35] Distortion is there-

33. This view will be found to be extensively employed by Kardiner, Horney, Fromm, Sullivan, Dollard, *et al.* It does not necessarily involve acceptance of Freud's notions on topography, "mental anatomy," etc.

34. *The Interpretation of Dreams,* p. 110. *Cf.* also C. G. Jung, *Contributions to Analytical Psychology* (tr. H. G. and C. F. Baynes, New York: Harcourt, Brace, 1928), p. 324.

35. *The Interpretation of Dreams,* p. 149. The theory of dreams was always undergoing revision at Freud's hands. It is perhaps especially interesting to follow his attempts to fit anxiety dreams into the mold of the wish-fulfilment theory; but, for a late general statement, see his *New Introductory Lectures,* ch. i.

fore common, and Freud even insists that there occurs in dreams a "transvaluation of psychic values." However the details may be,[36] the general insistence upon the limitations on self-perception is shared by others than Freud who differ seriously in other respects, and the limitations are by no means thought to be confined simply to the mentally ill.

In consequence, the proposition that "foresight is very keen," insofar as it bears, say, on the question of the personality's own future, will be looked at askance by Freud and others. We adduce one small item in this connection: "Nervous breakdowns" can be and often are altogether unexpected affairs from the point of view of the persons experiencing them, who may have previously imagined themselves free of all irrational traits.[37] We have, however, been speaking of phenomena that may seem to be largely characteristic of "neurosis." But it has been ably argued that certain basic trends are liable to be found not only in isolated individuals who may be said to be "neurotic," but in virtually all the personalities in a given culture.[38] The line of demarcation between "normal" and "abnormal" is notoriously difficult to fix, and it would be strange indeed if even fairly unique mental experiences had no continuity with other experiences within a human community. Thus, Faris and Dunham suggest that

> such hallucinations as "hearing voices" and "seeing visions" may result not only from sensory disturbances, but also from the inability of the seclusive person to communicate. Some investigations have revealed that patients who claim to "hear voices" may admit on further questioning that it is a "quiet voice" or "not really a voice, nor even a whisper, but a sort of silent whisper." Many such persons have some basis in their experience for such a belief. A patient who had spent a period in jail believed people

36. *Cf. The Interpretation of Dreams, passim,* wherein Freud examines fully the factors that in his view control dream-formation, such as condensation, displacement, regard for representability, and secondary elaboration.

37. Irrational, that is, in terms of the life organization of the individual. Rationality is relational in character. Given the fact that a "neurosis" is present, an individual may in a sense act "rationally" within the bounds and limitations it sets down. Thus, if he is susceptible to great anxiety when faced with tasks performed with relative ease by "normal" persons, withdrawal from circumstances which will enforce or require the performance of those tasks is in a definite sense "rational." But this does not negate the fact that the existence of the anxiety may prevent executive activity that would bring vital satisfactions, whether there is awareness of this or not.

38. Kardiner, *ibid.,* pp. 413–419; also Kardiner, *The Psychological Frontiers of Society* (New York: Columbia University Press, 1945).

were calling him "jailbird." A school-girl patient who had been the victim of a rape believed that people were talking about her. For isolated persons who feel that they could not know directly what persons might be whispering, such thoughts are not entirely unreasonable. The powerful feeling of embarrassment, disgrace, and helplessness may give rise to the conviction that other persons are discussing them. The statement that they hear voices may be in the nature of a metaphorical means of expression, used because it is felt that such a means is the only way to communicate the strength of the feeling.[39]

But even aside from this, one may say that the psychoanalytical view does not imply with respect to "normal" persons that they have anything like perfect or very considerable self-knowledge or foresight or insight with regard to the self. They may be quite deficient in these respects and yet quite "normal."

The views remarked above are not peculiar to Freud or to orthodox Freudians. Stripped of their association with Freudian instinct theory and the like, they are held by many others, as the examination of Horney's concept of "basic anxiety" or Kardiner's notion of "basic personality structure," or Sullivan's view of "parataxis," when the ramifications of each of these are worked out, reveals. As already noted, the entire Freudian psychology has a definitely anti-rationalistic bent. There is a further relevant feature of that psychology: its emphasis on the personality's insusceptibility to change in some respects and under certain circumstances—an emphasis sometimes rendered by speaking of "rigidity." Certain basic aspects of the personality are conceived to be laid down, usually quite early in life, and subsequently, even if unconsciously, one may react to persons (and even to non-human phenomena) quite in the same way as one reacted to important figures in the original familial constellation. This fact is indeed in some ways the basis of psychoanalytical therapeutic procedure, since the psychoanalyst cannot do significant work with his patient unless the latter's reactions to him are a fair sample of his reactions to other people, as, the analyst would say, they must be. There is encountered here a residue of unconscious "notions" with respect to other persons, what they are like, what they expect of one,

39. *Mental Disorders in Urban Areas* (Chicago: University of Chicago Press, 1939), p. 174. *Cf.* also the view that "mental abnormality . . . must be defined in terms of the relationship between actions and situations." *Ibid.*, p. 156. *Cf.* Freud, *Collected Papers*, vol. III, pp. 387–470.

etc. These "notions," often highly unrealistic and irrational, may nevertheless persist despite all evidence that might invalidate them. (They would ordinarily have to be raised to consciousness before any hope could be entertained of overcoming them, unless new and "happy" conditionings "made over" a personality in such fashion that the "preconceptions" no longer appeared implicit in behavior.) Something of this sort is implied in Dollard's criterion that "the continuous related character of experience from childhood through adulthood must be stressed,"[40] as also in Kardiner's assertion that the ego "is integrative in its development, which means that all adaptive processes are based on those which have proved expedient in the past."[41]

Rationalism and hedonism have often enough gone together, and a question arises about the extent to which the Freudian psychology is hedonistic. The whole bent of this psychology must cast some doubt on the degree of success that may be attained in the search for pleasure, even if pleasure were a primary aim. Yet Freud himself spoke much of the "pleasure-principle," and it formed an important item in his thinking, especially up to 1920, the date of the appearance of *Beyond the Pleasure Principle.*[42]

In this volume, Freud tells us almost at once that "it must be affirmed that it is not strictly correct to speak of the supremacy of the pleasure-principle over the course of psychic process . . . one can only say that a strong tendency towards the pleasure-principle exists in the psyche."[43] He then notes two "checks" on the pleasure-principle. Firstly, the "reality-principle" comes in, through the ego's in-

40. John Dollard, *Criteria for the Life History* (New Haven: Yale University Press, 1935), p. 8 and *passim.*

41. Kardiner, *The Individual and His Society,* p. 19. In view of our use, above, of terms like "unrealistic," "irrational," Kardiner's use of the term "expedient" may appear paradoxical. But "expedient" should be understood to mean "expedient" within a *given context,* and not necessarily "expedient" from the point of view of the total life organization of the personality. The prime exemplification of the integrative character of the psyche that Kardiner has thus far worked out is contained in his analysis of Alor, in *The Psychological Frontiers of Society,* pp. 101–258.

42. A brief conspectus of his views on pleasure–and reality-principles, prior to 1920, is found in his *General Introduction to Psychoanalysis,* pp. 297–312.

43. *Beyond the Pleasure Principle* (tr. C. J. M. Hubback, from the second German edition, London: International Psycho-Analytical Press, 1922), p. 4.

terest in self-preservation, and this reality-principle, "without giving up the intention of ultimately attaining pleasure yet demands and enforces the postponement of satisfaction, the renunciation of manifold possibilities of it, and the temporary endurance of 'pain' on the long and circuitous road to pleasure." Secondly, a no less important source of "pain" or pleasure renunciation arises from "the conflicts and dissociations in the psychic apparatus during the development of the ego towards a more highly coordinated organization." Having made this statement, Freud then briefly reviews his theory of "neurosis," and finally says: "The details of the process by which repression changes a possibility of pleasure into a source of 'pain' are not yet fully understood, or are not yet capable of clear presentation, but it is certain that all neurotic 'pain' is of this kind, is pleasure which cannot be experienced as such." One may ask just how far this qualification of the pleasure-principle, by Freud himself, may reach. "Neurosis" certainly does not readily suggest hedonistic endeavor. The goals of security or satisfaction that some modern analysts so frequently postulate are far enough removed from pleasure, and, in "neurosis," certainly anything but the "pleasurable" is attained. If, as is claimed by some, the covert intent of the personality is primarily to attain a feeling of safety especially when the person is under the pressure of "neurosis," a very large doubt must be cast on the pleasure-principle. But if Freud's psychology remains to an extent formally hedonistic, it does so under his own, not minor or trivial, qualifications. Nevertheless, he still avers: "The two sources of 'pain' here indicated still do not nearly cover the majority of our painful experiences, but as to the rest one may say with a fair show of reason that their presence does not impugn the supremacy of the pleasure-principle." [44]

In this volume also, Freud notes the tendency of sufferers from traumatic "neurosis" to live over their frightening experiences in dreams; indicating, too, that this raises a problem with regard to the wish-fulfilment theory of dreams.[45] He then abruptly switches to the theme of the play of children, hesitating, since the favoring evidence is inconclusive, over the possibility that such play may be interpreted

44. All quotations, *ibid.*, pp. 5 and 6.

45. *Ibid.*, pp. 8–10. *Cf.* also "Revision of the Theory of Dreams," first lecture in *New Introductory Lectures.*

in the light of an "impulse to obtain the mastery of a situation (the 'power' instinct)." He notes that, in psychoanalysis, the patient "repeats," instead of "recollecting," what is repressed. Divested of the elements of the libido theory that cling to Freud's presentation, the point may be adequately rendered by saying that the patient in relation to the physician reproduces "neurotic" behavior all over again. Having an eye to the element of repetition (and presumably also to the compelling character of the repeated behavior), Freud speaks of a "repetition-compulsion" that appears in the psychoanalytical treatment of "neurosis." He thinks that "the unconscious" has a kind of upward thrust (a tendency to come to expression), and resistance does not come from it. Rather, "the resistance in the treatment proceeds from the same higher levels and systems in the psychic life that in their time brought about the repression." And the "repetition-compulsion," he tells us, "must be ascribed to the repressed element in the unconscious." [46]

Now comes this important statement: "There is no doubt that the resistance of the conscious and preconscious ego subserves the pleasure-principle; it is trying to avoid the 'pain' that would be aroused by the release of the repressed material, and our efforts are directed to effecting an entry for such painful feeling by an appeal to the reality-principle." [47]

It is implied that "our efforts" must be very genuinely persuasive. "Neurosis" is seen here as an attempt, indeed, to get rid of "pain," but one which fails in that the result is in any case very painful. Freud is in effect repeating his former qualification of the pleasure-principle. Yet he says: "It is plain that most of what is revived by the repetition-compulsion cannot but bring discomfort to the ego, for it promotes the bringing to light of the activities of repressed impulses; but that is a discomfort we have already taken into account and without subversion of the pleasure-principle, since it is 'pain' in respect of one system and at the same time satisfaction for the other." [47]

What claims his attention at this point is the "new and remarkable fact" that "the repetition-compulsion also revives experiences of the past that contain no potentiality of pleasure, and which could at no time have been satisfactions, even of impulses since repressed." Yet these experiences are repeated under the insistence of "a powerful

46. *Beyond the Pleasure Principle*, pp. 14, 18, 19. 47. *Ibid.*, p. 20.

compulsion." An "endless repetition of the same" is in fact remarked by Freud as pervading even the lives of non-"neurotics." Freud finally ventures "to make the assumption that there really exists in psychic life a repetition-compulsion," which may explain something of the phenomena of play in children as well as of the dreams of shock-patients. The repetition-compulsion appears to him "more primitive, more elementary, more instinctive than the pleasure-principle which is displaced by it." [48]

It may be parenthetically remarked that something of the significance of Freud's adoption of the notion of repetition-compulsion may be seen in the manner in which he applies the notion to the dreams of persons suffering from traumatic "neurosis." Ordinarily, his theory of dreams would require that a wish-fulfilment in the service of the pleasure-seeking character of the mind should be worked out by the dream. But now he suggests that "before the pleasure-principle can begin its sway," another function is fulfilled in traumatic-"neurotic" dreams, namely, that of an attempt to regain the control and organization that were disrupted by the stimuli that impinged on the organism without allowing for an intervening apprehension that might have prevented the "neurosis." This attempt is compulsively repeated.[49] The connection of this with his former reference to a "power" or "mastery" impulse is clear. Some, at least, of contemporary analysts consider this a very important line of thought, and regret that Freud did not develop it further.[50]

The rest of this book, in which Freud speculates on "life" and "death" instincts, is not important for our purposes. The pleasure-principle, however, comes to the fore once more in the shape of an ingenious speculative reconciliation: "Our recognition that the ruling tendency of psychic life, perhaps of nerve life altogether, is the struggle for reduction, keeping at a constant level, or removal of the inner stimulus tension (the Nirvana-principle, as Barbara Low terms it)—a struggle which comes to expression in the pleasure-principle—is indeed one of our strongest motives for believing in the existence of death-instincts." [51]

48. All quotations, *ibid.*, pp. 20, 22, 23–25.

49. See *ibid.*, p. 37.

50. *Cf. e.g.*, Meyer Maskin, "Psychodynamic Aspects of the War Neuroses: A Survey of the Literature," *Psychiatry* IV (1941), 97–115.

51. *Ibid.*, p. 71. *Cf.* also *ibid.*, pp. 81 and 83.

Since the attainment of pleasure is always conceived by Freud as closely connected with the reduction of (painful) tension, it is clear that he has enlisted the pleasure-principle in the service of the death-instinct. His speculative interest has won a clever triumph, and he has gone "beyond the pleasure-principle," but only in the sense that he has tried to seek out presumptive biological elements that lie "below" it. He has not gone "beyond the pleasure-principle" in the sense that he has abandoned it. The shift achieved, as just seen, throws more emphasis on the "death-instinct" (which derives from the "repetition-compulsion," for if that is sufficiently pervasive Freud thinks it justified to postulate conation on the part of life to return to an inanimate state), but the latter continues to be catered to by the pleasure-principle.

Two essential points have emerged. Firstly, "neurosis" means "pain"; the behavior of "neurotics," to put it mildly, does not fall into a pattern unqualifiedly hedonistic. This, Freud admitted from the beginning. Secondly, the pleasure-principle is not fundamental. A kind of biological primacy falls to the "death-instinct" and related phenomena "beyond the pleasure-principle." Even if the latter is retained as a significant term by an ingenious tactic, we must see that it is even for Freud no longer "supreme" in psychic life. It is clear by now that the Freudian psychology, as it comes from Freud, is, in effect, hedonistic only after some rather serious qualifications. Many contemporary analysts qualify the hedonism even more, for they place much more stress on the first of the two points mentioned in this paragraph. This is inevitable in view of their emphasis on the concept of "security" and its implications; and this emphasis in turn is allied with a different perspective from Freud's on the scope and importance of sexual and non-sexual factors in human personality. But this different emphasis and perspective warrant further treatment.

### III. FREUDIAN AND NEO-FREUDIAN PERSPECTIVE

Much of Freud's writing, we note in review, was shaped by his concept of the pleasure-principle. He contended that individual human behavior went on under the dominance of a striving to attain pleasure and avoid pain. This principle, however, did not work unchecked. The sheer following out of pleasure strivings would involve the organism in grave difficulties with the environment, and consequently Freud postulated the existence of a reality-principle to which were attached the "ego-instincts," as contrasted with the "sexual instinct," to which pleasure strivings were strongly attached. But major interest centered in the sexual instincts and the pleasure-principle. As is well known, Freud held from a very early time in his researches and speculations that the "neuroses" had a sexual etiology, in the sense that the repression of certain sexual impulses (though not necessarily "normal" ones [52]) was ultimately responsible for them. The repressed impulses did not disappear, but manifested themselves in disguised ways through symptoms apparently idle and meaningless, but which Freud thought had a definite (sexual) significance. A central item in this view, therefore, was the defeat of the aims of the pleasure-principle, or, rather, there was a compromise with its aims, since symptoms were interpreted as indications that the aims were simultaneously being partly carried out and partly defeated. A symptom was indeed called a "compromise formation."

In his development of these views, Freud appealed to constitutional factors, which in their variation from one person to another might work out to comparative weakness in one constitution and comparative strength in another.[53] There were also environmental factors that might exercise a frustrating effect and co-operate with an unfortunate constitutional predisposition to produce illness. Freud's "environment," as has been pointed out by F. H. Bartlett, is always a rather abstract general environment, an environment "skinned, cleaned, and boned." It is of course actually impossible to live in an "environment" without living in a specific one of a determinate character. But Freud makes of constitution and environment a general formula, which he summarizes under the rubric, "demon and chance." The fact, however, that Freud conceives environment in the manner indicated [54] is, we would suggest, not without relation

52. *Cf.* his *Three Contributions to the Theory of Sex,* in A. A. Brill (tr. and ed.), *The Basic Writings of Sigmund Freud* (New York: Modern Library, 1938), pp. 553–629, at pp. 553–579.

53. The view that "neuroses" have a constitutional foundation is maintained as late as the *New Introductory Lectures* of 1933.

54. As Bartlett puts it, the "concession to a thin, colorless and static 'reality'

to his notion and peculiar use of the pleasure-principle. But a further pertinent point is that when Freud deliberately discusses social factors at all, when as in his later work for example he introduces the concept of the superego, he contends in effect that id and ego are developed independently of the social order. Social influences begin to prevail only after the very earliest years, when the superego begins to operate.[55] So there emerges a picture of a biological organism *versus* the "environment." It is only tardily that the relationship between organism and environment is conceived to become other than this, when there takes place the process of "introjection."

What would human nature be like if it were not always involved in a social matrix? Would it be aptly described, at least in part, by Freud's idea of the pleasure-principle? Perhaps; perhaps not. The question inevitably seems idle, for contemporary sociologists and psychologists are at one in telling us that human nature is always and unavoidably involved in a social matrix. If this is so, then from the beginning of life social influences are operative and molding. They afford conditionings, goals, aspirations, without which there would be no human nature, and which have nothing in particular to do with the pleasure-principle. But in that case, a distinctive kind of personality structure must be in process of (socially conditioned) development from the beginning. Our suggestion, tentatively offered, is that the less such a structure is kept in mind, the more plausible or the more possible it becomes to operate with the notion of a pleasure-principle, since that—at least in Freud's apprehension—is a datum

---

can easily be and often is withdrawn. Freud believes that it is not even necessary for the same circumstances to persist. If the child's own experience does not provide sufficient material in which the inborn pattern may express itself he will reach out beyond his own individual life to the experience of his ancestors. 'He fills in the gaps in individual truth with prehistoric truth.'" (See *Collected Papers,* vol. III, p. 577). Bartlett, "The Limitations of Freud," 78; see also *Sigmund Freud: A Marxian Essay,* p. 90.

55. The superego, Bartlett indicates, is conceived by Freud as the condition of repression. Hence, repression should not occur until the formation of the superego. But Freud has said that this is not the case, "that, in fact, when the Oedipus complex develops, 'repression has already begun in the child and has withdrawn from him some part of his sexual aim.'" (See Freud's *General Introduction to Psycho-Analysis,* p. 289). Here Freud is involved in "an insoluble dilemma." He is driven back to the postulation of "organic repressions." Bartlett, "The Limitations of Freud," 93; see also *Sigmund Freud,* pp. 109–110.

derived from pure organism. In this sense, Freud's failure to conceive environment as specific social environment may be closely connected with his comparative emphasis on the pleasure-principle. In any case, a burden of proof is placed on him in that he must be able to show that there is a constitutional organization so definite, so precrystallized, as it were, that it becomes valid to say that "civilization" as a whole, and quintessentially, represses instincts. This is not to deny the possibility that social prescriptions may sometimes be sheerly biologically frustrating. It is often claimed that this is true of the social mode of handling infantile sexuality in American society.[56] It is, however, an anthropological commonplace that sexuality is quite differently handled or treated in other societies.

For Freud there is no mixture, as it were, of subjective stuff and what comes from "outside." Rather, the relation of the latter to the former is one of superimposition. This is why he often comes so close to an anarchistic view of society and civilization. Did he not recognize in these latter the workings of a "libido" with unifying or uniting effect operating in the interests of "eros," the proximity of his position to anarchism would be even greater. One source of this typical view of his is surely his manner of conceiving human nature. His human beings appear to be born "wound up," and with birth it is as if a spring is released that usually hurtles them through "oral," "anal," "phallic," and "genital" phases. Definite crystallizations are present at almost any time *vis-à-vis* environment. The organism has relatively fixed qualities, impulses, instincts. Environmental factors are not merely different from, but often enough actively opposed to, the subjective factors. If the social environment is not congenial to Freud's "natural man," that is largely because the natural man is already conceived to be so sharply and arbitrarily constituted that a very considerable number of the rules to which he will find himself forced to comply will at once appear as unwelcome impositions. The poor fellow must obey, but Freud sometimes nostalgically writes almost, if not quite—never quite—as if it would have been better to let him alone.

56. See, *e.g.*, Dollard *et al.*, *Frustration and Aggression* (New Haven: Yale University Press, 1939), ch. iv.

The investigations of modern psychiatry and sociology make it increasingly difficult to accept such descriptions. And especially doubtful is Freud's view of human nature as a set of fixed qualities that operates over against another set, the environment. The point of view that seems to organize best the available evidence relates the subjective sphere, the sphere of "motives," very intimately to the sphere of situations. Situations can be said to evoke motives. To say nothing else, this greatly changes our conceptions of characterological traits. We are used to saying: "This man is jealous, envious, avaricious, inconsiderate," etc. Ordinary linguistic habits induce a view that the man is characterized by a fairly fixed set of traits. Perhaps even the path to looking for a biological explanation in terms of instincts is made easier when we think in this way. But jealousy, envy, avarice, may obviously be evoked at some times and not at others. They are relational or "interpersonal," and cultural realities. What reaction occurs will depend upon the situation, or perhaps one should say upon the situation and how it is interpreted, thereby introducing an element that many investigators apparently find indispensable. Motives will then appear to be potential reactions, and they or dissimilar motives will be evoked according as (interpreted) situations change. It is unnecessary to make doubtful biological appeals, since the situational analysis can be employed genetically. Some persons, observed clinically or under ordinary conditions, will manifest a certain sameness of response to situations in which others will show a variety of response. But this "rigidity" may be explained by pointing out that in the life histories of some organisms, often though not necessarily in very impressionable years, situations were constantly faced that for various reasons were so overwhelming in their effect, so "impressive," that they put their stamp on virtually all subsequent situations. One way of expressing the result of this is to say that the range of possible interpretations of situations becomes very limited because of the disciplinary effect of a special set of situations from the past. This special set, we say, puts its stamp on others, so that the particular characteristics of new situations as they arise can then be "seen" or studied only in a very circumscribed manner; and interpretations of situations have an effect of being *a priori*. One aspect of what the psychoanalysts mean by "neurosis" can then be rendered by speaking of an incapacity for "seeing" differences among different situations.

But even if one thinks of the matter in this way, it is not necessary to relinquish emphasis on emotional factors. The above paragraph, for example, owes much to Harry Stack Sullivan's elaboration of the "conceptions of modern psychiatry."[57] Sullivan certainly does not under-emphasize emotional factors. He attempts a kind of clinical rationale of the general picture presented above, and while he may not make a Freudian use of the concept, say, of "libido," nevertheless his own concept of "parataxis" indicates that he does not neglect the emotional bases of behavior, vision (in the widest sense), interpretation, etc. Patient and psychiatrist, he tells us, may be proceeding smoothly and in a manner mutually intelligible, when an "incomprehensible" element in the patient's behavior or attitude, an element not rationally understandable in terms of the immediate situation, appears. The element is, as it were, obtruded upon the situation. It may involve an assumption by the patient about the psychiatrist's attitude, the consequence of which appears in the patient's behavior or statements. The consequence once observed, the assumption upon which it rests needs clear and explicit statement. Why the "unwarranted assumption"? Sullivan's hypothesis always runs to the effect that it has been emotionally ingrained through contact with influential persons in the past. He refers to such obtrusions as "parataxic" formations or integrations, and they are conceived to have arisen from "interpersonal relations," the field of which, for him, is the field of psychiatry. Much the same kind of thing that Sullivan seeks to illumine by means of a clinical rationale is explored by Kardiner by means of comparative anthropological data. Kardiner especially looks for data that reveal correspondences to, and consequences of, a certain "basic personality structure," in the sphere of fantasies and religious life:

> . . . as it is "logical" for an individual who has learned from the beginning of his life to believe that if he submits to certain arbitrary disciplines which deprive him of pleasures he will continue to enjoy protection, so it is logical for him to deprive himself of pleasure in order to please a deity. Once the relation between impulse control and an ulterior gain becomes

57. See his work under that title, esp. 45 *sqq.*

experientially established, this syndrome becomes a part of his reality sense —a part of his common sense.[58]

But in analysis of this kind what comes to the fore and is of central interest is the concept of a character structure, the elements of which have been in the building since earliest days. The essential question asked with respect to this character structure is whether it functions to effect "security"—that is, of course, psychological security. The absence of security is marked by the appearance of amounts of apprehension, anxiety or fear that are "disproportionate" in the light of what may be expected when factors of cultural situation, age, etc. are taken into account.[59] So important in the theory is the concept of security that it is contended that various motivations that might seem independent are actually subordinate to the end of obtaining security. Thus, even sexuality may be treated in this way, as when sexual activity is interpreted as undertaken in order to gain a preoccupation so demanding that it will obviate the possibility of doing work, about which there is a covert but considerable discomfort or fear; or when it is interpreted as undertaken in order to live up to the requirements of a conventional picture of "manliness." The ostensible motive, in these cases, may not be the genuine one, and the widespread practice in psychology and social science of naming motives from the objects around which they center is likely to be misleading. On the whole, when the concept of security becomes thus central, it seems that much of the older psychoanalytical theory comes in for revision.[60]

Abstractly, and to put the matter in a very simplified yet perhaps revelatory way, there are two theoretical possibilities that emerge from two kinds of orientation, one closely connected with the concept of the pleasure-principle and one closely connected with the con-

58. *The Individual and His Society,* p. 128. *Cf.* also "Security, Cultural Restraints, Intrasocial Dependencies, and Hostilities," in *The Family* XVIII (1937), 183–196; and "The Concept of Basic Personality Structure as an Operational Tool in the Social Sciences," in Ralph Linton (ed.), *The Science of Man in the World Crisis* (New York: Columbia University Press, 1945), pp. 107–122, as well as *The Psychological Frontiers of Society, passim.*

59. Horney, *The Neurotic Personality of Our Time* (New York: Norton, 1937), ch. i.

60. An excellent example of this, with particular reference to the concept of "narcissism," is to be found in Erich Fromm's "Selfishness and Self Love," *Psychiatry* II (1939), 507–523.

cept of security.[61] The first possibility, that connected with the concept of the pleasure-principle, will derive such phenomena as "neuroses" from various elements in sexual development. Thus, the line of argument, highly curtailed, may be roughly as follows: Biologically grounded sex urges are felt toward some person in the environment. But it soon becomes clear that these urges are not welcomed by that person or by others. They may in fact be actively disapproved. Also, there may emerge some apprehension that the continued attempt to satisfy these urges will result in punishment or intolerable deprivations. The urges can then be repressed, though they do not thereby disappear, and this repression may be fraught with psychological consequences. Even when the person takes over the attitude toward his own urges originally taken by influential agents in the environment, there will be, as it were, always a "part" of him that will be in revolt, yet checked by another "part" that is

61. The connection of the first orientation with the pleasure-principle is historical, for the pleasure-principle as a purely formal conception could be retained by the sociologically oriented psychoanalysts. It may be asked therefore why so much is made of the opposition between "pleasure-principle" and "security." The answer is that certain crucial views of Freud's, different from those of the neo-Freudians, were actually worked out by him in close connection with discussion of the pleasure-principle. The opposition, then, while not formally exact, has a certain historical truth, and is also convenient for purposes of contrast. [This historical connection persists, as for example in John Dollard's contention that work is natively uncongenial to the human organism, which would find pure idleness much more conformable with the pleasure-principle. *Caste and Class in a Southern Town* (New Haven: Yale University Press, 1937), ch. vi.] Kardiner sees the essential issue as one of opposition between "affect" and "executive maneuver." His view is an operational one: conflict, for example, means executive failure, whereas by Freud it was seen as due to preference for a repressed goal. *Cf.* Kardiner, *The Traumatic Neuroses of War* (New York: Paul Hoeber, 1941), pp. 5–6. But if failure of executive maneuver or executive incapacity signalizes conflict, that does not obviate the question as to the further specification of conflict. Why does executive incapacity occur? The opposition therefore seems to lack sharpness, and the one above has been retained as equally convenient, despite its formal inexactness.

In the above, we have used the term "character structure" in a general sense clear from the context. It is worth noting that the term "character" is now used by Kardiner to mean individual psychological structure in contrast with the modal or "basic" personality, which is an institutional precipitate. See, in Cora DuBois, *The People of Alor* (Minneapolis: University of Minnesota Press, 1944), ch. xviii, Kardiner's "Conclusions to the Autobiographies," and *The Psychological Frontiers of Society.*

also powerful. Hence the elements of a conflict. There are "difficulties" in the sexual sphere. But the sexual sphere is often conceived as a kind of "model" for what is likely to occur in other spheres of behavior (*Vorbildlichkeit*). Various other elements may be introduced to help out the construction and present the sexual etiology as a convincing and a sufficient basis for the totality of behavior presented. One illustration may be given. Freud discusses the phenomenon of a tortured incapacity to make decisions that is found in obsessional "neurosis." He has this, among other things, to say:

> But this indecision will not confine itself for long to a single group of actions. For, in the first place, what actions of a lover are not brought into relation with his one principal motive? And, secondly, a man's attitude in sexual things has the force of a model to which the rest of his reactions tend to conform. And thirdly, it is an inherent characteristic in the psychology of an obsessional neurotic to make the fullest possible use of the mechanism of *displacement*. So the paralysis of his powers of decision gradually extends itself over the entire field of the patient's behavior.[62]

The second theoretical possibility postulates a certain type of character structure or personality, usually conceived to develop quite early in life. Though the notion of a character structure has a wider range than that of "neurotic" personality, which is only a special case, or a set of special cases, under the more general category, it can be given this special reference, just as can the notion of a "basic personality structure"; and when "parataxic" formations are spoken of, the special reference to "neurotic" personality is usually also definitely intended. But the character structure is a totality; a "neurosis" is a comprehensive way of life. If we choose to speak in valuational terms, we may say that it is a "misconceived" way of life, that may well bring to grief the organism holding to it. But,—and here the divergence from some of the older views becomes clearer—the personality is thought to be so organized that it, so to speak, carries itself along in whatever it does. Certain trends are seen no matter what the character of the activity engaged in. Thus, sexuality, for example, becomes in theory simply one sphere of behavior, in which are likely to be manifested trends similar to those that may be manifested in other

62. *Collected Papers,* vol. III, pp. 375-376.

spheres of behavior.[63] The character of the motivation therein resembles the character of the motivation found elsewhere. As for the effective factors that are conceived to underly the whole character structure, dynamisms such as repressions are still considered to be of the utmost importance, but there is much more emphasis on the total nature of the environment, with an eye especially to its general effect in the evocation of anxiety or hostility. This is, by way of example, the line of attack adopted by Karen Horney. In a generally "bad" kind of environment, especially where there is lack of affection or warmth and genuine respect for a child as a human being, she tells us that "there are several reasons, effective in various degrees and combinations, why a child . . . will repress hostility: helplessness, fear, love or feelings of guilt." [64] She affords brief descriptions of how each of these works out. Thus, in the case of helplessness, the underlying feeling, the "motto," is: "I have to repress my hostility because I need you"; in the case of fear: "I have to repress my hostility because I am afraid of you"; etc.[65] "In various combinations any of the factors mentioned may bring a child to repress his hostility and eventually produce anxiety." [66] This is of course only a very slight indication of the general point of view.

Those who advocate the second point of view have various arguments against the first. Sometimes the arguments take a clinical form, and the libido theory is directly challenged.[67] Sometimes they take a form that brings them more directly within the province of the anthropologist or sociologist. Thus:

> Now we have a hypothesis which seems to prove that sexual restraints are one source of unconscious, repressed hostilities. A corollary to this

63. "Freud stated that the sexual pattern . . . was the prototype of all life patterns. . . . There is little doubt that this sexual pattern is only part of a more fundamental life pattern." Alexander Reid Martin, in the *Kenyon Review* II (1940), "The Legacy of Sigmund Freud: Therapeutic," 140.

64. *The Neurotic Personality of Our Time*, p. 85.

65. *Ibid.*, pp. 86–87. But a kind of special emphasis on sexuality is not excluded by analysis of this type, in the sense that a type of treatment by parents that is likely to evoke feelings of insecurity may fall especially heavily on the sexual sphere. Thus Horney contends: "In our culture the sexual sphere is the one in which guilt feelings are most frequently stimulated." *Ibid.*, p. 87.

66. *Ibid.*, p. 87. *Cf.* also, *ibid.*, ch. v.

67. *Cf. e.g.*, Horney, *New Ways in Psychoanalysis*, ch. iii.

would be that where there are fewer sexual restraints, there would be no repressed hostilities.

I am afraid that this theory of ours is all wrong. We would be led to expect, if it were true, that in a society where there are no sexual restraints in the early formative years, the ego of the resulting individual will be strong, confident, assertive, and free from envy, and will enjoy a high self-esteem. If we look at Trobriand society from this point of view we must conclude either that our theory is wrong, our facts are wrong, or that we have made some essential errors of omission. In this society the individual is exposed to no cultural restraints as regards sex except object incest taboos, which include mother and sister. But . . . all females apart from sister and mother are sexually accessible to him to do anything and everything he wishes. The culture limits the choice of objects, but encourages the sexual aim in every way. After marriage, however, fidelity is expected. Do these people enjoy a high degree of personal security and confidence? No. They are notably unaggressive and devoid of stamina. They are usually weak in the handling of envy and rivalry situations. One can gauge the amount of intrasocial tension from the universal fear of sorcery and frequency of suicide, the fear of sorcery being of course the fear of other people's evil wishes, and hence an indicator of one's own repressed hostility to others.[68]

Evidence of this kind is especially valuable from the social scientist's point of view. And the psychiatrists who are willing to adduce and accept this sort of evidence escape many of the strictures on the Freudian system that the social scientist would have to express. A certain emphasis on the concept of security and a willingness to take into account the influence of social factors, not merely in the sense of prescriptions that enforce "impulse renunciation"—these two features are prominent in the work of the contemporary psychoanalysts we have mentioned. The concept of security, in close connection with that of character structure, is highly amenable to a partly sociological analysis. "Systems of security" as they are built up in different cul-

68. Abram Kardiner, "Security, Cultural Restraints, Intrasocial Dependencies, and Hostilities," in *The Family,* XVIII (1937), 187. Kardiner here also attempts to explain the Trobriand situation. Bearing in mind the peculiarities of Trobriand social structure, he suggests that "where the emotional lines of force of loyalty, obedience, authority, and obligation all run away from the actual individuals who comprise the family, a centrifugal tendency is created, which I suspect leaves the individual very insecure." *Ibid.,* 193. *Cf.* also the account and analysis of Marquesan culture, wherein considerable anxiety is remarked despite a certain "impulse freedom" in respect of sexuality from childhood on. *The Individual and His Society,* pp. 137–250.

tures,[69] and differences in character structure as they appear in one culture or even one social class as contrasted with another,[70] can be readily analyzed. There is no need for the presumption that certain biological factors will enforce uniform types of personality development in all cultures. This, however, does not mean, either, that all possibilities of psychological resemblance from one culture or class to another are eliminated. Some biological "needs" may be universally found, and it may be that certain dynamisms, such as repression, both occur everywhere and can be provoked everywhere under similar situations or stimulations. The sociologist can at least say that here he does not have to impose such strictures as are necessary with regard to the old Freudian theory. Furthermore, the study of motivation takes on a somewhat different appearance now. Motives may be studied in very close connection with social situations.

It thus becomes clear to the sociologist that there is no necessary incompatibility between at least certain types of psychoanalytical theory and a sociological orientation or sensitization to psychological data. We reserve the further discussion of this theme.

## IV. THE VALUE OF THE FREUDIAN PSYCHOLOGY

In our first chapter, we indicated that there are three questions that must be addressed to any psychology purporting to be relevant to analysis of the social order: What is the character and scientific value of the psychology itself? Is it applicable to social analysis? If so, how may the application be worked out? In the foregoing, answers to the second and third questions have been only very partially indicated. The purpose of this section is to give an answer to the first, for the Freudian psychology, deferring answers to the others.

The distinction between psychoanalytical *method* and the *doctrine* of Freud, which has been sharpened by Roland Dalbiez, is primary. Many features of the original Freudian doctrine are extremely du-

69. "The security system of the individual can be defined as that system of adaptations which insures the individual acceptance, approval, support when necessary, esteem, and maintenance of status." Kardiner, *The Individual and His Society,* p. 110. *Cf.* also Ruth Benedict, *Patterns of Culture* (Boston: Houghton Mifflin, 1934), *passim.*

70. *Cf.* Erich Fromm, *Escape From Freedom,* esp. the Appendix, "Character and Social Process"; also Fromm, "Die Psychoanalytische Charakterologie . . ."

bious today. Especially dubious is the underlying philosophy of "pure" or "radical" empiricism, which tends to lead Freud into perhaps the greatest of his difficulties, *viz.,* the "reduction" of distinctively human, institutional, normative phenomena to by-products of biological activity. Freud's sociological theory is, in consequence of this, unmistakably anarchistic. All this constitutes a crucial *general* difficulty of Freudian doctrine.[71] Instead of listing other such difficulties, however, we may profitably take a *specific example* of doctrine and outline the major critical reactions to it.

Some of the strictures that the sociologically oriented psychoanalysts have to make with regard to the Oedipus complex have been noted. The criticisms that Kardiner and others make have either an anthropological or a clinical foundation, or both. There is of course nothing sacrosanct about Freud's ideas, and if clinicians claim that on the basis of practical experience they must modify the theory of the Oedipus complex in one way or another, there is no *a priori* justification for thinking them wrong. As far as anthropological evidence goes, ever since Malinowski exhibited the peculiar directions of the emotional lines of force in the matrilineal society of the Trobriands, there has been reason for a certain skepticism about the Oedipus complex. It is not that Malinowski even attempted to deny the existence of emotional stresses of the *type* which the Freudians had pointed out. He conceded and even affirmed the existence of such stresses, but successfully demonstrated that their direction and even their precise significance in the life of the individual were contingent upon social structure. Thus, he insisted on the value to the Trobriand male of meeting the maternal uncle as an important personality relatively late in life. In Trobriand society, the two functions of the modern Western father as giver of affection and representative of authority are separated. The maternal uncle, who carries out the second function of representing authority, is importantly encountered only after considerable experience with the father, who tends to be only a giver of affection. The peculiar emotional and social difficulties and complications arising from the Western father's assumption of both functions, and precipitating the Oedipus complex, are thus avoided. At

71. On Freud's radical empiricism and its connection with his anarchism, see Dalbiez, *ibid.,* esp. vol. I, p. 108 and ch. vii and vol. II, ch. vi.

the same time, Malinowski recognizes in his very treatment of, and disagreement with, the Freudian theory, the need to examine the patterning of the emotional relations of the new-born male to his male (and female) relatives, in the form of bonds of love and authority.[72]

Further evidence or argument with regard to the Oedipus complex, from an independent source, is pertinent and welcome. Dalbiez distinguishes three cases in his discussion of the Oedipus complex—the genital complex, the sexual complex, and the filial complex. We may simply note that the genital complex in its various forms involves a terminal genital reaction, whereas the sexual complex does not. It is in what Dalbiez calls the *filial complex* that our largest interest centers. His statement requires rather full quotation:

> Are we justified in asserting the presence of the sexual Oedipus complex when its symptomatology is absent? The orthodox Freudians answer "yes"; we have no hesitation in answering "no." The Oedipus complex must be proved, not assumed. Once more we shall recall the principle which governs our whole work; psychoanalysis must be a method, not a doctrine. If there are no indications of sexuality in the little boy's psychic attitude towards his mother, we shall quite simply regard that attitude as non-sexual. This does not imply that that non-sexual attitude towards his mother may not (often decisively) condition the child's future psychosexual conduct. But such conditioning, which in the case of both genital and sexual Oedipus complex is effected by means of homogeneous continuity, is, in the instance we are discussing, effected by means of heterogeneous continuity. . . . In order to understand this point of view, we have merely to recall one of the most striking results of Pavlov's work.

72. See Malinowski, *Sex and Repression in Savage Society* (London: Harcourt, Brace, 1927), *passim,* but esp. pp. 263–273. Kardiner has already been quoted on the Trobriand situation (see footnote 68 in Section III, above) to the effect that "where the emotional lines of force of loyalty, obedience, authority, and obligation all run away from the actual individuals who comprise the family, a centrifugal tendency is created," which Kardiner suspects leaves the individual "very insecure." Malinowski on the other hand has insisted that there is positive value to the Trobriander in having the maternal uncle, or representative of authority, outside the family. A more intensive analysis than has yet been undertaken might possibly show that some aspects of the Trobriand situation confirm Kardiner's view and others Malinowski's. This is a mere possibility. But what is quite clear is that the familial constellation in Trobriand society structures the emotional lines of force in a manner distinctively set off from what holds in the modern West, and that characteristic emotional "complexes" differ significantly under the different types of social structure.

. . . If, for example, a dog has two separate conditioned stimuli, one auditory and the other visual, inhibition by differentiation of the auditory stimulus is found to affect the visual as well.[73] No one dreams of concluding from this that visual stimulation is auditory, or vice versa. It would be scarcely more judicious to claim that, in cases in which inhibition of the filial sentiment later entails psycho-sexual stunting, this relation of conditioning is enough to prove the originally sexual character of the filial attitude. The sexuality or non-sexuality of the psychic attitude of a particular small boy towards his mother is . . . a problem . . . which must be resolved by the close examination of each particular case. . . . If we are asked what is the relative frequency of the genital, sexual and simple filial Oedipus complex, our reply will be easy: we know nothing whatever about it. All that we do know is that the methods hitherto applied to the study of the question of the Oedipus complex are devoid of all scientific accuracy.[74]

It should be noted that these are the remarks of a practicing psychoanalyst as well as philosopher. Dalbiez has formulated his conception of the filial complex quite independently of the neo-Freudians, and it is logically entirely compatible with their point of view at the same time that it is independent. The context indicates that by the filial complex is meant a psychic formation which arises out of a *general* (not sexual) relation to the mother, one of the consequences of which is what Dalbiez calls "psycho-sexual stunting." This is entirely compatible with explanations of the type that Horney, for example, has advanced. Thus, the relation of a mother to a son may be so devoid of genuine affection on the part of the former, with consequences of serious lack of confidence on the part of the latter, that the boy's psycho-sexual activity will, like the rest of his activity, show marked inhibition because it is one sphere of *his* (generally stringently limited) activity. An element from another, peculiarly pervasive, series,

73. If a conditioned stimulus is developed—say by using a note of 1,000 vibrations per second—many other notes whose vibration ratio varies upwards or downwards from that of the original note acquire, within limits, the same conditioning quality. In other words, a conditioned reflex easily gets *generalized.* It may be *specialized* by using or operating stimuli which closely resemble the conditioned stimulus, but without reinforcement by the absolute stimulus (*i.e.,* without giving food, for example, since an absolute stimulus is, one to which the organism responds in virtue of "innate" forces, without conditioning). These un-reinforced stimuli soon stop provoking salivary reaction. This stoppage Pavlov calls "inhibition by differentiation." *Cf.* Dalbiez, *ibid.,* vol. II, p. 57.

74. *Ibid.,* vol. II, pp. 178–179.

comes in to affect the sexual series: substantially, this pervasion from another series is what Dalbiez means by "heterogeneous continuity." Kardiner has made essentially the same point in the following statement about personality determinants in the lives of the Alorese:

As regards sexual discipline, the early conditions of their lives favor a strong attachment to the mother, notwithstanding the many frustrations she causes. Sleeping with the mother and observing parental intercourse would tend to enhance these attitudes. However, the implied discipline in connection with sex is apparently very powerful. *This implied discipline does not refer to sexual activity; its inhibiting influence is created by making the object from which gratification is expected into one to be feared.* The attachment to the mother must therefore have a unique character. It is a strong attachment but one filled with hatred because she is both a gratifying and a frustrating object. *In view of the systematic way in which the mother teases and cheats the child, a very poor basis is laid for strong, tender relations first with the mother and later with women generally.*[75]

Mention should also be made of the interesting and relevant criticism of Alfred Adler. For Adler, generally, the sexual in psychopathology is a mere jargon, a *modus dicendi,* as he puts it; sexual manifestations in a "neurosis" are for him merely a disguised rendering of the genuinely operative motives, which have to do with the achievement of a goal of superiority in accordance with a life-plan aiming at maximizing power and ready to enlist sexuality and its modes in the service of that plan.[76] Adler, like Dalbiez in his analysis of the filial complex, contends that the sexual symptoms of the Oedipus complex are *derivative,* in that their source is not sexual but lies in a certain type of *general* relationship to the mother. In fact, aside from a characteristic special emphasis on "pampering," Adler's view is remarkably consonant with that of Dalbiez.[77] Although Dal-

75. Kardiner, in DuBois, *The People of Alor,* p. 178. Our emphases. For the ethnographic background of Kardiner's statement, *cf.* the account of DuBois, *ibid.,* chapters ii through viii.

76. For the application of this view to the Oedipus complex specifically, see Adler, *The Neurotic Constitution* (tr. B. Glueck and J. E. Lind, New York: Moffat, Yard & Co., 1917), esp. p. 64 and pp. 194–207.

77. This is very clearly brought out in the concise popular statements afforded in Adler's *What Life Should Mean to You* (ed. Porter, Boston: Little, Brown & Co., 1931), at p. 54 and pp. 126–127. Some of the relevant views of Jung on Freud's position with regard to sexuality in general are incidentally indicated in the treatment of Jung below, ch. v, Section II.

biez never mentions Adler he may have known of his work and might conceivably have been influenced by it, although there is no indication of this whatever. Some of the neo-Freudians have been influenced by Adler; [78] however, much of their criticism of Freud's conception of the Oedipus complex and his related formulations on sex has foundations (for example, in various anthropological sources) that were quite unavailable to Adler. And there can be little or no doubt of the independence of the work of Dalbiez and of the neo-Freudians. A significant convergence of independent strains of thought has taken place.

The Freudian conception of the Oedipus complex and of certain features of theory connected with it have been treated in order to exemplify the serious (convergent) criticisms to which a crucial portion of the Freudian doctrine is exposed. There are other portions of the doctrine on which there is very widespread agreement. It is significant that some of these—*e.g.,* strict psychic determination, the conceptions of the existence, influence and importance of the "unconscious," the conception that spontaneous psychic products reveal definite "themes" or emotional tendencies that make up ascertainable patterns—are very closely connected with the *method.* Conceptions of this kind are indeed the presumptions on which the method rests and without which it could not operate. But the distinction between doctrine and method is in principle quite clear. Modern Freudian literature already affords ample proof that many of the original Freudian theories have either been abandoned, toned down or modified, while the substance of the method has been retained. A considerable core of basic propositions both self-consistent and consistent with those advanced by others may be found in the literature today.[79] Examination of this literature also reveals that agreement extends even beyond presumptions or conceptions very intimately tied up with the method, however important these may be. An instance of

78. *Cf., e.g.,* Horney's *Neurotic Personality,* pp. ix–x.

79. One might, for example, compare in the light of this statement Dalbiez' *Psychoanalytical Method and the Doctrine of Freud,* Kardiner's *Psychological Frontiers of Society* and Sullivan's "Conceptions of Modern Psychiatry." An empirical science of course has to satisfy not only the criterion that it have a basic core of self-consistent propositions but also the criterion that those propositions have reference to some sector of "reality."

this is afforded by the positive sides of the convergence between the thought of Dalbiez in his analysis of the filial complex and the thought of the neo-Freudians in the general sphere of the revision of the old Freudian sexual theory. Both these strains of thought imply a marked tendency to take *general* character structure as a very significant and not necessarily sexually derivative datum.

Aside from the scientific merits of the Freudian theory in its orthodox or "revisionist" forms, that theory has a characteristic which is at once obvious and important. It goes directly to the heart of intimate human motives and impulses. It is on its medical side a "clinical" psychology that deals directly with emotions of love and hate, with conflicts of motives and values, with issues that involve the evaluation of alternative courses of conduct, etc., in fact, with a whole range of everyday phenomena closely bound up with virtually everyone's practical interests. The imaginative, theoretical and practical handling of such matters had been largely outside the scope of science and had been left to literature, religion, etc. But it is perfectly plain that the scientific handling of such a subject-matter must be of very large interest to social science. On the level of norms or institutions and social structures at which the latter operates, a clinically oriented psychology is of much greater relevance than any other.[80]

Certain major points made in this chapter may be selected for summary emphasis:

1) The psychoanalytical psychology generally affords poor support to views of human nature that ascribe to the latter a high degree of rationality or foresight or a comprehensive calculating faculty.

2) Since an excessive rationalism, and hedonism, have appeared together historically, it is worth noting that Freud himself finally adhered only to a very qualified hedonism, and the hedonistic bias of the neo-Freudians is even slighter than his.

3) The neo-Freudian theory is already seen, potentially, to allow of a much better integration with the structure of modern social theory than does the theory of Freud. This is true in virtue of the following:

80. *Cf.* Kardiner's *Psychological Frontiers of Society,* ch. i, and ch. v of this study.

a) The abandonment of a theory of *opposition* between pure organism and social environment;

b) The associated emphasis upon the intimate relationship between motive and situation, such that motives are seen to be relational, "interpersonal" and cultural phenomena;

c) The shift from a presumption that certain nuclear, largely biologically given, sexual drives either afford a kind of model for the rest of the personality's conduct or determine the main outlines of the latter to an orientation involving stress upon the concept of a character structure in process of development within a social and cultural matrix from the earliest days. With this orientation there is associated a general bias toward seeing the sexual sphere as one among others, as one that is likely to exhibit characterological traits also found in others, and as contingent, like others, on a basic character structure;

d) An abandonment of the attempt to make the facts of culture and society fit into the framework of a dogmatic biologistic psychology. This particular point will come out more clearly subsequently;

e) A much slighter emphasis than Freud's on "reduction" to, and derivation from, presumed biological (characteristically, sexual) sources, of many kinds of distinctively human phenomena. This statement is designedly left in this loose general form, since for the moment the major concern is to emphasize the implied independence of *valuational* elements in human conduct.

4) In spite of divergences, there is a certain core of agreement and a historical continuity between the views of the old and new Freudians.

5) But this is rather too general a statement, and it is useful to adopt the distinction between psychoanalytical method and the doctrine of Freud. The psychoanalytical method remains substantially intact and should allow of further development. The doctrine of Freud, on the other hand, contains much that must be rejected. The most crucial *general* tendency that must be rejected in that doctrine consists in Freud's radical empiricism whose most serious consequence, sociologically, appeared in his anarchism, and which other-

wise involved him in an unacceptable "reductionism." A *specific example* of an item in the original Freudian doctrine that must be rejected is the theory of the Oedipus complex as it came from Freud. The clinical views of modern analysts like Horney, anthropological demonstrations like those of Malinowski, the combined anthropological and clinical evidence of investigators like Kardiner, the criticisms of philosophers and psychoanalysts such as Dalbiez and the consonant critique of Alfred Adler—all these converge to undermine the probability of the theory of the Oedipus complex in its original form taken as an example of Freudian doctrine.

6) A close examination of modern Freudian literature shows a common core of self-consistent propositions referring to a sector of "reality." Many of the most important of these propositions are closely associated with conceptions that arise from a common method, but there has also emerged some true agreement in "doctrine" as well.

7) Quite aside from the scientific merits of Freudian theory, the *subject matter* of that theory makes it of highest relevance to social science.

# 3. An Approach to the Veblenian View of Human Nature

## I. CRITIQUE OF OTHER THEORIES

THORSTEIN VEBLEN throughout his life was chronically a member of the "opposition."[1] He did not care much for the amenities of the "higher learning," he was sharp in detecting difficulties in arguments about "economic harmonies," and above all, for the present purpose, he was an acute critic of what he conceived to be the psychological underpinnings of economic theory.

Veblen is in his way no more hospitable to rationalistic views of human nature than are the Freudians. His critical reaction to certain aspects of the economic theories preceding his own shows this very well.

He contended that an animistic (or anthropomorphic) bias or preconception informed much theoretical writing. In the light of modern science, economic and social phenomena are parts of a neutral and "colorless" sequence. There is no propensity, conceived on a human model, which orders and constrains the sequence. But, "to meet the high classical requirement, a sequence—and a developmental process especially—must be apprehended in terms of a consistent propensity tending to some spiritually legitimate end."[2] The great anthropologist, Tylor, had said that "animism characterizes tribes very low in the scale of humanity, and thence ascends, deeply modified in its transmission, but from first to last preserving an unbroken continuity, into the midst of high modern culture";[3] and

1. The standard source for the facts of Veblen's life and intellectual background is Joseph Dorfman's *Thorstein Veblen and His America* (New York: Viking, 1934).

2. *The Place of Science in Modern Civilization,* p. 61.

3. Edward B. Tylor, *Primitive Culture* (seventh ed., New York: Brentano's, 1924), vol. I, p. 426.

Veblen inclined to see in economic theory (surely a phase of "high modern culture"), in varying degrees (and with the exception of cases of "taxonomy for taxonomy's sake") the intrusion of patterns of thought reminiscent of primitive habits of mind. For the classical economists, the "ground of cause and effect is not definitive." [4] They look to a "natural law" which shall be a final term in the systematization of knowledge and shall bend observed data to the line of its own bias. The pedigree of the "natural law" is not in doubt, as far as Veblen is concerned. Already in primitive communities there are two ranges of knowledge, one animistic and personal, "the picturesqueness of which has drawn the attention of all observers," and the other impersonal and matter-of-fact. The industrial side of life enforces a matter-of-fact habit of thought, but the large ranges of "social, civic, military, and religious interests come in for their share of attention," [5] and these enforce an apprehension mainly animistic.

The background of thinking, as Veblen conceives it, involves emphasis on the conditioned nature of social science theory. Economists, like others, are creatures of their time and place. The British economics of the eighteenth century is appreciably less animistic, less given to searching out a teleological strain in phenomena, than the French economics of the same time. "The scheme of thought or of knowledge is in good part a reverberation of the scheme of life." [6] And the British community in the 18th century, by contrast with the French (or the German, for that matter) was already characterized by "greater resort to mechanical contrivances . . . and larger scale of organization" [7] in the industrial sphere, besides which, in the light of the character of religious, civil, and military institutions, "relatively, it may be said that the sense of status, as a coercive factor, was in abeyance in the British community." [8] The "sense of status" is conceived to induce a personalistic or animistic interpretation of phenomena at large.

The psychological background of this has been postulated as follows:

4. Veblen, *ibid.*, p. 61. 5. *Ibid.*, pp. 102–103. 6. *Ibid.*, p. 105.

7. *Ibid.*, p. 111. *Cf.* also *Imperial Germany and the Industrial Revolution* (New York: Viking, 1939), p. 82 *sqq.*

8. *The Place of Science*, p. 111.

Each individual is but a single complex of habits of thought, and the same psychical mechanism that expresses itself in one direction as conduct expresses itself in another direction as knowledge. The habits of thought formed in the one connection, in response to stimuli that call for a response in terms of conduct, must, therefore, have their effect when the same individual comes to respond to stimuli that call for a response in terms of knowledge. . . . So that, after all has been said, it remains true that with the growth of industrial organization and efficiency there must, by selection and by adaptation, supervene a greater resort to the mechanical or dispassionate method of apprehending facts.[9]

We are not so much interested in the fact that Veblen is, in effect, in the passage quoted and elsewhere,[10] affording the elements of a kind of "sociology of knowledge," as in the simple point that he contends for a determination of large items of knowledge by cultural or institutional circumstances. His "thinker" or "speculator" is not isolated and not self-propelled. He is rather strictly determined: his apprehension is neither "haphazard" nor independent of circumstances. And what holds for the thinker in this respect will hold also for the "common man."

This leads directly to another criticism of the older economists. By and large they operated with a psychological theory that Veblen found quite unacceptable. On this point, he is at his most insistent and most incisive. Few thinkers in social science have been so "psychology-conscious" as Veblen, and he invariably sought to expose the psychological underpinnings of the theories with which he dealt. It might be thought that even if one admitted that economic or social theories contain psychologies, the relation between the general theory and its psychological components is not intrinsic. Perhaps a casual modernization of the psychological features would do, while the rest of the theory was left intact. But Veblen, in effect, denies this, and the following passage is quoted to illustrate the deep connection that in his view psychologies in social science have with the ostensibly non-psychological components of the theoretical scheme:

It has already appeared above that the second great article of the metaphysics of classical political economy—the belief in a meliorative trend or a benign order of nature—is closely connected with the hedonistic conception of human nature; but this connection is more intimate and organic

9. *Ibid.*, p. 105. 10. *Cf. e.g.*, *The Place of Science*, pp. 1–31 and 32–55.

than appears from what has been said above. The two are so related as to stand or fall together, for the latter is but the obverse of the former. The doctrine of a trend in events imputes purpose to the sequence of events; that is, it invests this sequence with a discretionary, teleological character, which asserts itself in a constraint over all the steps in the sequence by which the supposed objective point is reached. But discretion touching a given end must be single, and must alone cover all the acts by which the end is to be reached. Therefore, no discretion resides in the intermediate terms through which the end is worked out. Therefore, man being such an intermediate term, discretion cannot be imputed to him without violating the supposition. Therefore, given an indefeasible meliorative trend in events, man is but a mechanical intermediary in the sequence. It is as such a mechanical intermediate term that the stricter hedonism construes human nature.[11]

Psychological issues are therefore of central interest for Veblen. His own human agents, as has been seen, are to an important extent the creatures of institutional circumstances, by contrast with the human agent envisaged in the hedonistic conception, who "has neither antecedent nor consequent."[12] It is true that a teleological element in human nature is not to be denied.[13] But both classical and marginal utility theory abstract this element, allowing it (together with a capacity to discriminate pleasure and pain and to prefer the former to the latter) to stand independently of all circumstances as a final and all-important trait in human make-up on the basis of which virtually everything in (economic) conduct may be explained. In the rationalistic-hedonistic view, man exercises his forethought and discretion to influence the course of the economic process in such a way as to make his pleasures balance (or overbalance) his pains. Intelligence is, as it were, subject to no corruptions. It stands aside from given institutional circumstances; it is not affected by them, except as, with different circumstances, the variables that have to be taken into account may differ: the exercise of intelligent forethought and the adjustment of actions to get the "best" results do not differ. Institutions are not conceived to mold human beings in any significant way. Thus, in the line of theory of which Veblen speaks, the institution of ownership figures in this way: "All pecuniary notions arising from

11. *The Place of Science*, p. 157. 12. *The Place of Science*, p. 73.

13. *Cf.* "The Limitations of Marginal Utility," in *The Place of Science*, esp. p. 238.

ownership are treated simply as expedients of computation which mediate between the pain-cost and the pleasure-gain of hedonistic choice, without lag, leak or friction; they are conceived simply as the immutably correct, God-given notation of the hedonistic calculus." [14]

It follows that human nature must always be the same. In the economic sphere, under different institutional circumstances, different notational schemes may have to be used. The material objects in which the rational calculator deals may also be different. But he himself is always substantially the same, whether he uses wampum and shells or money, whether the products of the current technology are physically slight or massive. Hence the "conjectural history" of the economists, and hence the need for taking many among them to task for gaps in general information "on Digger Indians, Eskimos, and palæolithic society at large." [15] It should also follow, at the very least in the economic respect, that if in some manner a Digger Indian or Eskimo could be transferred to the circumstances of modern economic life, he should have no difficulty in working out an adequate economic destiny as soon as he had learned some new terms and familiarized himself with new objects and qualities. His rational human nature should presumably carry over and work intact (institutionally uncontaminated), and was presumably intact in the first place.

But Veblen finds this view of human nature entirely unacceptable. The very fabric of human civilization consists in a scheme of institutions, and the "ways and means" of this fabric consist in the response of human nature

> to exigencies that vary incontinently, cumulatively, but with something of a consistent sequence in the cumulative variations that so go forward,—incontinently, because each new move creates a new situation which induces a further new variation in the habitual manner of response; cumulatively, because each new situation is a variation of what has gone before it and embodies as causal factors all that has been effected by what went before; consistently, because the underlying traits of human nature (propensities, aptitudes, and what not) by force of which the response takes place, and on the ground of which the habituation takes effect, remain substantially unchanged.[16]

14. *Ibid.*, p. 245. Veblen speaks also of "that gift of appraisement and calculation which is the hypothetical hedonist's only human trait." *Ibid.*, p. 223.

15. *Ibid.*, p. 185.

16. *Ibid.*, pp. 241–242.

The theoretical schemes of which Veblen is critical abstract from the features of variation and cumulation, and are therefore left only with the feature of "consistency": so that it happens that they "can reach statical results alone." [17] An institutional account, on the other hand, is given terms by which change may be explained. Unless institutional factors are rather fully considered, not even the human nature of individuals can be adequately understood, to say nothing of the fortunes of communities. For even if one allowed the hedonistic view of human nature to be correct, for purposes of argument, it is nevertheless true that institutions impinge on individuals, and before any pure impulse derivative from an unsullied hedonistic source could work itself out in action there would appear (intervene) the counterpart of the institution as it manifests itself in the life of the particular person.[18] This would appear as an interpolation by way of the individual's habituation in terms of arbitrary local conventions.

In his paper on marginal utility, Veblen indicates the larger bearing of his views by distinguishing between "sufficient reason" and "efficient cause." [19] The former emphasizes the exercise of discretion and forethought, and its focus is on the teleological character of human conduct.[20] But the ground of efficient cause must come in for large consideration also in human affairs, and in fact is of "graver interest" from the point of view of modern science.[21] This ground cannot be formulated in terms of teleology, or rationality, or calculation, or choice. It can only be understood in terms of an impersonal, undirected "sequence of cause and effect." It is of course institutional variation and development that are referred to. The ways involved in institutions, we may add, are not deliberately and calculatingly adopted by individuals, and there is no collective organ functioning for the community as a whole that continually sifts them for subtle purposes of its own, whatever those might be.

17. *Ibid.*, p. 242. 18. *Ibid.*, p. 244. 19. *Ibid.*, p. 237.

20. The paper cited deals with the *limitations* of marginal utility. "It is," says Veblen, "of course, true that human conduct is distinguished from other natural phenomena by the human faculty for taking thought, and any science that has to deal with human conduct must face the patent fact that the details of such conduct consequently fall into the teleological form. . . ." *Ibid.*, pp. 238–239.

21. *Ibid.*, p. 239.

The consequences that such a view as this has may be instanced in Veblen's discussion of the "institution of property." In hedonistic economics, "the theory is confined to the ground of sufficient reason instead of proceeding on the ground of efficient cause." The pecuniary substance of property thereby comes in for consideration only as the peculiar set of terms in which for the time being the hedonistic calculus works itself out. But "the modern economic situation is a business situation," in which considerations of price loom so large that they even invade "non-pecuniary ramifications of modern culture," with the consequence that at length persons themselves are rated in pecuniary terms. If the price system and the habits of thought it engenders are of such significance even outside the business or commercial sphere proper, what shall be said of their effects *within* the business sphere? The marginal utility economists admit "that preoccupation with commercial interests has 'commercialized' the rest of modern life, but the 'commercialization' of commerce is not admitted." [22] Veblen puts the matter positively in giving his sense of the modern business situation, thus:

> Variations of capitalization, *e.g.*, occur without its being practicable to refer them to visibly equivalent variations either in the state of the industrial arts or in the sensations of consumption. Credit extensions tend to inflation of credit, rising prices, overstocking of markets, etc., likewise without a visible or securely traceable correlation in the state of the industrial arts or in the pleasures of consumption; that is to say, without a visible basis in those material elements to which the hedonistic theory reduces all economic phenomena. . . . The hedonistically presumed final purchase of consumable goods is habitually not contemplated in the pursuit of business enterprise.[23]

Money is not, therefore, necessarily a measure of benefits. While the producer gives neither more nor less and the consumer gets neither more nor less, variations in valuation may nevertheless occur. There are changes on the money level, but there need be no traceable concomitant changes on other levels.[24]

22. *Ibid.*, pp. 237, 245, 247. 23. *Ibid.*, p. 249.

24. In speaking of the "money level" and "other levels" we have had in mind Wesley C. Mitchell's distinctions of the "money level," the "commodity level," the "level of sensations" (pleasure-pain), and the "level of general welfare." *Cf.* the first volume of his unpublished lectures on the development of economic

The concrete character of Veblen's institutionalism is exemplified better by few elements in his thought than by his views on money. Since, further, Veblen's views on "money in society" will be of considerable interest to us at a later point, it is well to set them briefly in perspective. J. S. Mill had contended that money is only desirable for its uses, namely, to facilitate the distribution of the produce of industry according to the convenience of those among whom it is shared. "Money, as money, satisfies no want. . . . The difference between a country with money and a country altogether without it, would be only one of convenience . . . to mistake money for wealth is the same sort of error as to mistake the highway which may be the easiest way of getting to your house or lands, for the house and lands themselves." [25]

In this way of looking at the matter money becomes a kind of "glass" through which the percipient student will look to see other and more important phenomena. But for Veblen, money has, so to speak, thicknesses of its own; it has dimensions that must be taken account of in their own right. Money is an institution. It figures as such both in the business sphere and outside the market-place. The money level does not automatically reduce to, say, the pleasure-pain level. Its institutional, conventional character is attested in such phenomena as the "putative stability of the monetary unit." [26] Instead of being simply a wise and convenient device, money becomes one of the most substantial phenomena in the modern business situation. Veblen's analysis of credit and allied phenomena is closely connected

theory, in the Columbia Library, especially on Ricardo. *Cf.* also his "Role of Money in Economic Theory," in *The Backward Art of Spending Money* (New York: McGraw-Hill, 1937), and "The Rationality of Economic Activity: II," in *Journal of Political Economy* XVIII (1910), esp. 205–215. With regard to the connections of the various "levels," it is interesting to remark that even Alfred Marshall admits that in a dynamic economy ("in an age of rapid changes") there is but a "loose connection between supply price and real cost of production." *Principles of Economics* (eighth ed., London: Macmillan, 1920), p. 347. We understand "real cost" in this phrase, of course, in a hedonistic sense.

25. J. S. Mill, *Principles of Political Economy* (fifth London ed., New York: D. Appleton & Co., 1870), vol. I, "Preliminary Remarks."

26. *Cf. The Theory of Business Enterprise,* ch. v, and *Absentee Ownership* (New York: Viking, 1938), ch. v.

with this insight. The analysis may be thought of as one of "money in business."

But aside from "money in business," one may speak of "money in society." The acquisition of money, Veblen contends, is far removed from any consideration of "pleasure." He then says, in terms inevitably reminiscent of *The Theory of the Leisure Class:* "Indeed, it may . . . be true . . . that the contemplation of a wealthy neighbor's pecuniary superiority yields painful rather than pleasurable sensations as an immediate result. . . ." [27]

Veblen concludes his paper on the limitations of marginal utility by saying:

> It is not simply that the hedonistic interpretation of modern economic phenomena is inadequate or misleading; if the phenomena are subjected to the hedonistic interpretation in the theoretical analysis they disappear from the theory; and if they would bear the interpretation in fact they would disappear in fact. If, in fact, all the conventional relations and principles of pecuniary intercourse were subject to such a perpetual rationalized, calculating revision, so that each article of usage, appreciation, or procedure must approve itself *de novo* on hedonistic grounds of sensuous expediency to all concerned at every move, it is not conceivable that the institutional fabric would last over night.[28]

Thus Veblen turns his attention to the institutional dimensions of the phenomena treated in abstraction from those dimensions by "orthodox" economic theory. And those are the dimensions most substantial for him. Veblen's emphasis is therefore on the non-rational (in our second sense) or traditional.[29] This emphasis is very closely bound up with his criticism of the psychology of the orthodox economists as unsound. He introduces a non-rational component which others would tend to exclude from the strictly economic sphere. But traditional or institutional forms mold individual behavior, and thereby have psychological consequences. It should be noted once again that Veblen speaks of the *limitations* of marginal utility, conceiving that a limited amount can be done on marginal utility presuppositions; but he leaves little doubt that he thinks that more can

27. *The Place of Science*, p. 246.
28. *Ibid.*, pp. 250–251.
29. See above, p. 16.

be done in the way of explaining obtrusive economic phenomena by means of his own theory.[30]

Our interest has made for a somewhat uneven and partial review of Veblen's criticisms of economic theory. We have focussed attention mainly on the critique of the animistic preconception itself, on the notion of the strict cultural determination of knowledge, and (most emphatically) on the criticism of rationalism and hedonism. The last especially, as we have seen, leads into the whole issue of institutions, their meaning, their consequences, which will be of constant importance.

Veblen's views have not escaped criticism.[31] The most serious criticism, however, rests upon different methodological orientations. From the point of view of attempts to formulate an "abstract analytical economics," economics needs no particular psychological theory and no hypothesis about motives. Institutional elements may then be defined as "non-economic," and Veblen accordingly criticized for trying to make economics an "encyclopedic sociology."[32] However that may be, Veblen's economics is in the nature of an attempt

30. On the basis of the perspective suggested in distinguishing between "money in business" and "money in society," much of Veblen's work will be seen to fall, in a rough way, into an examination either of the ramifications of money in its first or economic dimension ("money in business") or in its second or sociological dimension ("money in society"). Thus, considerable parts of *The Theory of Business Enterprise* and *Absentee Ownership* may be considered as studies in the first pecuniary dimension. From the same point of view, *The Theory of the Leisure Class* is a study in the second pecuniary dimension. *Imperial Germany and the Industrial Revolution,* in its analysis of the penalty of "taking the lead" suffered by the English in consequence of the heavy encrustation of business and corporate practices (with their technologically inhibitive effect) and of the "conspicuous consumption" that had grown up in the English community, is a study in both dimensions at once. This is aside from the fact that Veblen's absorbed interest in the question of actual production and technological potentialities may lead him to an attempt to show that both pecuniary dimensions ultimately have an inhibitive effect on technology and production.

31. See, *e.g.,* A. K. Davis, *Thorstein Veblen's Social Theory,* unpublished doctoral dissertation (Harvard University, 1941), p. 171 *sqq.,* and *passim;* and Talcott Parsons, "Sociological Elements in Economic Thought," in Barnes & Becker, *Contemporary Social Theory* (New York and London: Appleton-Century, 1940), pp. 601–646, esp. pp. 615–620 and 642–644. A considerable debt of suggestiveness and stimulation is owed to Davis' study.

32. See Talcott Parsons, *Structure of Social Action* (New York: McGraw-Hill, 1937), p. 173.

to explain "concrete economic reality," and to such an economics a consideration of "psychological" and other "non-economic" elements is indispensable. That is the only important consideration for us. It is quite beyond our scope to define the nature of economic science.

### II. VEBLEN'S VIEW OF HUMAN NATURE

What view of human nature did Veblen adopt himself? In the light of his criticisms, we should expect to find that his own work has a distinctive psychological underpinning. The expectation arises directly out of the character of his challenge to the orthodox types of theory.

Among the most obtrusive psychological elements which Veblen introduced into his theoretical scheme are the "instincts," and he inclined to give a primary place to the "instinct of workmanship," defined in one of his early papers.[33] All men, he tells us, have a "quasi-æsthetic sense of economic or industrial merit, and to this sense of economic merit futility and inefficiency are distasteful. In its positive expression it is an impulse or instinct of workmanship; negatively it expresses itself in a deprecation of waste." [34] The significant opposite of the instinct of workmanship appears as the "irksomeness of labor," which is a purely conventional phenomenon. The instinct of workmanship has been settled upon the race by the selective action of biological forces. It is part of man's native endowment, and consequently the convention that labor is irksome appears as an institutional growth opposed to an instinctive endowment. This sort of opposition —between instinct and institution—is quite characteristic of Veblen's thought.

The instinct of workmanship is again treated in *The Theory of the Leisure Class,* substantially in the same terms in which it had been treated in the earlier paper:

> As a matter of selective necessity, man is an agent. He is, in his own apprehension, a center of unfolding impulsive activity—"teleological" activity. He is an agent seeking in every act the accomplishment of some concrete, objective, impersonal end. By force of his being such an agent he

33. "The Instinct of Workmanship and the Irksomeness of Labor," reprinted in *Essays in Our Changing Order* (New York: Viking, 1934), pp. 78–96.

34. *Essays in Our Changing Order,* p. 81.

is possessed of a taste for effective work, and a distaste for futile effort. He has a sense of the merit of serviceability or efficiency and of the demerit of futility, waste, or incapacity. This aptitude or propensity may be called the instinct of workmanship.[35]

But Veblen's interest is, by his own account, not purely or mainly biological. He was, as in the case of *The Instinct of Workmanship,* primarily concerned with "a genetic inquiry into institutions," and such an inquiry "will address itself to the growth of habits and conventions, as conditioned by the material environment and by the innate and persistent propensities of human nature; and for these propensities, as they take effect in the give and take of cultural growth, no better designation than the time-worn 'instinct' is available."[36] The propensities "as they take effect in the give and take of cultural growth"—these, then, are the center of interest. Wesley C. Mitchell also, in a paper largely following and expanding certain of Veblen's points, speaks of "tracing the processes by which habits and institutions have grown out of instincts."[37] The instincts are, then, supposedly dealt with only because they presumably bear upon "cultural growth," and therefore a genetic inquiry into institutions will have to deal with them.

But just what is the instinct of workmanship? It has been defined as distaste for futile effort and satisfaction with productive effort, most briefly. Veblen opposed it to a convention, that of the "irksomeness of labor." The notion that labor is low, menial, degrading, he regards as the outgrowth of specific cultural conditions.[38] This notion is in opposition to the frame of mind that should theoretically be rendered by an instinct. The suspicion arises that the instinct of workmanship may not be an "instinct" at all, or at least may contain non-"instinctive" components. This has in fact been urged by some of

35. *The Theory of the Leisure Class* (New York: Vanguard Press, 1928), p. 15.

36. *The Instinct of Workmanship* (New York: Viking, 1937), pp. 2–3.

37. "The Rationality of Economic Activity: II," in *Journal of Political Economy* XVIII (1910), 216.

38. In this connection, it is interesting to note an incidental comment of Marx's. Adam Smith, he says, treats the expenditure of labor power "as the mere sacrifice of rest, freedom, and happiness, not as . . . the normal activity of living beings. But, then, he has the modern wage-labourer in his eye." *Capital,* vol. I, p. 54, footnote.

Veblen's critics. For example, A. K. Davis repeatedly insists that the instinct of workmanship includes two norms—doing a job well for its own sake, and the goal of maximum productivity of material goods.[39] A somewhat similar position is taken by Talcott Parsons,[40] who relates the instinct of workmanship to the concept of "calling" in Max Weber's sense. The (acceptable) implication in each case is definitely that the complex phenomenon that Veblen called the instinct of workmanship at least in part contains institutional components.

It is true that Veblen deliberately defined "instinct" loosely. But this cannot save him from criticism. He suggested that the instincts or "distinguishable propensities" could be analyzed into, or broken down into, "simpler constituent elements, of a quasi-tropismatic or physiological nature," but for the purposes of social science they could be "handled as irreducible traits of human nature." [41] For a sociologist or economist interested in how instincts take effect in the "give and take of cultural growth," it will appear legitimate to take the propensities or instincts as "irreducible," but Veblen does claim that they could, for other purposes, be resolved into tropisms or cognate physiological elements. This should hold for the instinct of workmanship.[42]

The significance of this point can be indicated only by making appeal to some of the ostensibly non-psychological components in Veblen's thought. T. W. Adorno speaks of the relationship in Veblen's sociology "between his positivism and his Rousseauist ideal of the primitive," and states:

> As a positivist who does not acknowledge any other norm but adaptation, he sardonically raises, in one of the most advanced passages of his work, the question of why one should not also adjust oneself to the givenness of the principles of waste, futility and ferocity which according to his doctrine form the canon of pecuniary decency: "But why are apologies needed? If there prevails a body of popular sentiments in favor of sports, why is not that fact a sufficient legitimation? The protracted discipline of prowess to which the race has been subjected under the predatory and quasi-peaceable culture has transmitted to the men of today a temperament

39. *Cf. e.g.*, Davis, *ibid.*, p. 130.
40. *Structure of Social Action*, p. 529.
41. *The Instinct of Workmanship*, p. 3.
42. *Cf.* the slight qualification of this in *The Instinct of Workmanship*, p. 10.

that finds gratification in these expressions of ferocity and cunning. So, why not accept these sports as legitimate expressions of a normal and wholesome human nature? What other norm is there . . . ?" Here Veblen's reasoning brings him close to the danger of capitulating before the mere existent, before "normal barbarism." His solution is surprising: "The ulterior norm to which appeal is taken is the instinct of workmanship, which is an instinct more fundamental, of more ancient prescription than the propensity to predatory emulation." This is the key to his theory of the primitive age. The positivist permits himself to think the potentiality of man only by conjuring it into a given; in other words, conjuring it into the past. He allows no other justification of non-predatory life than that it is supposed to be even more given, more positive, more existent than the hell of existence. The golden age is the positivist's *asylum ignorantiae*.[43]

Veblen is thus represented as asking, in effect: Why not make one's peace with what actually is? and his answer is that there is a more basic "is." The instinct of workmanship is "more fundamental, of more ancient prescription than the propensity to predatory emulation." Veblen has introduced an ethical norm by the back door, by making it appear as given in man's native endowment. Such and such activity is therefore criticizable because it is "contrary to nature." It is obvious that this interpretation also involves skepticism about the "instinct" of workmanship.

The question of the nature of the instinct of workmanship now broadens into the whole question of man's native endowment, as it is represented by Veblen. He presented a scheme of stages of social evolution in which the "savage state" came as the first great stage, to be followed by the stage of "predatory culture," which subdivides into a "barbarian state" characterized by a warlike, directly pugnacious state of predation and a "pecuniary state" which is, rather, quasi-peaceable. The latter in turn may be divided into the handicraft era and the era of the machine technology.[44] (This deliberately neglects some of the niceties, such as the distinction between "higher" and "lower" barbarism). Veblen is greatly interested in the human nature that presumably characterizes man in the savage state, as judged by his repeated preoccupation with the theme.[45] He admits

43. T. W. Adorno, "Veblen's Attack on Culture," *Studies in Philosophy and Social Science* IX (1941), 405.

44. This classification is given by Davis, *ibid.*, pp. 34 and 39.

45. *Cf. e.g.*, *The Leisure Class*, pp. 6, 7, 18–19, 21, 27, ch. ix and *passim;*

at the beginning of *The Leisure Class* that "unequivocal instances of a primitive savage culture are hard to find," and adds that "few of those groups or communities that are classed as 'savage' show no traces of regression from a more advanced cultural stage." [46] Similarly, in the *Instinct of Workmanship,* after drawing on contemporary primitive cultures for illustrative purposes, he tells us that

> the evidence from these contemporary lower cultures bears only equivocally on the point of first interest here,—*viz.,* the antecedents of the Western civilization. What is more to the point, though harder to get at in any definitive way, is the prehistory of this civilization. Here the inquiry will perforce go on survivals and reminiscences, and on the implications of known facts of antiquity as well as of certain features still extant in the current cultural scheme.[47]

It is therefore a genuinely "primitive savage" culture that Veblen is looking for, a kind of first point in an evolutionary scheme. In fact, the evidence for his hypothesis about such a culture "is in great part drawn from psychology rather than from ethnology." [48] For his purposes in *The Leisure Class,* Veblen takes as fair representatives of the primitive savage culture certain extant communities "without a defined leisure class," and describes them as follows:

> They are small groups and of a simple (archaic) structure; they are commonly peaceable and sedentary; they are poor; and individual ownership is not a dominant feature of their economic system . . . it is to be noted that the class seems to include the most peaceable—perhaps all the characteristically peaceable—primitive groups of men. Indeed, the most notable trait common to members of such communities is a certain amiable inefficiency when confronted with force or fraud.[49]

Veblen again refers to the "peaceable or ante-predatory variant," and "this variant is taken to represent the ancestors of existing civilized man at the peaceable, savage phase of life which preceded the predatory culture, the régime of status, and the growth of pecuniary emulation." His discussion of this variant is accompanied by some

---

*The Instinct of Workmanship, passim; Imperial Germany,* pp. 44–51 and *passim; The Place of Science,* pp. 1–31; *Essays in Our Changing Order,* pp. 200–218; *The Nature of Peace* (New York: Huebsch, 1919), ch. ii.

46. *The Leisure Class,* p. 6.
47. *The Instinct of Workmanship,* pp. 100–101.
48. *The Leisure Class,* p. 21.
49. *Ibid.,* p. 7.

very dubious speculation about the presumed hereditary characteristics of the "dolicho-blond," "brachycephalic-brunette" and other types, the "dolico-blond" type being thought to show "more of the characteristics of the predatory temperament—or at least more of the violent disposition." [50] The whole development of human characteristics, in fact, in the ninth chapter of *The Leisure Class,* as well as elsewhere, is treated by Veblen with many biological flourishes and much vague talk about "selection," social and biological senses of which term he never distinguishes.[51]

In *The Instinct of Workmanship,* Veblen gives a further description of the "primitive savage" or genuinely archaic culture:

> This savage mode of life, which was, and is, in a sense, native to man, would be characterized by a considerable group solidarity within a relatively small group, living very near the soil, and unremittingly dependent for their daily life on the workmanlike efficiency of all the members of the group. The prime requisite for survival under these conditions would be a propensity unselfishly and impersonally to make the most of the material means at hand and a penchant for turning all resources of knowledge and materials to account to sustain the life of the group.[52]

It is clear that under the conditions of the "savage mode of life," the instinct of workmanship would be quite strong and unmitigated, as witness the "propensity . . . to make the most of the material means at hand." A certain benevolence is also suggested in the terms "unselfishly" and "impersonally." Indeed, Veblen speaks of a "parental bent." He tells us that

50. *Ibid.,* pp. 215 and 217; *cf.* also p. 225.

51. *Cf. e.g., ibid.,* pp. 225 and 229; *The Instinct of Workmanship,* pp. 119–120. Veblen has with some justice been called a "social Darwinist," on which matter see Pareto, *Mind and Society,* vol. I, p. 492, and vol. IV, p. 1481, footnote 7; Parsons, *Structure of Social Action,* pp. 219–228; Davis, *ibid., passim.* Abram Harris, discussing the institutional theories of Marx, Veblen, and Mitchell, makes reference to "neo-Darwinism," and, referring to the "neo-Darwinian principles of selection, variation, and survival," says of them that they are "not scientific—that is to say, empirical. . . . They are simply analogies drawn from biology and anthropology." Harris, "Types of Institutionalism," *Journal of Political Economy* XL (1932), 741, footnote. Note also his interesting comment that these principles perform "much the same function as the Hegelian dialectic does in the Marxian system." *Ibid.,* 742. *Cf.* also Harris, "Economic Evolution, Dialectical and Darwinian," *Journal of Political Economy* XLII (1934), 34.

52. *The Instinct of Workmanship,* pp. 36–37.

it is difficult or impossible to say how far the current solicitude for the welfare of the race at large is to be credited to the parental bent, but it is beyond question that this *instinctive disposition* has a large part in the sentimental concern entertained by nearly all persons for the life and comfort of the community at large, and particularly for the community's future welfare.[53]

Moreover,

like other innate predispositions the parental bent continually reasserts itself in its native and untaught character, as an ever resilient solicitude for the welfare of the young and the prospective fortunes of the group. As such it constantly comes in to reenforce the instinct of workmanship and sustain interest in the direct pursuit of efficiency in ways and means of life.[54]

Together, the instinct of workmanship and the parental bent conduce to the material welfare of the group, and in fact bring it about when undisturbed by the working of alien elements. The parental bent "will have had wide and free play in early times, when the common good of the group was still perforce the chief economic interest in the habitual view of all its members." The men and women of the "early neolithic time" "took instinctively and kindly to those activities and mutual relations that would further the life of the group. . . . They took less kindly and instinctively to such activities as would bring damage and discomfort on their neighbors and themselves."[55] The "primitive savage" culture is therefore peaceable,

53. *Ibid.*, pp. 26–27. Our emphasis. Veblen again returns to the question of the reducibility of his "instincts" to tropisms, or visceral stimuli. He now says: "All that is matter for the attention of those whom it may concern." Referring again to the instinct of workmanship, as an "expression," he comments: "The expression may as well be taken to signify a concurrence of several instinctive aptitudes each of which might or might not prove simple or irreducible when subjected to psychological or physiological analysis. For the present inquiry it is enough to note that in human behavior this disposition is effective in such consistent, ubiquitous and resilient fashion that students of human culture will have to count with it as one of the integral *hereditary* [our emphasis] traits of mankind." *Ibid.*, pp. 27–28. Veblen finally decides that what "marks off the instinctive dispositions from tropisms is the indirection of intelligence. It enters more largely in the discharge of some proclivities than of others; but all instinctive action is intelligent in some degree. This is what marks it off from the tropisms and takes it out of the category of automatism." *Ibid.*, pp. 30–31.

54. *Ibid.*, p. 48.

55. *Ibid.*, ch. ii and pp. 89, 120.

fecund, solidary, benevolent; its members are richly endowed with the instinct of workmanship; the culture is characterized by the relative absence of predation and ownership.

Except for some vague biological argumentation,[56] Veblen gives very little evidence for the existence of this first evolutionary stage of the "primitive savage" or "archaic" culture. This is the "Rousseauist" strain in Veblen which T. W. Adorno has remarked, and which has also been noted by A. K. Davis.[57]

Veblen writes that the "surveillance" of the instinct of workmanship and the parental bent "has not always been decisive . . . ; human culture in all ages presents too many imbecile usages and principles of conduct to let anyone overlook the fact that disserviceable institutions easily arise and continue to hold their place in spite of the disapproval of native common sense." [58]

The two benevolent instincts would obviously conduce to the best welfare of the race, but since their "selective control" is "neither too close nor too insistent," "imbecile usages" and "disserviceable institutions" arise, and the primitive simplicity of the savage state is undone. There is a definite implication that mankind would fare well under a dispensation where only the two benevolent instincts were operative.

Veblen indeed postulates a kind of general opposition between instinctive endowment and cultural or institutional set-up. There is some sort of initial congruity between culture and instinctive endowment, which increasingly becomes incongruity or disparity as institutional change goes on. This is well illustrated in the following:

In the course of cultural growth most of those civilizations or peoples that have had a long history have from time to time been brought up against an imperative call to revise their scheme of institutions in the light of their native instincts, on pain of collapse or decay; and they have chosen variously, and for the most part blindly, to live or not to live, according as their instinctive bias has driven them. In the cases where it has happened that those instincts which make directly for the material welfare of the community, such as the parental bent and the sense of workmanship, have

56. *Cf. e.g., The Leisure Class,* ch. ix.
57. Davis, *ibid., e.g.,* pp. 11, 12, 45, 53.
58. *The Instinct of Workmanship,* pp. 48–49.

been present in such potent force, or where the institutional elements at variance with the continued life-interests of the community or the civilization in question have been in a sufficiently infirm state, there the bonds of custom, prescription, principles, precedent, have been broken—or loosened or shifted so as to let the current of life and cultural growth go on, with or without substantial retardation. But history records more frequent and more spectacular instances of the triumph of imbecile institutions over life and culture than of peoples who have by force of instinctive insight saved themselves alive out of a desperately precarious institutional situation, such, for instance as now faces the peoples of Christendom.[59]

In the light of this and like passages, one student goes so far as to suggest that institutions are for Veblen "exploitative mechanisms and hypocritical frauds" that defeat the aims postulated by the savage instinctive endowment.[60]

In discussing Graham Wallas' *The Great Society,* Wesley C. Mitchell comments critically:

Perhaps we have no original capacities which the cave man had not; but before we start in school, still more before we begin to earn our livings and to vote, our numberless unlearned capacities have grown into certain more or less stereotyped combinations utterly different from the combinations of the cave man. It still remains true that "neither our instinctive nor our intelligent dispositions [even as thus made over] find it easy to discover their most useful stimuli" in the Great Society. . . . But happily the disharmony is not that between the original instincts of cave men and the requirements of civilization. It is the disharmony between the requirements of the Great Society and a human nature composed of cave man elements combined with one another in definite forms derived from generations of farmers, handicraftsmen, and petty shopkeepers.[61]

Accordingly, it is not surprising to find the following remarks in Mitchell's review of *The Instinct of Workmanship:*

There is one point . . . at which we may fairly ask Mr. Veblen to modify his language. Just as Mr. Wallas seems mistaken in saying that complex dispositions (in his usage) are free from acquired elements, so Mr. Veblen seems mistaken in saying that instincts (in his usage) are "hereditary traits." In making this statement I suspect that he has momentarily reverted from his own meaning of instinct to Mr. Thorndike's meaning. As

59. *Ibid.*, pp. 24–25. *Cf.* also p. 20.
60. Davis, *ibid.*, p. 16.
61. "Human Behavior and Economics: A Survey of Recent Literature," in *Quarterly Journal of Economics* XXIX (1914), 15–16.

parts of the original nature of man, instincts are inherited; but instincts "as they take effect in the give and take of cultural growth" have important acquired elements in addition to the elements which are inherited.[62]

This suggests that Veblen put "too much" into man's "original nature" or "archaic nature." If Veblen reverts to the meaning of instinct as part of the original nature of man, he makes himself liable precisely to this error of imputing too much to original nature as such. This makes possible the anarchistic strain that has been remarked in Veblen.

These quotations from Mitchell's paper should be compared with the following (still in review of *The Instinct of Workmanship*): "Now the great problems of cultural history arise from the fact that while 'the typical human endowment of instincts' changes but little, 'the habitual elements of human life change unremittingly and cumulatively.' Conflicts are thus frequently produced between the stable instincts and the evolving institutions." [63]

If instinct is here intended in the sense of equipment tied up with man's original nature (as the reference to "stable instincts" by contrast with "evolving institutions" would seem to indicate), then the same error is being committed for which Graham Wallas was so aptly criticized. If on the other hand by instincts are meant "complex dispositions" somehow compounded with "acquired elements" (presumably derivative from institutions) the force of the opposition is considerably weakened, and it becomes difficult if not impossible to see why instincts are labelled as "stable" by contrast with "evolving" institutions.

The anarchistic strain in Veblen's thought is not merely incidental. He carries it with him in many of his researches. *Imperial Germany* is a good example. In this volume, he never tires of emphasizing "the long-term bent and hereditary genius of the English and German peoples." [64] He speaks of "the drift of institutional development in western Europe in modern times," which has been in the direction of a lessening of the force of dynastic autocracy. He then suggests that this drift of institutional development has not so much been creative of or initiative of an "anarchistic" or "non-servile" spirit, "but rather has permissively harbored it, and so has allowed the native anarchistic

62. *Ibid.*, 22. 63. *Ibid.*, 25. 64. *Imperial Germany*, p. 44.

bent of these peoples to reassert itself in a measure, by force of the indefeasible resiliency that characterizes all hereditary proclivities."[65]

He seems time and again to be saying in effect that if only certain distinctive institutional furniture were removed or even if the whole institutional furniture were removed (with the exception of those portions in accord with "native hereditary bent"), there would ensue a blossoming of life and a material welfare unprecedented since the savage state. This is perhaps nowhere better illustrated than in the following passage, where Veblen is speaking of the "mechanistic" or scientific conception and "the modern drift toward free or popular institutions":

> This pervasion of modern communities by such a mechanistic conception and by a bias inimical to prerogative and personal government is, of course, to be taken as a matter of habituation and acquired bent, not a derangement or deflection of the underlying instinctive proclivities of human nature. Yet, the habituation leading to this mechanistic, matter-of-fact drift in Western civilization may presumably be better conceived as a disciplined obsolescence of habitual elements derived from the recent past and no longer enforced by current circumstances. . . . It would appear to be a work of divestment or riddance, quite as much as of investiture or inculcation of a new proficiency. *In the absence of, or under reduced pressure from discipline conducive to personal subjection and abasement, or to the interpretation of objective things and relations in the personalized terms of magical or occult forces, it may be conceived that human faculty will, in a sense atavistically, assert its native bent of matter-of-fact in both of these cognate directions.*[66]

The direct implication is that certain arbitrary institutional forms "discipline" man away from a "native" bias in favor of scientific or "mechanistic" thinking and democratic governmental forms. Many similar passages, with a similar meaning, could be cited.[67]

65. *Ibid.,* p. 68. 66. *Ibid.,* footnote, pp. 268–269. Our emphasis.

67. *Cf. e.g., ibid.,* "Preface," p. vii, pp. 13–14, 17, 102, 136, 166, 168. It is interesting to remark that this strain in Veblen's thought was noted by Henry A. Wallace in his "Veblen's 'Imperial Germany and the Industrial Revolution'" in *Political Science Quarterly* LV (1940), 435–445:

"Probably he [Veblen] was more anarchistic than socialistic in his thinking. He believed our minds and bodies were evolved under rather small farm and village conditions, and that Germans, Englishmen, Frenchmen, Americans and western Russians would all be happiest in living under those conditions." *Ibid.,* 441. *Cf.,* however, the qualified retraction, *ibid.,* 443, footnote 2. Veblen real-

With respect to the general problem of "instincts and institutions," we may review Veblen's work as follows:

He is decidedly vague about the character of the instincts themselves. One critic unequivocally avers that "the instincts are in part moral values, and not merely hereditary drives."[68] And this point becomes significant precisely because of its connection with Veblen's anarchism, for if enough content of a non-hereditary character is piled into the instincts, institutional forms can, quite obviously, become superfluous.

Veblen insists more than once that "of the several phases of human culture the most protracted and the one that has counted for most in shaping the abiding traits of the race, is unquestionably that of savagery."[69] We already know what human nature is like in the savage state, by Veblen's account: it is eminently characterized by the sway of the instinct of workmanship and the parental bent. If this state "has counted for most in shaping the abiding traits of the race," it would appear that beneath various superficial traits, man should manifest essentially peaceable, benevolent and cooperative traits. Yet Veblen spoke also of a "predatory instinct."[70] There is, however, a possibility of his extricating himself from this difficulty. Though he is still insistent, as always, on an initial peaceable stage, he nevertheless states in *The Leisure Class* that "some fighting . . . would be met with at any early stage of social development," and makes appeal to "the evidence from the well-known promptings of human nature."[71] The point in question, he tells us, does not relate to the occurrence of an "habitual bellicose frame of mind," and "the predatory

ized, of course, the dissolving effect of any considerable development of the machine technology and its concomitants on older "quasi-anarchistic" schemes of social control based on neighborhood organization, personal and informal contact, etc. *Cf. Imperial Germany,* pp. 46–47, *The Theory of Business Enterprise,* p. 51 *sqq.,* and *The Instinct of Workmanship,* ch. vii. On the same general question of institutions appearing as coercive overlay on a human nature that finds itself opposed to them, *cf. The Place of Science,* pp. 1–31 and *Essays in Our Changing Order,* pp. 200–218. *Cf.* also Ogburn, *Social Change* (New York: Huebsch, 1922).

68. Davis, *ibid.,* p. 162. Davis, following, as we do, Durkheim and Parsons, thinks of institutions as normative patterns, patterns that are moral from the point of view of the actor, and that serve to define the actor's goals and means.

69. *The Place of Science,* p. 24.

70. *Cf. e.g., The Leisure Class,* p. 29.

71. *The Leisure Class,* p. 19.

phase of culture is attained only when the predatory attitude has become the habitual and accredited spiritual attitude for the members of the group." He says, farther on, that "the predatory instinct and the consequent approbation of predatory efficiency are deeply ingrained in the habits of thought of those peoples who have passed under the discipline of a protracted predatory culture." [72] The "predatory culture" may therefore by its peculiar discipline positively encourage the "predatory instinct," which might then be interpreted as having been latent in men's nature during the savage state. In this way, in any case, a contradiction could be avoided, but again it does not help the precision of Veblen's conceptions of human nature to speak of "predatory instinct" and "predatory impulse" and "predatory animus," as if the terms were interchangeable.

Veblen never gave an adequate solution to the problem of how instincts "take effect in the give and take of cultural growth." His solution was simply of a common-sense, essayistic or verbal nature. This may be briefly instanced in some of the passages of *The Leisure Class*. It is convenient to divide the problem into two: (1) psychological elements, not instinctive, as they "take effect in cultural growth"; and (2) instincts, as they "take effect in cultural growth." With regard to the first, Veblen claims that "the institution of a leisure class is the outgrowth of an early discrimination between employments, according to which some employments are worthy and others unworthy." [73] It is not quite clear how an "institution" can arise from a "discrimination," especially since the latter term is not specifically defined. Again, speaking of "marriage resting on coercion" and of "the custom of ownership," Veblen says that "the two institutions are not distinguishable in the initial phase . . . both *arise* from the desire of the successful men to put their prowess in evidence. . . ." [74] Again, it is not made clear how an "institution" can "arise" from a "desire." "The motive that lies at the root of ownership is emulation." Now it is a "motive" that lies at the root of an institution, in this case ownership. This is in effect repeated in the view that "the dominant incentive [to ownership] was from the outset the invidious distinction attaching to wealth . . . no other motive

72. *Ibid.*, pp. 19, 29–30.
73. *Ibid.*, p. 8.
74. *Ibid.*, pp. 23–24. Our emphasis.

has usurped the primacy at any later stage of the development." [75]

Successively, then, Veblen has spoken of a "discrimination," a "desire," a "motive," and an "incentive" as lying at the roots of institutions. If this may perhaps be set down as pardonably loose usage, what do we read when Veblen makes use of his own peculiar terms, such as "the instinct of workmanship"?

> Wherever the circumstances or traditions of life lead to an habitual comparison of one person with another in point of efficiency, the instinct of workmanship works out in an emulative or invidious comparison of persons.
>
> That propensity for purposeful activity and that repugnance to all futility of effort which belong to man by virtue of his character as an agent do not desert him when he emerges from the naive communal culture. . . . When he enters upon the predatory stage . . . this propensity goes with him still. . . . The propensity changes only in the form of its expression and in the . . . objects to which it directs the man's activity.[76]

If these statements are in some sense intended for an indication of how instincts "take effect in cultural growth," to say that "the instinct of workmanship" works out "in an invidious comparison of persons" is to give a purely verbal solution if there is no specification, as there is not, of the precise mechanics of the working out.

The general manner in which instincts appear in relation to institutions in *The Instinct of Workmanship* has already been indicated to some extent. However, reference should at least be made at this point to Veblen's chapter on "Contamination of Instincts in Primitive Technology." [77] He makes his discussion of the presumptive "contamination" appear "psychological" partly by the very simple device of retaining his distinctive term, "the instinct of workmanship." By the contamination of instincts Veblen means that man projects his own workmanlike bent and more or less conscious creative bias onto the materials with which he works and the objects which surround him. This has an inhibitive technological effect, especially where the items technologically dealt with are farthest removed from any possession of distinctively human traits—purely physical materials and such. The contamination of instincts will do least technological damage where the items dealt with bear a larger resemblance to humans,

75. *Ibid.*, pp. 25–26.
76. *Ibid.*, pp. 15–16, 33.
77. *The Instinct of Workmanship*, pp. 38–102.

as in the case of plants, and more especially of the domestic animals. Veblen states his view succinctly at one point by reference to an "instinctive bias to colour, distort and derange the facts by imputing elements of human nature," and further remarks that this "will unavoidably act to hinder and deflect the agent from an effectual pursuit of mechanical design."[78]

The universal character of Veblen's generalization should be remarked. He stated a somewhat similar point of view later, in connection with his brilliant hypothesis of the "merits of borrowing," in *Imperial Germany.* There, he also claimed rather unqualifiedly that "magical" and "religious" usages cohering around technological expedients necessarily had an inhibitive or impairing effect on technology itself. He made these magical and religious usages analogous in their inhibitive effect to encrustations of conventional usage that had a technologically inhibitive effect in the case of expedients used in modern cultures.[79]

The "functionalists" in anthropology have certainly cast doubt on such a view, especially when it is stated in the more or less unqualified form in which Veblen stated it. According to their evidence, magical and "animistic" techniques come in at the point where scientific control ends, and are neither substitutes for nor derangements of practical technological applications of knowledge where such exist. The Trobriand Islanders, for example, apply what scientific knowledge they have to the cultivation of their gardens. They do not sit back and content themselves with magical activities to make their gardens fruitful without their own work. But their knowledge and control are limited, and, where they end, magical practices come in. Magic has the function of providing people with a specific, ritualized set of activities to perform, in a critical situation where to do nothing would be tremendously disorganizing, since it would enforce the realization of helplessness. Magic also has a cathartic function for the individual, as when he points a bone at a distant enemy to the accompaniment of considerable alleviating vehemence. The function is not to change external circumstances but to change the individual, and the effects may be seen in the change in the individual's perception, which tends to become more "optimistic" after such magical per-

78. *Ibid.*, p. 74.

79. *Cf. Imperial Germany*, pp. 19–43.

formance. Most important for the matters that Veblen was discussing, magic, as in the case of Trobriand boat-building, has the effect of introducing a technologically valuable rhythm into the work of production. There are intermittent stops for magical procedures, which are said by the natives to strengthen the boat. No doubt, literally taken, that statement is untrue, but the magic nevertheless effects an important periodicity and set of breaks in the productive work.[80]

Quite conceivably, magic may not always function in the manner for which the functionalists have given evidence, and "animistic" and "religious" fringes might sometimes have the technologically inhibitive effect that Veblen claimed for them. But Veblen's *generalizations* on this matter are unquestionably dubious. Moreover, no distinctive psychological contribution emerges from his treatment of this theme.

To the vagueness of the category of instinct and the attendant confusions and to the failure to solve the problem of how instincts mesh with cultural growth, we may add the anarchistic strain itself, and thus attain a full view of Veblen's weaknesses in dealing with the question of "instincts and institutions" that he set for himself.

Thus far, we have discovered in Veblen no distinctive or systematic psychological theory; we have rather found definitely challengeable views, and common-sense views simply. Did Veblen, then, ever manage to achieve more than this? This question is best answered in the context of the more general issues as to how he treated the whole matter of institutions.

Veblen was persistent in his attempt to find a thread running from instinct to institution, and our account has not explicitly included at least one other general statement that needs attention at this point. In *The Instinct of Workmanship,* Veblen defined instinct in such a way as to allow the inclusion of "intelligence," in varying degrees. Thus, "all instinctive action is intelligent in some degree. This is

80. *Cf. e.g.,* Bronislaw Malinowski, *Argonauts of the Western Pacific* (London: G. Routledge and Sons, 1922), *passim.* A kind of support for Veblen's view may be found in such a volume as Lucien Lévy-Bruhl, *Primitive Mentality* (New York: Macmillan, 1923), with which should be compared a representative critique like that of Alexander A. Goldenweiser, *History, Psychology and Culture* (New York: Knopf, 1933), pp. 179–185.

what marks it off from the tropisms . . . ," and "all instinctive action is teleological." [81] Again:

All instinctive behavior is subject to development and hence to modification by habit. Such impulsive action as is in no degree intelligent, and so suffers no adaptation through habitual use, is not properly to be called instinctive; it is rather to be classed as tropismatic. In human conduct the effects of habit . . . are particularly far-reaching. In man the instincts appoint less of a determinate sequence of action, and so leave a more open field for adaptation of behavior to the circumstances of the case. When instinct enjoins little else than the end of endeavor, leaving the sequence of acts by which this end is to be approached somewhat a matter of open alternatives, the share of reflection, discretion and deliberate adaptation will be correspondingly large. The range and diversity of habituation is also correspondingly enlarged.[82]

Therefore, the "looseness" or flexibility of instincts allows for the introduction of other psychological elements that are decreasingly of a definitely hereditary nature, and the further course of Veblen's argument allows for the introduction of even "conventional," cultural or institutional elements. He thus begins with a set of non-rational instinctual elements, and finally introduces a set of non-rational institutional components.[83] He never explicitly distinguishes "habit" from "institution," and in fact inclines to define the latter in terms of "widespread habits of thought." [84] Technically, this definition is certainly subject to criticism.[85]

No one has ever demonstrated that any institutional scheme, such as the system of business enterprise or a scheme of social stratification, holds together on the basis of "habits," literally understood. Habits as such have no social sanctions behind them, and are not collective,

81. *The Instinct of Workmanship,* p. 31. 82. *Ibid.,* p. 38.

83. This, however, hardly constitutes a distinctive contribution to the question of how instincts take effect in the "give and take of cultural growth." Veblen's position, as stated here, with its postulate that man has a highly plastic hereditary nature, which enables "learning," has long been a socio-psychological commonplace.

84. Compare the material on Veblen in Mitchell's unpublished lectures on the history of economic theory, in the Columbia University Library.

85. *Cf.* MacIver's criticism of Dewey's comparable definition of customs as "widespread uniformities of habit," in *Society* (New York: Farrar and Rinehart, 1937), pp. 370–371.

*i.e.*, they are not held as common values by the members of some group. The "violation" of habit carries with it simply the penalty of individual discomfort over the discontinuing of a periodic, usual activity. Customs or institutions may have habitual counterparts, but if they were merely habits they could not exercise the compulsive or "constraining" effect (in Durkheim's sense) that guarantees that a society will be held together. Customs, mores or folkways in Sumner's sense, institutions—these are not simply habits. The importance of the point arises from the cohesive effect of institutions and the norms or collective or shared values they involve. Habits as such do not have such an effect, and the problem of how a society holds together or maintains its regular, more or less predictable and limited and characteristic activities, cannot be solved by appeal to the factor of habit alone.

Veblen himself sometimes dealt with institutions in such a manner that it became perfectly clear that he had gone far beyond their definition in terms of habit. A highly important example of this type of treatment is to be found in *The Leisure Class*. For our present purpose, Veblen's treatment of such matters as conspicuous consumption, pecuniary success, etc. may be subdivided into his emphasis on normative elements; his emphasis on the "constraining" character of the normative elements which, so to speak, reach down, to constrain individuals; his emphasis on the pervasion of other classes in the community by the norms of the leisure class.

With regard to the first point—the emphasis on normative elements —it is true that Veblen says that "a standard of living is of the nature of habit," [86] but the context of his chapter on the "pecuniary standard of living" indicates that this is simply loose usage (though it might conceivably be misleading), since Veblen's usage of habit here brings it very close to the notion of norm, or socially established and sanctioned standard. Departure from a norm or standard in this sense would mean not only a purely private discomfort deriving from the lapse of a usual, repetitive procedure, but it would mean also a "discomfort" deriving from disapproval for a "moral lapse" on the part of the members of a community sharing certain values. In addition, in the case of a full-fledged norm there would also be the "twinge of

86. *The Leisure Class*, p. 106.

conscience" experienced by the derelict individual. The putting in evidence of pecuniary prowess is systematically treated as an *obligation* incumbent on the members of the community, and it may well be that when Veblen uses the phrase, "pecuniary decency," he is more than a little in earnest. To be "pecuniarily decent" is to live up to the moral requirements, and the word "moral" also may here be understood in a perfectly serious sense: morality is undoubtedly involved from the point of view of the agents or actors involved. "Any retrogression from the standard of living which we are accustomed to regard as worthy . . . is felt to be a grievous violation of our human dignity." [87]

But Veblen's appreciation of the normative character of institutions is perhaps even better brought out by the second emphasis we have mentioned—that on "constraint." This was an aspect that Veblen saw clearly and sharply in *The Leisure Class:*

The institution of a leisure class has an effect not only upon social structure but also upon the individual character of the members of society. So soon as a given proclivity or a given point of view has won acceptance as an authoritative standard or norm of life it will react upon the character of the members of a society which has accepted it as a norm. It will to some extent shape their habits of thought and will exercise a selective surveillance over the development of men's aptitudes and inclinations.[88]

Individuals are therefore trained in pecuniary norms, and will show a certain conformity to them. In fact,

such human material as does not lend itself to the methods of life imposed by the accepted scheme suffers more or less elimination as well as repression. The principles of pecuniary emulation and of industrial exemption have in this way been erected into canons of life, and have become coercive factors of some importance in the situation to which men have to adapt themselves.[88]

In such passages, Veblen makes perfectly plain the normative and constraining character of institutions. Also, through the emphasis placed upon the individual's being constrained to the adoption of the social norms, Veblen attains his greatest success in the attempt to give different "psychological" foundations to his theory. We have seen the difficulties arising from his peculiar attempts to work in with one

87. *Ibid.,* p. 156.

88. *Ibid.,* p. 212.

another instincts and institutions, but here his position is much stronger. Individual character is affected by the incorporation within the individual ("internalization") of the norms or systems of values current in his community, and consequently a *definite kind* of individual, the product of specific cultural circumstances, goes to work as an economic agent in one community or another.

Lastly, the pecuniary norms pervade the community. There are of course forces that work against this. The exposure of the industrial workmen to the impact of the machine technology in its most recent and most developed forms, Veblen claims, induces in them a "habit of mind" that does not find congenial leisure class standards and criteria. Despite this, the position and prestige of the leisure class (which is "conservative" because "the exigencies of the general economic situation of the community do not freely or directly impinge upon the members of this class" [89]) still give it a tremendous influence over the other classes in the community. Veblen speaks of the *"imperative* example set by the upper class in fixing the canons of reputability." Again, it sets a *"prescriptive* example of conspicuous waste and of conservatism." [90] In other words, the norms found flourishing "on top" seep downward through the rest of the community, even in the face of the counter-values derivative from another source (that is, from the "habituation" that occurs in connection with the discipline of the machine technology).

The pecuniary norms therefore organize the community and hold it together in its present form. As long as they are accepted by the members of the "lower classes," to the accompaniment of the phenomenon of "strain" to reach the "heights," [91] as long as the institutionalization of the scheme of life represented by the leisure class maintains itself, the classes will be held together in one solidary community. Only the definite repudiation by large elements in the community of the norms of the pecuniary class will break down the present cohesion. That this view of the matter is held by Veblen is in fact indirectly verified by his treatment of the presumptive effects of the machine discipline.[92] If those effects could go far enough and be sufficiently unmitigated by effects from other sources (leisure class

89. *Ibid.*, p. 198. 90. *Ibid.*, pp. 204, 205. Emphases ours.
91. *Cf. ibid.*, p. 103.
92. *Cf. The Theory of Business Enterprise*, pp. 302–373.

sources, sources inducing a "bellicose habit of mind" through chauvinistic indoctrination), it is clear that a reconstitution of the community would follow, preceded by a rejection of the values or norms upheld by the pecuniary classes and sustained, in degree, by the rest of the community.

In view of the emphasis on norms, on their constraining character, and on their cohesive effect, it will be seen that Veblen was able on occasion to realize very well the character of institutions. He also recognized the molding of motivation by institutions, and in this way was able to advance what was probably his strongest point in the way of the development of "psychological" components.[93]

### III. THE VALUE OF THE BACKGROUND PSYCHOLOGY

Veblen's psychological theory has some patent limitations. It is logically possible, however, that these limitations are due to Veblen's treatment rather than to the resources of the psychology he employed. We must revert to the psychology of Veblen's day in order to get adequate answers to the three questions we constantly pose for any psychology purporting to be relevant to the problems of social science. What sort of psychology, then, did Veblen actually use, and on examination of it what answers do we obtain to our three questions?

The psychology Veblen used was the psychology of instinct and habit being vigorously pursued in the decade before and after the turn of the century, among whose prominent representatives were men like William James, William McDougall, Jacques Loeb and Lloyd Morgan. These particular men, in fact, had an obvious and acknowledged influence upon Veblen. It was William James who, in a familiar passage, assigned to habit much of what he should have assigned to custom and thereby perhaps helped to preserve in Veblen's work a certain unclarity about the two: "Habit is . . . the enormous fly-wheel of society, its most precious conservative agent. It alone is what keeps us all within the bounds of ordinance, and saves the children of fortune from the envious uprisings of the poor."[94] Moreover, in James as in the others, one can see clearly why Veblen undertook

93. The treatment of Parsons, *Structure of Social Action, passim,* is fundamental to this section; *cf.* also Davis, *ibid., passim.* We do not, however, unqualifiedly accept the Parsonian view on Veblen.

94. *Principles of Psychology* (New York: Holt, 1890), vol. I, p. 121.

the ambitious enterprise of finding out how instincts take effect in cultural growth. The work of the psychologists abounded in efforts to get beyond the discussion of instinct in frogs and chicks to a discussion of instinct in man, to a further discussion of the relation of instinct to habit and distinctively human traits. When Veblen sought to extend the study of instinct to the analysis of culture, he was not engaging in an entirely novel task. His own citations indicate that men like Graham Wallas, in his *Human Nature in Politics,* and McDougall, in his *Introduction to Social Psychology,* were engaging in a substantially similar task.

Our first question deals with the scientific value of the psychology that Veblen employed. In a way, it may be answered quite easily. Without doubt, it had scientific value. This is especially true when it remained close to physiological ground. When it departed from this, it became less and less scientifically trustworthy. But the general statement that it had scientific value needs qualification. Thus, William James, almost at the very beginning of his discussion of instinct, noted an error common among the psychologists, who, in analyzing instincts, proceeded "by naming abstractly the purpose they subserve, such as self-preservation, or defense, or care for eggs and young—and saying the animal has an instinctive fear of death or love of life, or that she has an instinct of self-preservation, or an instinct of maternity and the like." [95] In this statement, James came close to seeing a rather fundamental pattern of thought in much of the work on instinct, and one which vitiates some of the work on motivation generally even today: noting a goal, purpose or object, inferring that there exists a drive or impulse toward it, and naming the latter accordingly, with the net result that nothing is learned about motivation as such.[96]

95. James, *ibid.,* vol. II, p. 383.

96. In a sense, the phrase "pecuniary motive" may be criticized on this basis. The object of pursuit referred to in the phrase is obviously money, which may equally obviously be pursued for a variety of motives. Generally, the same objects may be pursued for a variety of motives, and a variety of objects for the same motives. The Freudian psychology abounds in clinical evidences for this. It should be said, however, that for purposes of economic discussion, a phrase like "pecuniary motive" may still have utility, although it really points to a similarity of objects or goals pursued by different agents. "The motive is pecuniary" merely means that it is money which is sought, and in itself really says nothing about motive.

But James himself devoted the larger part of his chapter on instinct to a listing of instincts, with very loose empirical descriptions, in fact almost belletristic accounts, of each of them.[97] He concedes that his list may be too large or too small: "With the boundaries of instinct fading into reflex action below, and into acquired habit or suggested activity above, it is likely that there will always be controversy about just what to include under the class-name." [98]

If James consoles himself by an affirmation of faith in his physiological method, it should still be decidedly difficult to be complacent about the unity of, and control of, a list that ranges, as his does, from fear to cleanliness. Inconvenient discrepancies do arise in this matter in the work of the various students of instinct. An example interesting from the point of view of Veblen's work is the instinct of curiosity. James lists such an instinct, but states that "with what is called scientific curiosity, and with metaphysical wonder, the practical instinctive root has probably nothing to do." [99] McDougall also makes room for an instinct of curiosity, but states that "to its impulse we certainly owe most of the purely disinterested labours of the highest types of intellect. It must be regarded as one of the principal roots of both science and religion." [100] Such discrepancies inevitably suggest the purely verbal nature of much of the work on instincts.

There was also a good deal of disagreement in the psychological literature to which Veblen had recourse on some rather basic matters of philosophical or methodological orientation. Thus McDougall constantly affirmed that "there is every reason to believe that even the most purely instinctive action is the outcome of a distinctly mental process, one which is incapable of being described in purely mechanical terms." [101] And he insisted that in all mental processes a cognitive, as well as an affective and a conative, aspect was discernible. On the other hand, Jacques Loeb characteristically stated that investigations in the physiology of the brain had been made difficult in virtue of a bias toward "metaphysical conceptions," such as soul,

97. *Ibid.*, vol. II, pp. 403–441.
98. *Ibid.*, vol. II, p. 440.
99. *Ibid.*, vol. II, pp. 429–430.
100. McDougall, *An Introduction to Social Psychology* (Boston: J. W. Luce & Co., 1921), p. 61.
101. *Ibid.*, p. 27.

consciousness, will, etc. "One part of the work of the physiologist must consist in the substitution of *real* physiological processes for these inadequate conceptions." [102] Loeb's confusion in philosophical matters is here sufficiently evident.

The implication that consciousness is "unreal" is plain. Loeb's sympathetic biographer, Osterhout, thus summarizes his outlook on "the fundamental problem of psychology":

> The fundamental problem of psychology is the mechanism of associative memory and the manner in which stimuli are transmitted; the method of attack is to try to discover what properties of colloids make such phenomena possible. For the solution of these problems we must use the methods of physical chemistry, particularly as employed in the study of protoplasm.[103]

McDougall characteristically pushed his inquiries "upward," into human data and social relationships and, so far from attempting to reduce instincts to chains of reflexes or tropisms or the like, sought to discover in them, even on the lowest animal levels, the germs of "consciousness" or "intelligence" or "will." Loeb, on the other hand, pushed his inquiries "downward," and sought to "reduce" the data of physiology and even of psychology to the terms of physics or physical chemistry.[104] This kind of discrepancy in outlook may easily have created difficulties for Veblen in his attempt to trace the influence of instinct in cultural growth. A sense of the very real nature of norms or institutions plus a haunting feeling that perhaps after all they were not so very remote from instinct or tropism or reflex could well have resulted precisely in the situation we find in Veblen's work: much that is genuinely institutional is given recognition and made

102. *Comparative Physiology of the Brain and Comparative Psychology* (London: J. Murray, 1901), "Preface," p. v.

103. W. J. V. Osterhout, "Biographical Memoir of Jacques Loeb," *Biographical Memoirs of the National Academy of Sciences*, vol. XIII, paged pp. 318–401, n.d., p. 334. Osterhout quite properly comments with regard to Loeb that "faith in mechanism became the religion to which he devoted his life." *Ibid.*, p. 320.

104. *Cf.* the repeated statements in *Comparative Physiology of the Brain, passim,* to the effect that living organisms are machines and can only be explained on the principles used by the physicist. *Cf.* also the characterization of Loeb as a brilliant experimentalist but poor biological thinker in the philosophically well balanced Erik Nordenskioeld's *History of Biology* (New York: Tudor Publishing Co., 1935), p. 606.

to count in the treatment of human relationships, but with a fumbling biological hand that puts norms into the sphere of instincts.

There were, then, some serious limitations upon the scientific value of the psychology of instinct and habit. It contained some discrepancies which indicated an area of ignorance or mere verbal play, and others which indicated a divergence in philosophical or methodological tendency that could scarcely be reconciled. Such divergence in itself certainly does not detract from the scientific character of a field of investigation; but it was accompanied in this case by a good deal of sheer fruitless polemicism, as witness Loeb's metaphysics of mechanism, which constituted, in effect, a substitute for close analysis of the problem in which, after all, a majority of the psychologists were mainly interested—the workings of instinct and habit in man and the relationship of his animal to his human endowment.

Could this psychology be useful for sociological purposes? The question has a historical and a logical side: Was it actually shown to be useful for sociological purposes? If it failed, historically, can its potential utility for social science nevertheless be demonstrated from the nature of the psychology itself? Historically, Veblen did not find a great deal to help him in his attempt to construct a socially or culturally useful theory of human nature, at least not in the psychologists whom he knew. Graham Wallas was in Veblen's day making an attempt along similar lines, but the only professed psychologist known to Veblen who was ostensibly doing work, in any systematic way, toward relating the theory of instinct to the theory of society, was William McDougall. The poverty of McDougall's resources when he comes to the crucial points of his work, those at which he assesses "the operation of the primary tendencies of the human mind in the life of societies," throws a very favorable light, by contrast, on Veblen's efforts in *The Instinct of Workmanship.*

McDougall began his work with a courageous statement that holds as true today as when he made it:

> The department of psychology that is of primary importance for the social sciences is that which deals with the springs of human action, the impulses and motives that sustain mental and bodily activity and regulate conduct; and this, of all the departments of psychology, is the one that has re-

mained in the most backward state, in which the greatest obscurity, vagueness and confusion still reign.[105]

Like Veblen, McDougall is very skeptical of hedonism and rationalism. He even reverses a question that Henry Sidgwick had posed as to why men "*sometimes* act unreasonably and otherwise than they ought to act." He contends staunchly that "men are moved by a variety of impulses whose nature has been determined through long ages of the evolutionary process without reference to the life of men in civilized societies," and the question becomes for him, then: "How can we account for the fact that men so moved ever come to act as they ought, or morally and reasonably?" [106] In consonance with this, he observes in criticizing the psychology of the classical economics that "mankind is only a little bit reasonable and to a great extent very unintelligently moved in quite unreasonable ways." Interest is enhanced when McDougall states that "it is the fundamental and all pervading character of their influence upon the social life of mankind which alone gives the consideration of instincts its great practical importance." [107]

It would be pointless to give a full account or criticism of McDougall's psychology, but a few high points need to be mentioned. McDougall's psychology provides a framework for questions like: Is *x* an instinct or not? What are its cognitive, affective and conative aspects? Is *y* a primary or a secondary emotion? There does not emerge a theory of human nature, except for the bare rudiments of such a theory as are given by (1) the recognition that man has some kind of hereditary endowment and some biological kinship with the animals; (2) the enunciation of a few useful "principles" common in the psychology of the day; (3) the statement of haphazard psychological insights. The discussion of the instincts usually proceeds by an assertion that they are instincts, agreement or disagreement with some other psychologist who has also given an opinion about them, and a descriptive passage making appeal to common experience or common knowledge.

105. *Introduction to Social Psychology*, pp. 2–3.
106. *Ibid.*, p. 10. There is perhaps something of an implication in McDougall's question of a sheer opposition between "nature" and "society."
107. *Ibid.*, p. 11 and p. 31, footnote.

Where McDougall does render a fairly effective account of certain aspects of human nature, as in his discussions of socialization and the moral tradition,[108] it is most significant that substantially the same treatment as he gives could be given without the use of any particular theory of instinct. A few slight verbal changes would make no one conscious that McDougall held to any such theory. Scattered statements on institutions prior to McDougall's formal treatment of the instincts and emotions in society do not bode well for that treatment. Thus, for example, he makes the comment on "revenge" and "moral indignation" that they are "the main roots of all justice," although neither would suffice to secure the efficient administration of the latter.[109] Nor would both together suffice. This is, in principle, the same sort of error as Veblen committed when he spoke of a "discrimination" or a "desire" or a "motive" or an "incentive" as lying at the roots of institutions. At another point, McDougall shows some awareness that it is not possible to derive institutions directly from emotions, that there is need for intermediaries of some sort. In connection with Shand's conception of sentiment as a more or less "organized system of emotional dispositions centred about the idea of some object," he observes:

> The growth of the sentiments . . . is the organization of the affective and conative life. In the absence of sentiments . . . all our social relations and conduct, being based on the emotions and their impulses, would be correspondingly chaotic, unpredictable and unstable. It is only through the systematic organization of the emotional dispositions in sentiments that the volitional control of the immediate promptings of the emotions is rendered possible. Again, our judgments of value and merit are rooted in our sentiments, and our moral principles have the same source, for they are formed by our judgments or moral values.[110]

There is at any rate some recognition in this passage of the need for the introduction of "higher" terms, closer to the normative level than instinct or emotion, before man as a member of society can be effectively dealt with by the psychologist. Unfortunately, McDougall makes no effective use whatever of the conception of sentiment in his discussion of the "primary tendencies" in the "life of societies."

108. *Ibid.*, chs. vii and viii. 109. *Ibid.*, pp. 148–149.
110. *Ibid.*, pp. 164–165.

Some social Darwinism, some haphazard anthropological and historical information, some "conjectural history," much discursiveness and a liberal use of the term "instinct"—these are the major ingredients of his treatment of "the operation of the primary tendencies of the human mind in the life of societies." The general tenor of the treatment can only be given by some quotation from it, since there is simply no sustained analysis that could be given serious or systematic consideration. He thus summarizes his treatment of the "gregarious instinct":

> We may briefly sum up the social operation of the gregarious instinct by saying that, in early times when population was scanty, it must have played an important part in social evolution by keeping men together and thereby occasioning the need for social laws and institutions; as well as by providing the conditions of aggregation in which alone the higher evolution of the social attributes was possible; but that in highly developed societies its functions are less important, because the density of population ensures a sufficient aggregation of the people; and that, facilities for operation being so greatly increased among modern nations, its direct operation is apt to produce anomalous and even injurious social results.[111]

We should expect that an "instinct" whose effect is to keep men together would do so. The contribution made by the discussion of the gregarious instinct is palpably very small. The following is a fair extract from a discussion of the "instinct" of acquisition:

> The importance of the instinct of acquisition . . . is due to the fact that it must have greatly favored, if it was not an essential condition of, that accumulation of material wealth which was necessary for the progress of civilization beyond its earliest stages.
>
> There are still in existence people who support themselves only by hunting and the collection of wild fruits, having no houses or fixed places of abode, nor any possessions beyond what they carry in their hands from place to place. Among them this instinct would seem to be deficient; or perhaps it is, that it never is able to determine the formation of a corresponding habit owing to their wandering mode of life. Among pastoral nomads the working of the instinct is manifested in the vast herds sometimes accumulated by a single patriarchal family.[112]

This scarcely requires any comment except the obvious one that it is social thinking at its very poorest. The full value, such as it is,

111. *Ibid.*, p. 308.

112. *Ibid.*, p. 329.

of McDougall's treatment of instinct in society would have been preserved without any reference whatever to instinct psychology. The only possible conclusion is that the instinct psychology, in his hands, is virtually a complete failure when it comes to discussion of phenomena that are properly of interest to the social scientist.

Graham Wallas, who was not a professional psychologist, made a plea for the re-introduction of questions of human nature into the science of politics in the same year (1908) in which McDougall published his *Social Psychology*. He also felt that there had been excessive rationalism in the older English psychology: indeed, he begins his work with the statement: "Whoever sets himself to base his political thinking on a re-examination of the working of human nature, must begin by trying to overcome his own tendency to exaggerate the intellectuality of mankind."[113] This tendency to "exaggerate the intellectuality of mankind" is the target of Wallas' repeated criticism, and his own corrective for it is the attempt to think about politics in the terms rendered by the psychology of instinct and habit, although, like Veblen, he scarcely denies that "men can and do reason."[114] He undoubtedly saw clearly the relevance of the limitations of rationality to the general problems of democracy and based some intelligent discussion on this insight.[115] But his book gives little or no reason for thinking that as enlightened an exposition of politics as his could not have been given without the apparatus specifically afforded by the instinct psychology. It may be that, historically, in the development of English psychology, the rise of the theory of instinct gave particular stimulation to men like Wallas and sharpened for them the "intellectualism" of classical psychological propositions, but there is no reason to assume that the theory of instinct is the sole possible antecedent for a general insight into the limitations of rationality. That theory does undoubtedly, in a general way, suggest such limitations, but the claim to a special contribution to social science is weakened if other, independent formulations have a similar effect. Thus, at about the same time as Wallas was writing, Robert Michels' empirical studies of German and Italian social democracy were affording him insights into the limitations of rationality in politics at least as

113. *Human Nature in Politics* (London: A. Constable & Co., 1908), p. 21.
114. *Ibid.,* Pt. I, ch. iv.
115. *Ibid.,* Pt. II.

effective as those of Wallas, and without benefit of the particular psychology which the latter employed.[116]

The limitations of the theory of instinct as a psychology for social science purposes are evident from the nature of the theory itself, even apart from the historical failure noted. The theory was at its best and strongest at the points of its origin, when it remained close to the facts of animal behavior. It lacks adequate terms to make a transition to social behavior. The attempt to make it useful for the purposes of social science inevitably bogs down in purely verbal formulations or in a neglect of specifically social or institutional phenomena. In the absence of intermediate terms to make the transition to social phenomena, which the theory does not even suggest except dimly in such of its portions as stimulated analysis of habit and sentiment in man, it is small wonder that Veblen found so few resources to his hand. McDougall failed in his attempt; Graham Wallas did not succeed in showing that the theory had any special utility for the purposes of social science; Jacques Loeb was a brilliant physiologist whose mechanistic pronouncements from the point of view of social science were at best programmatic; William James' discussions of instinct and habit terminated in purely practical and pedagogic suggestions. Since the answer to the second of our questions addressed to theories of human nature—whether they can be utilized for the purposes of social science—is in the negative for the theory of instinct, our third question need not be raised.[117]

116. Robert Michels, *Zur Soziologie des Parteiwesens in der Modernen Demokratie* (Leipzig: W. Klinkhardt, 1911).

117. We answer the second question in the negative, not because the theory of instinct is completely useless for the purposes of social science, but because it is not a systematic theory of human nature that may, at least potentially, be significantly integrated with the body of propositions of social science.

# PART TWO

# *Clinical Psychology and Social Theory*

# *4. Reason and Anarchism*

PART II carries forward the analysis of the effect of a psychology upon an associated social theory. It begins with an analysis of "reason" and rationality, and of anarchism, in Freud and Veblen. This analysis will pose some basic questions. Even when we treat of the variants in clinical psychological theory represented by Adler and Jung and neo-Freudianism, the purpose is to keep a firm grip on the distinctive character of each of the psychologies dealt with and to pose clearly the question of what place is given to normative elements in the treatment of the individual and in such treatment as there may be of social structure. The design is to indicate what paths may be and actually have been followed for a fruitful integration of clinical psychology and social theory. Many questions previously raised are raised again in order to give them fuller treatment. A basic premise is that the concept of norm or value must be taken as central and organizing in both clinical psychology and social theory as a condition for the development of significant relations between the two.

## 1. THE MEANING OF REASON

We have previously emphasized the relational character of both rationality and irrationality. Their relational character is a fundamental if not quite explicit point in the psychology of Freud. In order to state clearly the issues centering around the status of reason in both Freud and Veblen, it is necessary to raise a few philosophical points. In our previous and preliminary treatment of rationality, we noted the intimate connection of the concept of the irrational with the notion of an intrusion of an alien, "distorted" element. This needs further consideration.

Irrationality has been indicated to have a close relationship to conflict of purposes, and Freud's theory obviously puts great emphasis on conflict. Logically, conflict involves a polar concept, such as "balance" or "harmony" or "equilibrium." In Freud's view, mind actually consists in or is determined by an interplay of emotional forces. But all the "forces" or elements in the "abnormal" are also present in the "normal" mind. Normality or abnormality is a question of the relative "strength" or "quantity" of the various elements or forces. Conflict itself arises from exaggeration. Many of the terms that Freud and the Freudians use are, it is true, somewhat metaphorical expressions taken from the language of physics, but in the absence of others they are useful in roughly indicating the character of the phenomena that the clinical psychologists attempt to describe. Whatever the value of the various terms used, however, there can be no doubt of the fundamental place of the conception of conflict, and about this term it is essential to be quite clear. But if conflict is fundamental, its polar opposite (whatever term we apply to it—balance, harmony, equilibrium) is equally so. It is important to notice that a concept or term like balance or harmony would not be particularly significant in a psychology like that of Janet, for whom mental illness is much more a "deficiency" phenomenon than one of conflict.[1]

The connection between conflict and irrationality, as the clinical psychologist deals with them, is fairly plain. Conflict is emotional conflict, and its results or manifestations in behavior are characterized as irrational. But what, precisely, enables the psychologist to characterize a mode of conduct or a modality of thought as irrational (or "distorted")? Irrationality as a concept, obviously, logically involves the concept of rationality. At least an implicit appeal is made to reason when something is characterized as irrational. The psychologist may say to a patient that to refuse to work is irrational, that such a refusal is even in a sense a form of suicide: refusal to work in the absence of support from others might have serious objective consequences. But it is irrational only in relation to a set of purposes that the patient is presumed to have. It is irrational only if he wishes to attain certain goals which a refusal to work might tend to defeat.[2]

1. For an effective contrast of the deficiency and conflict views, see Dalbiez, *ibid.*, vol. I, pp. 189–191.

2. In orthodox Freudian discourse there is a marked tendency to speak of a conflict of instincts, rather than one of purposes or goals. To avoid constant qualifications in our treatment, this tendency is not particularly emphasized.

From this point of view, the problem of therapy is to achieve greater consistency among purposes, some of which are unconscious. Or if we note the plain tendency in Freud's psychology to pose the problems of mental health in terms of the energy quantities that accrue to different instincts or instinct-systems, the problem of therapy is one of the redistribution of energy. Whether energy in the psychic system be conceived as general "libido" in the sense of Jung, or as specifically sexually originated libido, it remains true that one kind of energy distribution will result in behavior that the psychologist will mark as rational and another in behavior that he will mark as irrational.

If so, the conception of a balance or harmony among the energies is posited by implication, and is intimately associated with the concept of rationality. Or else, balance or harmony among purposes is posited. We may henceforth refer mainly to conflict of purposes and, without abandoning the conception of the unconscious, we may say that the individual in conflict has "choices" and must "make up his mind" what goals he will finally adhere to. His major goals or purposes are such that he cannot follow them out or realize them all at the same time.

Conflict precipitates irrationalities. Balance or harmony is manifested in rational behavior. It is useful to recall that in the history of philosophical thought, the term reason has had at least three distinguishable meanings: (1) It has been used to refer to a certain order in things: "nature" shows some conformity to "law"; it is not utterly arbitrary or haphazard, and to that extent manifests "reason." (2) The term has been used to refer to that human faculty which typically enables the apprehension of such phenomena as that of a certain order in things. (3) It has been used to refer to what we have so far termed balance or harmony. The first meaning is of no particular interest to us, but the second and third are. It is in its second historical meaning, rationality or reason *as faculty,* that the term has been most familiarly used in social science. Veblen's attack on the psychology of the economists was an attack on the large scope given to reason in this sense. Reason as faculty enables apprehension of order in things, but also enables calculation of chances, shrewd gauging of alternatives, etc. The third meaning underlies the clinical psychological conception of irrationality and is of real importance even outside clinical psychology, in the realm of social science.

When we say that any psychology presumes a great deal of rationality, the reference is to the view taken of the scope of a concrete human *faculty,* but when we speak of reason or balance in mental constitution (or in other systems) the reference is to an abstract *form.* Thus, "neurosis" is not incompatible with the existence of acute "intelligence," although that "intelligence" may be severely bounded in that it will not extend into substantial insight into the nature of the self. We are inevitably brought back to the question of relationships among important goals or purposes held by the same individual. Conflict of goals or purposes results in irrationality, in specific modes of behavior or lines of thought that the clinical psychologist will unhesitatingly call irrational. If we revert to the language of "energies" for a moment, a balance of energies or forces is not itself in any sense a concrete *force,* but only a type of ordered *relationship* among forces. But, whatever language be employed, we must, if we are to avoid a psychology metaphysical in the worst sense, always refer to the actual constitutions of individuals. If we attempt to show that the concept of rationality or reason (as form) is inseparable from that of balance or harmony, great care is needed to demonstrate that we are talking about a balance among elements really present, not attributed or projected.

As any individual turns out in any particular culture, or in any particular social class, he will have a particular moral constitution. If there are elements in the totality of that moral constitution in conflict with one another a problem of resolution of conflict is presented to the clinical psychologist. The psychologist, however, can only deal with what is actually or potentially present in the individual. He deals, say, with a "middle-class" American, not with an upper-caste Hindu or someone else. He has to achieve resolution of conflict in terms of the moral imperatives present in the individual confronting him. Balance or resolution of conflict has reference to the bringing about of consistency among these moral imperatives or among purposes and goals in the individual's total universe of goals.[3]

3. To speak of "moral constitution" at this point conveniently organizes our materials. For fuller perspective on our use of this term, *cf.* ch. v.

Let us say that the psychologist deals with a "middle-class" individual whose marked alcoholism leads to "shame" and "unhappiness." Investigation reveals a fairly typical pattern of recoil from serious work and responsibility because of fears from an unconscious source. A considerable part of therapeutic procedure must then consist in a detailed demonstration of the incompatibility of the *results* of alcoholism with the goals *otherwise* held by the individual.[4] Appeal must be made to the individual's own sense of the irrationality of his behavior. Irrationality appears, even superficially, as an absence of harmony between a set of purposes (avowed or unavowed) and a set of results (in clinical theory also ultimately reducible to something like "purpose.") The course of clinical investigation reveals that the individual's revolt against work and responsibility is connected with a refusal to be stereotyped, to be made a cog in a machine. The individual has real potentialities for independence; the revolt against work as such is seen, however, to have been "mistaken" (always in terms of what the individual *himself,* however obscurely, "wants") and exaggerated. Hence, irrationality. Greater rationality is achieved when the "valid" element in the revolt is precipitated out and adhered to, and the "invalid," "infantile" element abandoned. The individual was "confused" and "defeated himself," not in that he was pursuing a line of conduct radically without "value," but only in that he was exaggerating a line of conduct which to an extent had a perfectly "sensible," understandable background in terms of the kind of individual he was. "Exaggeration" must also refer to the individual's own constitution.

The following remark by Dalbiez is significant: "Freud is certainly no philosopher, but he has grasped, with an extraordinary lucidity, the application in the limited field of the neuroses of a metaphysical principle unknown to him, that the ultimate root of evil lies in the opposition of goods."[5]

In our hypothetical case, it is a "good" to desire not to be de-personalized or made into an automaton performing meaningless work. In

4. To underline "results" is to be neutral and behavioristic. Clinically, the "results" may nevertheless be shown to be "desired ends" in the sense that they are the outcome of a system of "unconscious purposes," which would then be in conflict with overt purposes.

5. *Ibid.,* vol. I, p. 201.

any case, the individual's value system might hardly enable him to give up this desire. It is also a "good" to accept responsibility and perform work. In any case, the individual is capable, actually or potentially, of holding to such a view. "Evil" arises from the "opposition" occasioned by such an emphasis on the first "good" as to leave no room for the second; "evil," finally, would be eliminated by establishing a balance between the two "goods." [6] The individual's behavior would cease to manifest various irrationalities. A new type of relationship among the components of his moral make-up would supervene. The psychologist would now characterize his behavior as much more *rational,* and the reference would clearly not be to the individual's ability to reason or calculate or manipulate in a narrow sense, but rather to the form of a relationship among moral-constitutional components.

In principle, there need be no moral "legislation" in this. Certainly no one has directly "legislated" the individual's illness. His own constitution or make-up has been determinative. Although the psychologist must always address himself to particular moral constitutions, this does not exclude the possibility of finding common denominators in different constitutions; and whatever the concrete problems presented by an individual, as long as conflict is present, then, just as conflict itself is an indispensable general conception, so its polar opposite (balance, harmony, equilibrium) is an indispensable general conception, in principle applicable to all cases. When the form which we note by some such term as balance is present, rationality or reason in the third historical meaning noted is also present.

With regard to the need for applying the conception of rationality or balance to analysis in terms of elements actually present, it is patent that to different agents, even within the same culture, actions of various types have a quite different significance. Theft, for example, may arouse "shame" or damage "self-respect" in one person and not in another, or it may function to arouse these sentiments in quite different degree in one person and another. In the prescriptions of goals and of the limited ways to attain them that are involved in every cul-

6. An acute analysis of reason and balance in the field of ethics is afforded in the five volumes of George Santayana, *The Life of Reason* (New York: Scribners, 1905).

tural system, disjunctions arise frequently, so that at certain levels in the social structure the goal prescriptions are retained while the prescriptions with regard to means of attaining them lose hold.[7] This suggests that the clinical psychologist might easily go astray in expecting to find among individuals of different social strata precisely the same moral components. Insofar as structural differences occur and goals-means disjunctions appear, they should be reflected in moral constitutions. The problem of balance or the incidence of balance would obviously be generically the same only for generically similar individuals.

It should be noted as an abstract possibility that there may be individuals with "superegos" so weak that there could be virtually no point of sympathetic moral contact between them and others, while at the same time they were free of conflict. Such evidence as we have suggests the rarity of such individuals.[8] But if they existed, even if they were "anti-social" there could be no question of a psychologist's finding irrationality or convincing them of its presence so long as conflict was genuinely absent. There is nothing "sick" or "infantile" or "irrational" in a tiger let loose in a city street. "Irrationality" is meaningless unless it has reference to some such phenomenon as conflict of purposes and unless the purposes in conflict are actually present in the particular individual, not in some other. Another type of case suggests a theoretical difficulty rather readily resolved. The individual, say, persistently refuses to respond, but answers all demonstrations of the irrationality of his conduct by some equivalent of the colloquial "So what?" Despite his refusal to respond by a genuine acknowledgment of the presence of irrationalities, the individual may still be said to be involved in them if there is objective evidence

7. See Robert K. Merton, "Social Structure and Anomie," *American Sociological Review* III (1938), 672–682.

8. A recent study of a "psychopathic" individual is interesting in this light in that it implicitly reveals the susceptibility of the particular psychopath studied to at least *some* rather general moral appeals current in our culture. This is especially important because the author of the study specifically defines psychopathy in terms of inaccessibility to, and intolerance of, "the demands and pleas of the community," and regards the psychopath as having a "stunted" superego. See Robert M. Lindner, *Rebel Without a Cause: The Hypno-analysis of a Criminal Psychopath* (New York: Grune and Stratton, 1944), pp. 1–14 and *passim*.

of "conflict" in the form of "suffering," "unhappiness," etc. Although it cannot be too strongly emphasized that irrationality exists in virtue of elements in the individual's own nature, the criteria for establishing its existence are in principle quite objective.

Freud's analysis of the status of reason (as form) in human affairs [9] is, by and large, "pessimistic." Appropriate perspective is afforded by his familiar account of the beginnings of culture. In the "primitive" social situation there existed a "horde" ruled by a despotic father who prevented the access of his sons to the females. The fate of the sons "was a hard one; if they excited the father's jealousy they were killed or castrated or driven out." [10] Life in the horde must have seemed intolerable to the sons; indeed, "nasty, brutish and short." They therefore killed their father, but soon became embroiled in quarrels. However, they came to see the danger and futility of this behavior and achieved a "hard-won understanding" of the need to curb impulse:

> This hard-won understanding—as well as the memory of the deed of liberation they had achieved together and the attachment which had grown up among them during the time of their exile—led at last to a union among them, a sort of social contract. Thus there came into being the first form of a social organization accompanied by a renunciation of instinctual gratification; recognition of mutual obligations; institutions declared sacred, which could not be broken—in short, the beginnings of morality and law.[11]

This is Freud's answer to the form of the question of "abiogenesis" in psychoanalysis: how did the Oedipus complex originate in a human situation in which it was once absent? Freud responds by placing at the "beginning" of history a figure that looks suspiciously like certain middle-class Europeans of the mid-nineteenth century, a figure whose presence might indeed generate something like an Oedipus complex. But this obviously begs the question. In what purports to be an account of origins, we should expect something more. Yet the result is not surprising in view of Freud's presumption that the male infant has a biologically grounded sexual urge toward the mother.

9. The formal conception of reason is applicable beyond the psychological field.

10. *Moses and Monotheism* (tr. K. Jones, New York: Knopf, 1939), p. 128.

11. *Ibid.*, p. 129. *Moses and Monotheism* is quoted to indicate that Freud never abandoned these views, which he had set out long before.

Freud's history and anthropology then become merely extrapolated first terms that substantially resemble the terms of the description of the grounding of the Oedipus complex in the present. The Oedipus complex and related phenomena in fact afford a basis for Freud's entire theory of society: he takes institutions, for all practical purposes, as clinical psychological phenomena. Thus, he urges that there is a "psychological correspondence between taboo and compulsion neurosis." [12] Even where the facts he deals with, as in *Totem and Taboo,* are unequivocally social or cultural, his procedure is to "subject the facts as stated to analysis, just as if they formed the symptoms of a neurosis." [13] He never succeeded in bridging the gap between psychological and institutional phenomena except on condition of virtually completely psychologizing the latter.[14]

The significance of the fact that Freud treated institutional phenomena "just as if they formed the symptoms of a neurosis" consists in the perspective on reason in society that his view afforded him. His theory of society involves a projection on to another plane of precisely the same irrationalities that he finds in the clinically analyzed individual. In fact, the social plane is barely different from the individual. "The development of man up to now," he states, "does not seem to me to need any explanation differing from that of animal development," and hastens to anticipate an objection that distinctively human achievements might need some additional explanation by observing that "the restless striving towards further perfection which may be observed in a minority of human beings is easily explicable as the result of that repression of instinct upon which what is most valuable in human culture is built." [15] The very meaning of the terms "social" or "collective" is, in Freud's usage, obscure. He veers and shifts between a meaning in which the social or collective is simply what happens in the individual case multiplied many times, and a meaning in which something like a "collective psyche" or "group mind" (much like the individual psyche or mind except on a grander scale)

12. *Totem and Taboo* (tr. A. A. Brill, New York: New Republic, 1931), p. 63.

13. *Ibid.,* p. 87.

14. This failure is most conspicuous in *Moses and Monotheism, q.v.,* at pp. 85, 89, 126, 129, 134, 140, 145, 147, 208–209 and *passim.*

15. See *Beyond the Pleasure Principle,* pp. 52–53.

is to be inferred. The latter concept is simply not feasible; the first meaning does not allow for an adequate account of human interaction.[16] If we reject such concepts as "collective psyche" and "collective neurosis," Freud's scheme of theory is left with a minimal apparatus for analysis of the social plane, and it is understandable that he should have scarcely any other recourse than projection: in fact, the concept of "collective neurosis" is nothing but an inapplicable analogy from the one plane on which "neurosis" has some meaning.

Mental health, in the Freudian view, as we have seen, involves a delicate balance of forces, and rationality in the human being exists only in virtue of their harmony. The brothers, in the account of the primitive horde, having slain their father, are overcome with feelings of guilt and seek to wipe out the memory of their deed. With their feelings of guilt comes repression, and repression is therefore aboriginal as human institutions and prescriptions originate in the Oedipus complex. Emotional imbalance, or irrationality, is the primordial condition of the members of the race, and the scheme of relationships between the sons and their father in the horde is prototypical for all human relationships. Human society itself appears as somehow the mere preservation and continuance of a condition of mental illness. Moreover, there is no way out of this result in Freud's theory, since society or culture involves the renunciation or crippling of instinct, in the line of the action of the aboriginal brothers who in their guilt and contrition finally re-instituted a restrictive situation much like the one that had prevailed before they killed their father. The alternative would be to dispense with society or culture, and Freud, in a vivid passage, speculates on what the human situation would then be like:

One could choose any woman who took one's fancy as one's sexual object, one could kill without hesitation one's rival or whoever interfered with one in any other way, and one could seize what one wanted of another man's goods without asking his leave: how splendid, what a succession of delights life would be!—True, one soon finds the first difficulty: every-

16. This limited conception of the social or collective appears also in some of the newer socio-psychoanalytical work. *Cf. e.g.,* Dollard's *Caste and Class in a Southern Town,* pp. 60, 170, 174, 366, 382, 391, 404 and *passim.*

one else has exactly the same wishes, and will treat one with no more consideration than one will treat him. And so in reality there is only one single person who can be made unrestrictedly happy by abolishing thus the restrictions imposed by culture, and that is a tyrant or dictator who has monopolized all the means of power; and even he has every reason to want the others to keep at least the cultural commandment: thou shalt not kill.

Freud continues, showing that this alternative is not ultimately feasible:

But how ungrateful, how shortsighted after all, to strive for the abolition of culture! What would then remain would be the state of nature, and that is far harder to endure. It is true that nature does not ask us to restrain our instincts, she lets us do as we like: she destroys coldly, cruelly, callously, as it seems to us, and possibly just through what has caused our satisfaction. It was because of these very dangers with which nature threatens us that we united together [*sic*] and created culture, which, amongst other things, is supposed to make our communal existence possible. Indeed, it is the principal task of culture, its real *raison d'être,* to defend us against nature.[17]

The nub of the whole perspective on the status of reason or rationality in society is Freud's theory of human nature. Before ever society existed [18] the primeval sons lusted to kill their despotic father and indulge in an orgy, and socialized behavior for Freud is a pure overlay, shed like a raincoat. Underneath is an inveterate, changeless creature—the Freudian rascal—*by nature* fiercely aggressive, jealous, patricidal and cannibalistic. The theory of the superego modifies this view to an extent, but for the moment we wish to keep this strand in Freud's thought analytically separated from others. Because man has a specific nature *before* society comes into being, he can find society uncongenial and can regard it and culture as inimical. Given the description of man's specific nature before society comes into being, conflict between "nature" and "culture" becomes inevitable in Freud's theory. There is, incidentally, a logical relationship between the postulation of a rather full and specific endowment for the "natural man" and the idea that there was a definite pre-cultural human life:

17. *The Future of an Illusion* (tr. W. D. Robson-Scott, London: Hogarth Press and Institute of Psychoanalysis, 1934), pp. 25–26.

18. It is of course quite useless in itself to speculate about how society "began." Social relationships are, in logical language, series of the type without a first point.

the former lends the latter plausibility. The essence of the matter is that since there has to be a balance between biology and culture, and the two are really incompatible, human society is always precariously organized and the tenure of reason within it is likewise precarious. To live "naturally" would result in mutual destruction, but to live under "culture" involves grievous and maiming restrictions to the "natural man." Other than these, Freud's view of human nature allows no alternatives. Given this part of his theory by itself, there is no reason why from time to time "culture" should not seem so oppressive to some groups that they would attempt to revert to "nature," momentarily heedless that this would end in mutual destruction. The insecure status of reason in society is a matter of the sheer constitution of man and society.

Freud's theory, as we have seen, is certainly *anti-rationalistic,* and we have been concerned to show that this does not warrant calling it *anti-rational.* At this point, however, there is some justification for applying to it the latter term. It denies, in principle, the possibility of a harmonious, relatively stable scheme of social relationships, the denial being grounded in its view of human nature.

His theory of human nature also involves Freud in a paradox that has the effect of tending to negate his best and most characteristic insights. He states, as noted, that it was because of the threats of nature that we "united and created culture." The masterly exponent of an anti-rationalistic psychology, in other words, verges on a social-contract theory. It is even stated that the primeval brothers entered upon a "sort of social contract." To recognize the threats of nature and therefore to unite and create culture, to enter upon a social contract after achieving a "hard-won understanding" that without society life is mutually destructive—all this obviously presumes a tremendous amount of rationality (as faculty). Freud is virtually duplicating Rousseauist conceptions, such as that when men saw the inconveniences of being without language they assembled and invented it. Culture, for Freud, we see again and again, is a superimposition upon a fairly thoroughly pre-formed human nature, and the "natural man" now appears not only as fierce, cannibalistic and patricidal, but also as a shrewd calculator and even a very highly imaginative and far-sighted being who can anticipate the destructive effects of a mere following out of impulse and can compact a social and institutional system to prevent them.

The Freudian "man underneath," then, shows a striking resemblance to the "economic man." In fact, if man has a really discrete human nature, separate from a cultural scheme that is essentially a superimposition, then necessarily that culture does not profoundly mold him in its shape. He should be able to stand aside from it, be culturally "uncontaminated," intact, in a manner analogous to that in which the human agent envisaged by the thorough-going hedonists criticized by Veblen stands intact. It takes the argument scarcely a step further to contend that man has a good knowledge of his (intact) nature and of the precise character of his preferences and distates. If this element in the Freudian theory is abstracted from others, and its logical implications are developed, the Freudian man and the economic man come so close together that the difference in *objects* pursued (mainly sexual in the one case and mainly pecuniary in the other) fades into the background. It remains true, however, that the resemblance cannot be pushed indefinitely. Freud's rationalism is only one component in a total theory of human nature whose characteristically *clinical* components are in contradiction with it; also, there is an important qualification of the view of human nature as standing intact and apart from society as a kind of detachable phenomenon beneath culture in Freud's theory of the superego.

These aspects of Freud's theory, while very questionable, serve to bring out once more the distinction between reason as form and rationality as faculty. That primitive imbalance which is manifested by the Oedipus complex and, in the Freudian theory, projected onto the social plane, which marks the psychic wound of the race, liable to gape open at any time in particular ("neurotic") individuals, and likely to menace the foundations of society—that imbalance results in or is manifested in the absence of reason as form in the emotional organization of the individual and in the structure of society. At the same time, Freud, in his social-contract vein, attributes to man a really extreme rationality in the sense of faculty. Reason as faculty, as ability to estimate, calculate and foresee does not indeed extend to a self-understanding that would eliminate the bases of conflict: the Oedipus complex remains unpenetrated; but only that complex sets bounds, in this strain of theory, to reason as faculty, which is even presented as so acute and far-reaching in other respects that Freud's characteristic insights into the limitations of rationality tend to be denied. Man appears to have one basic irrationality and for the rest to be boundlessly rational. The role of cultural factors in the genesis of irrationalities is completely by-passed.

There is one connection between Freud's rationalism and his anarchism, already implied, which must be stated explicitly. On Freud's view, there is no really reliable "cement" to hold a society together, to effect cohesion. Insofar as man has, and is aware of, biologically grounded interests that run counter to the organization of society and culture, there is no reason why the latter should not be continually threatened. Actually, this is virtually the same point we noted when we remarked that, on Freud's analysis, the tenure of reason (intimately related to balance or order) must be precarious in human affairs. The only way in which Freud's theory can be saved from rather unqualifiedly anarchistic implications at this point is precisely by postulating a very considerable faculty of rationality: cohesion could continually be preserved on the hypothesis that human beings inclined to rebel, in their biological interest, against society and culture, would always anticipate the ultimately internecine effects of such rebellion and would therefore not initiate it. But, again, on Freud's more purely clinical analysis, human beings are not likely to possess so much rationality.

## II. STRUCTURAL IRRATIONALITY

Non-rational, traditional sources of cohesion and maintenance of order in society are largely omitted in Freud's social psychology, although to some degree his concept of the superego implies these. For conceptual clarity, it is necessary to indicate that the concept of reason in the sense of order or balance is applicable to a social scheme marked by the considerable scope of non-rational or traditional behavior. Everything depends upon the type of relationship among the elements of the traditional behavior. If the cultural prescriptions and definitions in the various spheres of behavior encompassed in the total cultural scheme are mutually consistent and "harmonious," in that sense reason is present, although behavior has largely non-rational or traditional sources. Folk sociology and rural-urban sociology, in fact, carry a suggestion that when reason in this sense is disturbed in a traditionalistic society, rationality in the sense of taking rather self-conscious thought about social circumstances tends to be stimulated.[19]

Reason in the sense of balance or order among cultural elements is a concept continually implied in modern sociological writing but seldom set forth explicitly. Karl Mannheim has made a useful and pertinent distinction between "substantial rationality" and "functional rationalization." He understands as substantially rational "an act of thought which reveals intelligent insight into the inter-relations of events in a given situation."[20] On the other hand, "functional rationalization" has reference to an organization of a set of actions in a systematized and definite way, so that a definite goal may be attained. Thus: "Whether a series of actions is functionally rational or not is determined by two criteria: a) Functional organization with reference to a definite goal, and b) a consequent calculability when viewed from the standpoint of an observer or a third person seeking to adjust himself to it."

So, the ordinary soldier may carry out whole series of functionally rational actions without having any idea of the connection of his action with the actions of others or of the goal to which the totality of actions leads. Functional rationalization, a scheme of order and a definite plan the terms of which are understood by *some,* is present in such a case, but there is very little substantial rationality.[21] This dis-

19. On the notion of consistency or harmony among non-rational traditional components see Edward Sapir, "Culture, Genuine and Spurious," *American Journal of Sociology* XXIX (1924), 401–429. "Genuine culture" is understood by Sapir precisely in the sense of a harmony among cultural elements. It is *logically* possible that cultural elements should be mutually consistent and harmonious and yet not give much scope to, or actually be repressive of, biologically grounded interests. Thereby the problem of reason in the social order in the sense in which Freud's theory raises it would remain unsettled, and at this level mere cultural consistency or harmony would not mean very much. The functionalists in anthropology have tried to show how cultural norms mesh with biological interests. *Cf. e.g.,* Malinowski's article, "Culture," *Encyclopedia of the Social Sciences,* vol. IV (New York: Macmillan, 1937), pp. 621–646.

20. *Man and Society in an Age of Reconstruction,* p. 53.

21. *Cf. ibid.,* pp. 54 and 58. It is of interest in relation to Veblen that Mannheim notes that in the case of the machine industry there is a tremendous

tinction would be quite sufficient if it did not omit a feature of social structure which is in fact present in Mannheim's own analyses.

Contemporary society presents the spectacle of the existence of both substantial rationality and functional rationalization in connection with a variety of goals that are incompatible *as goals,* and also, and this is at least as important, it presents the existence of *potentially* incompatible goals or purposes. This incompatibility or potential incompatibility of goals pursued at different points or in different areas of the same general social organization (with as much functional rationalization or even substantial rationality at each of the points or in each of the areas as one pleases) was already a very important element in the theory of Marx, as when he premised that capitalist enterprise would finally be eliminated because it could not justify itself by making full use of the possibilities of the means of production. Organization around the needs of the institution of capitalist ownership is thus perceived as not harmonizing with organization around the economic needs of the community. The same formal element is clearly seen in Karl Polanyi's thesis about modern economy and society, to the effect that the self-regulating market destroys the human and natural substance of society but that society, in instituting self-protective measures, tends to destroy the market.[22] The disruptive, disordering effects of such "contradictions," insofar as they exist, are quite plain. It is equally plain that such effects are quite widespread in our society, and present major problems. It is suggested that phenomena of this type might be referred to as structural irrationalities. It is an important point that structural irrationalities are rather clearly connected with conflicting or potentially conflicting goals, since this brings us back to the concept of reason in the sense of order or balance.[23]

If the only manifestations of, let us say, "inadequate" rationality in contemporary society derived from insufficient substantial ration-

---

amount of functional rationalization not paralleled by anything like an equal amount of substantial rationality.

22. *The Great Transformation* (New York: Farrar & Rinehart, 1944).

23. As indicated, Mannheim is not unaware of the existence of structural irrationalities (*cf.* also his later work, *Diagnosis of Our Time,* London: K. Paul, 1943), but he omits the concept (the term scarcely matters) in his formal analysis of the place of rationality in society.

ality or from the fact that at many points in social organization there exists *only* functional rationalization, social structure would be a much simpler affair than it actually is. In a sense, only "education" would be needed to supply a much more considerable amount of substantial rationality where mere functional rationalization now exists. And why would it be necessary for sociologists of a planning turn of mind, like Mannheim, to be quite so exercised over the fact that there is a great deal of functional rationalization at points where substantial rationality can be found only in a few strategically placed persons? Substantial rationality is particularly useful to the individual, and its lack particularly harmful, in a society in which there is considerable goal conflict, where choice and selection of goals and values must constantly be made. What makes mere functional rationalization "dangerous" from the point of view of the democratically inclined planner is precisely the existence of structural irrationality, which may at any time precipitate out strong movements oriented around goals objectively against the interests of large masses of a population.[24]

To arrive at the concept of structural irrationality, or to give a treatment of social phenomena that implies it, requires more serious attention to social phenomena than Freud gave. He was far too preoccupied with the attempt to demonstrate a radical disharmony between biological interests and culture. But structural irrationality is given much more earnest attention by Veblen. Thus, much of his analysis in Part I of *Absentee Ownership* is designed to trace the genesis of certain forms of structural irrationality, as when he attempts to demonstrate that, historically, "business" interests meshed fairly well with community needs but diverged from them in the course of time. An even more cogent instance is given by his analysis of modern Germany. The imperialist designs of modern Germany, in Veblen's analysis, can only be realized in the modern world by use of the machine technology. Therefore, Germany cannot get along without the machine technology. On the other hand, the machine technology involves the rise of an urban proletariat whose animus and general point of view tend to run counter to imperialist design. Therefore, Germany cannot get along with the machine technology.

24. *Cf.* the Addendum on structural irrationality.

This thesis is susceptible of restatement in unequivocally normative terms. The goals, values and purposes centering around imperialist design are incompatible with at least certain of the goals tending to emerge from the economic and political experience of an urban proletariat. As long as the machine technology is retained, the latter goals will continue to emerge. As long as imperialist design is maintained, the machine technology must be kept. The goal and value conflict marks a structural irrationality, which the adherents of imperialist design seek to eliminate by elimination of the other value system.

Veblen, however, is not always so clear as this on institutions and on the fact that it is norm or goal conflict that he is considering. It is necessary to go back to some of his psychological views in order to be quite sure of attaining to his perspective on reason as form and rationality as faculty. There are, as has been noted, two sets of instincts that are, for Veblen, determinative in man's native endowment. Typical of one set are the instinct of workmanship and parental instinct. Typical of the other is the predatory instinct. The consequences in society of the working out of the first two would be productivity and fecundity; what associated institutional apparatus would be like is unclear because of the tendency in Veblen's thought to regard these more "worthy" instincts as sufficient architects of society. The consequences in society of the working out of the predatory instinct are on the line of war and the subordination of others within the same community framework; associated institutional apparatus would be in the nature of class hierarchy and militaristic enterprise. But the first set of instincts somehow has, for Veblen, a higher biological authenticity. Veblen's "natural man" lives peaceably in a solidary and fecund community. The predatory instinct may be presumed to be latent in the savage state. There are two important implications. Firstly, life in the savage state would be quite "rational." Such instincts as would be in force and actively working, together with their consequences in social relationships, would harmonize with one another: workmanship and parental benevolence are scarcely incompatible. In this sense, there would be reason in the social structure, and there would even exist some rationality in the sense of a human faculty of taking thought and calculating and foreseeing, since this would be bound up with the instinct of workmanship and its terminus of mechanical efficiency. A "primitive savage" *balance* in the social structure is to be inferred. True, a very restricted, small-scale life might be lived, but that is something else.

Secondly, insofar as Veblen argues for the higher biological authenticity of the first set of instincts—which may therefore be called the primary instincts—he introduces a romantic, "optimistic" strain into his theory. Instincts that are more deeply ingrained, of greater antiquity, more "indefeasible," should "in the long run" triumph over other instincts. It is this element in Veblen's thought which warrants criticisms of the type that Harris and Adorno have made, and justifies the remark that the theory of instinct plays the same role in Veblen as the dialectic did in Marx. History and nature are on "the side of the angels," "good" instincts will triumph, and "reason" will come into its own as "bad" institutions are abandoned or allowed to lapse. This strain in Veblen is not, however, left unqualified. We have noticed that he was willing to entertain the possibility that "imbecile" institutions might triumph over "good" instincts or over the needs of life. There are many points in his writings where he does leave open the possibilities as to whether the outcome of modern social and economic enterprise will be in the direction of conforming or not conforming with the goals implicitly posited in the instinct of workmanship. His romantic optimism is not inflexible, but is tempered by a realistic sense that "good" instincts may be defeated. Moreover, Veblen is explicitly critical of the romantic optimism of Marx. He recognizes that "Marx, as a Hegelian—that is to say, a romantic philosopher,—is necessarily an optimist, and the evil (antithetical element) in life is to him a logically necessary evil, as the antithesis is a necessary phase of the dialectic. . . ." [25]

Veblen does not, therefore, grant that the course of history is necessarily a working out of goals that might be humanly desirable. The processes of history are, for him, more neutral, more "impersonal," and their working is not particularly heedful of human goals or desires. Why should capitalism not, indeed, assuming that Marx's economic analysis was correct, mean the end of the human race? What guarantee is there that the proletariat, at a crucial point when considerable misery has been generated for it, will necessarily take

25. *The Place of Science,* p. 430.

thought of its conditions, mark its oppressors, and make a change? Veblen assumes a "Darwinian" neutrality about what the capitalist process may lead to, a neutrality reinforced by his skepticism about the presumption of a crucially intervening rationality on the part of the proletariat, functioning to avert complete economic catastrophe when it threatens and to constitute the beginnings of a new economic system. Veblen had also been critical of what he took to be the "animism" of other lines of economic theory than the Marxian. In his formal criticisms, therefore, he will not accept *any* line of thought that loads "nature" or "history" or the economic process by assuming an inherent but extra-human bent in these ranges of phenomena which will necessarily make things ultimately come out "well." These are important qualifications, although Veblen does not himself altogether escape a criticism of the same general type as he levelled against the classical economists and Marx. It is simply that the terms chosen for the romantic component in Veblen are somewhat different. The benevolent constraint in "nature" appears under the guise of a presumed indefeasible and very ancient biological endowment of man.

In the "animism" of economic theory, in the Hegelian optimism of Marx and in Veblen's Darwinism, an identical element appears: a reading back of norms or values into history or nature. In all these cases, there is a tendency to presume that unequal balances will be redressed and "reason" will be victorious. If we follow out this particular line of thought, Veblen's psychology appears as if it should not be seriously taken as a psychology at all. It is rather a psychological jargon performing two functions: 1) It raises a presumption that what Veblen regarded as "bad" institutions, like business enterprise and the militaristic national establishment, have some chance of being ultimately abandoned because of the vitality and resilience of the ancient and primary instincts; 2) It gives Veblen a seemingly "neutral" position from which to assess these institutions, so that he can "impartially" note and analyze the discrepancies between them and the characteristics or needs of indefeasible human nature. The only way to have definitely avoided this statement of discrepancy between institutions and human nature (always made, it must be noted, to say nothing else, on the basis of a very dubious view of human nature) and still have retained some very important insights, Veblen did not quite take. This would have consisted in an analysis of structural irrationality and would have involved an examination of actual or potential goal discrepancies between, say, business enterprise and what Veblen called the "socialistic disaffection." He would then have clearly postulated tensions between alternative value schemes.

Since, however, he did not clearly and unequivocally take this road, for him, as for Freud, there is a certain incompatibility between biological interests and human social and cultural organization. In detail, of course, the manner in which the incompatibility is presumed in Veblen is different from what it is in Freud's case, and there are different consequences accordingly.

With Freud the irrationality found in the individual "neurotic" is projected on to social structure. Man cannot get along without culture, but neither can he get along with it. He is constitutionally and from the beginning a creature who cannot achieve reason or order in his social life, no matter which way he turns.

In Veblen's view of "beginnings," man was well endowed with the instinct of workmanship and the parental instinct, while the predatory instinct may be presumed to have been in a state of latency. Man was therefore biologically and socially in a rational or ordered and balanced state.

For the Freudian man, there is no way out of his tensions. They are unavoidable. For man, as Veblen saw him, there should be a way out, a way of resolving tensions. The presumption of incompatibility between biological nature and culture is toned down in Veblen by comparison with Freud. As we have seen before, by interpretation Veblen's view may be read as one according to which the predatory instinct was only latent in the savage state. There is nothing in Veblen's sketchy psychological theory to indicate that the predatory instinct must *necessarily* go from a latent to an active state, although his work suggests that it is rather easily aroused. There is therefore no *necessary* conflict between predatory and benevolent instincts. It is relevant that Veblen all along allows a certain looseness to the instincts, so that they may be to some extent compounded with cultural elements. This gives some plausibility to his view that the instinct of workmanship gets more closely and exclusively associated, in time, with the members of the class engaged in the community's industrial, material work, and the predatory instinct (or some refinement thereof) with the class engaged in the community's business, financial work. Man in the savage state, therefore, is not necessarily self-conflicted, and by a shrewd compounding of instinctual and cultural elements man even in an advanced state of civilization and the industrial arts may be free of self-conflict. This does not of course prevent conflict between classes, but should rather intensify it, as those ruled by different instincts understand one another less and less (since Veblen prefers to see class divergence as a result of different "habituations" to seeing it as the outcome of a rational calculation of where interests lie).

Insofar as class conflict is seen as the result of different "habituations" and the working out of different instincts, conflict has more or less "mechanical" or "impersonal" causes. Insofar as the norms of the different classes are brought into focus (and our view is that the whole instinct-habit terminology has the effect both of confusing Veblen so that he does not clearly see a divergence of norms, on the level of norms, and of enabling him to disguise the fact that he is talking about a potential conflict of value-systems) structural irrationalities in society and economy are implied. But in either case, tensions in the form of either a sheer mechanically, impersonally produced failure of the classes to understand one another (with a consequent drift apart in their sentiments and allegiances) or in the form of structural irrationalities, are theoretically resolvable. There is nothing in particular in human nature as such to inhibit a resolution. The classes could drift farther apart, and those engaged in industrial work, say, might reconstitute a society more or less exclusively based on the "impersonal" and "matter-of-fact" viewpoint (although a society would certainly appear to require further foundations). Or else, the incompatibility between such activities as "making money" on the one hand and "making goods" on the other could be seen to call for a recasting of institutions such that discrepancies of this type would be resolved in a community with greater unity of purposes or values or goals. The result in the latter case would be an elimination or toning down of structural irrationalities, of "distortions" produced by actual or potential goal discrepancies at the institutional level.

Veblen's view (though only to the extent that he adheres to it) that in the human endowment there is little of what Mannheim calls "substantial rationality" does not allow him to rely on this as a solvent of structural irrationalities. He had criticized Marx for ostensibly suggesting such a solution, within the context of the latter's Hegelian presumptions. This playing down of rationality as faculty is undoubtedly a factor that drives Veblen in the direction of his own brand of romantic optimism. If a humanly "favorable" outcome is insisted upon in a theory, and the faculty of human reasoning and calculation cannot be relied on to produce such an outcome, and if, moreover, structural irrationalities or their equivalents are postulated, there is little recourse except to a presumption that something in the "nature of man" constrains to the favorable outcome. Had Veblen been a perfectly consistent "Darwinian," and at times he almost was, he could have left out the romantic element in his thought, and society would have appeared as an utterly aimless, goalless process, *a priori* as likely to have one upshot as another.

By comparison with Freud, then, Veblen allows a larger place to reason in the sense of order or balance either among instincts at the biological level or among interests, goals and value-systems at the institutional level. The differences between the two have a *logical* source in their different views of human nature. The differences may be reviewed firstly with an eye to the distinctive romanticism of each. Freud's primeval man is self-conflicted: "evil" is inherent in his nature and projected by Freud on to the social structure: in the interest of this projection the social structure, with its distinctive elements, even tends to be dissolved. Every society, being a society, will "maim" human nature. Veblen's primeval man is "good" and not notably self-conflicted. For both Freud and Veblen, the primeval natural man persists beneath institutional variations (although more unqualifiedly and rigidly for Freud—aside from the theory of the superego—since Veblen allows some compounding of instinctual and cultural elements: the instincts are loose and may combine with other elements). Freud's implication is that the natural man may at any time disrupt social order and re-institute a culture-less anarchy. In Veblen's view, the natural man exercises a pull against "bad" institutions, and there is some presumption that if he ever gets the upper hand—and there is always a chance of this in view of the strength and antiquity of his pedigree—such institutions will dissolve. The result in either case would be to disrupt the institutional order. Freud's humans would then plunge back into a war of each against all, but Veblen's into a tranquil and fecund, if perhaps somewhat somnolent, state. The primeval, constitutional-biological irrationalities would not lapse, for Freud, but for Veblen an ordered and simple life would be restored.

Aside from the romanticism of Freud and Veblen, with the associated "pessimism" in the first case and "optimism" in the latter, Veblen's theory leaves much larger scope for resolutions that would bring about reason in the sense of order or balance in human affairs. It is true that it remains very unclear just how a society could exist without institutions and it is likewise unclear whether any institutional apparatus at all would be found in the savage state or whether a re-building in strict, exclusive accord with the instinct of workmanship would produce any recognizable institutional apparatus. But there are other elements in Veblen's complex theory. Insofar as he can be understood to be operating on a purely institutional level, he recognizes structural irrationalities as such. These really constitute Veblen's most significant problem in any case, in that he is constantly, if obscurely, noting the actual and potential incompatibility of goals or norms implicit in business enterprise or militaristic enterprise and goals or norms implicit in the "socialistic disaffection" and kindred phenomena. But incompatibilities or tensions of this type are at least theoretically resolvable, however difficult concrete and actual resolutions may be, whereas Freud's presumption of man's constitutional irrationality projected on to social structure puts any genuine resolution of tensions outside the bounds of possibility. Beneath all the complexities of each of the theories, the constraining influence of the view of human nature upon the position adopted with respect to the status of reason in human affairs is discernible. Further consideration of the problems raised in this section inevitably raises the already many times implied issue of anarchism.

But there is still another element in Veblen's views that must be dealt with. We have noted just above that his claim that rationality as a faculty has only small scope in human affairs does not allow him to place much reliance on rationality in this sense. At the same time that this is true there is another tendency in his thought that goes in quite a different direction. Among his speculations on the effects of the machine process, there is one line of a clearly psychological order. Briefly, the machine process builds and increases the rationality of the workman. In a passage in *Imperial Germany* Veblen compares the "habit of consuming printed matter" with "habituation to the machine process," and indicates that these "habits" both have an intellectually emancipating effect.[26] In an earlier work, again discussing the effects of the machine industry upon the workman, he states of the latter:

Insofar as he is a rightly gifted and fully disciplined workman, the final term of his *habitual* thinking is mechanical efficiency. . . . But mechanical efficiency is a matter of precisely adjusted cause and effect. What the discipline of the machine industry inculcates, therefore, in the habits of life and of thought of the workman, is regularity of sequence and mechanical precision; and the intellectual outcome is an habitual resort to terms of measurable cause and effect.[27]

The workman in contact with the forces given by the machine industry is trained to think in "matter-of-fact" terms, in "cause and effect" terms, and there is a carry-over of "matter-of-fact" thinking from its origins in the machine discipline to other types of activities.[28] This is rather definitely a psychological view of the effects of the machine process on the workman, and the outcome of that process is a rational, "scientific" workman. Veblen even presumes "transfer of training." It is hardly necessary to argue that there is little evidence for Veblen's view, taken at face value. Obviously the distinc-

26. *Imperial Germany*, pp. 74–75.

27. *Business Enterprise*, p. 309. There is another strain in Veblen's thought on this matter. "It is the part of the workman to know the working of the mechanism with which he is associated and to adapt his movements with mechanical accuracy to its requirement. This demands a degree of intelligence. . . ." *Instinct of Workmanship*, p. 307. He had also noted in his early paper on "Industrial and Pecuniary Employments" that the differentiation of employments may be selective rather than disciplinary of certain human types. (*The Place of Science*, p. 322.) But the strain emphasized above is a very constant, consistent one.

28. *Business Enterprise*, p. 308.

tion of substantial rationality and functional rationalization would weaken Veblen's argument considerably. It is at least as important to note that Veblen has here put a great deal into terms like "matter-of-fact." He does not simply mean an utterly neutral faculty of reasoning. The businessman, after all, reasons too, in the sense of calculating the main chance, yet Veblen is repeatedly contrasting "matter-of-fact" with "matter-of-imputation" or "pecuniary" or "animistic" or the like. Here also he has introduced a normative element. When the workman is infected by the canons of the leisure class, his "matter-of-fact" thinking lapses to that extent. Does his sheer reasoning faculty lapse? That is hardly the point. "Matter-of-fact" has reference to a normative scheme that, Veblen considered, somehow took its rise in the machine discipline. The workman's rationality is not only sheer reasoning power, but reasoning power definitely oriented toward anti-leisure class and anti-business norms.

This element in Veblen's theory does not harmonize with either his criticisms of Marxism or of classical economics. In itself, it definitely plays up rationality on the part of the workman, even if the rationality is assigned non-rational "habit" sources. Latently, also, it harks back to the norm-impregnated theory of instinct. The point is that Veblen never put his theory into sufficiently systematic shape to enable a clear estimate from it as to his views on the scope and function of human rationality. Despite his incisive criticisms, he affords no unequivocal view on this matter and makes no conclusive contribution to the assessment, in human affairs, of rationality as a faculty. Just as Freud recognized that factors of an emotional nature set limits on rationality as a faculty, so Veblen contended that institutional or traditional factors had an analogous effect in the range of the operations of business and industry. The contention that the effect of machine discipline is to make workmen rational agrees as little with important features of Veblen's general views as Freud's presumption of the rationality of the "natural man" agrees with his general theory. Each formally plays down the significance of rationality and presents positive evidence to fortify his position. Yet neither is content to let the matter go at that, but brings in a presumption of rationality at an unexpected point. This in itself would suggest that rationality has not been properly evaluated in either scheme of theory. But Freud did make a definitive contribution to its treatment on the clinical level.

We cannot, from the heritage left by Freud and Veblen, obtain a clear guide to the formulation of rationality as a faculty in human affairs, that is to say, aside from the clinical level and in the social structure. Freud's clinical perspective on the limitations of rationality as faculty by the bounds imposed by irrationality (as form) remains as a permanent contribution integrated into a systematic psychological theory. But Veblen's perspective on the limitations on rationality as a faculty through the effects of institutions and conventions, while it remains as an important insight, does not integrate into a systematic economic or sociological theory. Even severe critics of the main line of (orthodox) economic theory concede that "there has been ***no other economic theory*** in the sense of a precise and integrated system of abstractions." [29] What is mainly important for us, however, is the fact that Veblen's perspective on rationality in society does not finally lead to a clear, integrated and consistent estimate of it. This prevents us from making a lucid theoretical analysis of the relations between the limitations on rationality marked by the Freudians in the clinical sphere and those noted by Veblen in the institutional sphere. We can, however, investigate the relations between concrete non-rational, institutional forms analyzed by Veblen and irrational psychological trends of the type studied by the Freudians. A case study of this type is set forth in Chapter 7.

### III. ANARCHISM

At the risk of some repetition, a separate treatment of anarchism in Freud and Veblen is undertaken to sharpen our main problem: the relation of the individual, as seen by clinical psychology, to the social order, as seen by social theory.

The previous section has already raised the problem of "order" in society.[30] Freud was unable to solve this, and fell into anarchism. He could never quite rid himself of the notion of a discrete and rather fully endowed pre-social human nature, and this was the essence of his difficulty.

29. Soule, *The Strength of Nations,* p. 124.
30. See Parsons, *Structure of Social Action.*

Thus, in his work on *Group Psychology and the Analysis of the Ego*,[31] ostensibly devoted to elucidating the nature of the group bond, Freud makes a brave beginning that arouses high expectations, with the statement that "in the individual's mental life someone else is invariably involved, as a model, as an object, as a helper, as an opponent, and so from the very first Individual Psychology is at the same time Social Psychology as well—in this extended but entirely justifiable sense of the words." [32] But he soon tells us that

> in a group the individual is brought under conditions which allow him to throw off the repressions of his unconscious instincts. The apparently new characteristics which he then displays are in fact the manifestations of this unconscious, in which all that is evil in the human mind is contained as predisposition. We can find no difficulty in understanding the disappearance of conscience or of a sense of responsibility in these circumstances. It has long been our contention that "dread of society (soziale Angst)" is the essence of what is called conscience.[33]

The implication is clear. The universal, biological *Urmensch* is still present beneath the social camouflage, and would emerge were it not for his fear, which is here claimed to be the substance of conscience. Conscience is thereby more nearly an outcome of considerations of expediency (with all the rationalistic implications) than a matter of internalized norms or values.

Freud's anarchism is qualified by his contention that culture, however repressive, is after all necessary. There are also a few incidental qualifications. Thus, he speaks of the "narcissistic satisfaction provided by the cultural ideal," explaining: "True, one is a miserable plebeian, tormented by obligations and military service, but withal one is a Roman citizen. . . ." He comments: "Unless such relations, fundamentally of a satisfying kind, were in existence, it would be impossible to understand how so many cultures have contrived to exist for so long in spite of the justified hostility of great masses of men." [34] Art is also instanced as something which "offers substitute

31. (Tr. J. Strachey, London and Vienna: International Psycho-Analytical Press, 1922).

32. *Ibid.*, pp. 1–2.

33. *Ibid.*, pp. 9–10. In this volume Freud, incidentally, deals with the group bond in terms of libido-refinements or aim-inhibited sexual impulses.

34. *The Future of an Illusion*, pp. 22–23.

gratification for the oldest cultural renunciations." [35] But qualifications of this sort are definitely of minor importance by comparison with the importance attaching to the concept of the superego, which introduces a new strand into Freud's work, one that genuinely serves to modify his rationalistic anarchism.

Already in *The Future of an Illusion* Freud had partly answered the question as to why culture, which is so burdensome, is borne by human beings, by reference to the superego. He had there envisioned the superego as an instrument for the internalization of external compulsions, although he remarked that it neither worked in the same way nor with the same scope in everyone and that it was not always sufficiently strong to prevent outbursts of aggression and license.[36] In *Civilization and Its Discontents,* the question is again raised why man sustains such tremendous sacrifices of aggressive and erotic impulses in his induction into culture. The answer given is, briefly, that aggressiveness is introjected and directed against the ego as the superego is formed. The child takes toward his native impulses the same hostile attitude taken by his parents. He is induced to do this because, if he did not, he would lose countless gratifications. The answer to the question as to why men obey lies in "man's helplessness and dependence upon others; it can best be designated the dread of losing love." [37] A sort of general human "self-defeat" is brought about, although Freud does not specifically call it that. This point is significant. Although the concept of the superego marks an important departure in Freud's thought in relation to the matter of anarchism, the superego still appears to an extent to be only a device to hold in check the "natural man" persisting somewhere at the bottom. It is

35. *Ibid.*, p. 23.

36. *Ibid.*, pp. 18–19.

37. *Civilization and Its Discontents*, p. 107. *Cf.* the whole treatment of the superego, *ibid.*, pp. 105–122. It is worth noting that the superego, in Freud's view, is not necessarily a pure social construct. Not even here can he abandon the biologistic bent of his general theory, for side by side with the presentation of a social genesis of the superego there is a presentation of a biological genesis. This becomes intelligible when we remember that Freud believes in the existence of an aggressive instinct. Then, even a lenient or loving parent may foster the development of a strict superego, contrary to what would otherwise be the expectation, since the child's native aggressiveness—an energy sum that cannot perish—can only be turned inward when the parent clearly gives it love. See, *ibid.*, footnote, p. 118, and pp. 116–118, wherein Freud seeks to reconcile the two views on the genesis of the superego.

true that to emphasize the superego amounts to emphasizing checks that are now seen to come from internal pressures. But who with a functioning superego can really be "himself"? The superego appears in the first place only because man is dependent and helpless and must make sacrifices of instinct to gain the tolerance or love of his parents.

It is undeniable that Freud saw that each new generation cannot be indefinitely policed by purely external constraint, and that it is necessary to the economy and even existence of society that a mechanism like the superego function effectively. Each new generation, with its many individuals emergent from many homes, can thereby go to its life and work with a domesticated, internally regulated psychic structure. This insight qualifies the assumption of tremendous rationality that would otherwise be necessary, on the lines of the theory that social disruption is avoided as man foresees that a destruction of the social order would end only in his own ultimate destruction. From our point of view, also, it is not necessary to contend that the superego is the whole of human nature, but there is no warrant for the notion that the residue of human nature is a kind of undigested aggressive-cannibalistic-sexual lump. This criticism is borne out by evidence afforded by some of the neo-Freudian work, which at the same time attests the significance of the concept of the superego and invalidates Freud's anarchistic premises.

The evidence comes from the study of the society of Alor. Here, norms are relatively weak and cohesion is somewhat precarious. Strong and deep attachments are not conspicuously present. There is a marked tendency for individuals to wander from one group or residence to another, and even for children, when provoked, to run from parents to live with others. One woman, described by Dr. Oberholzer in a manner consistent with the ethnographic data on Alor, is said to be "self-contained, encrusted, and encysted. . . ." In fact, "she, like others of the Alorese women, reminds one of a dead volcano." [38] The Alorese, furthermore, say, "We die if people are fond of us." [39] This statement is perhaps a sufficient commentary on the character of personal relationships. The implications with regard to trust of

38. Oberholzer, in DuBois, *The People of Alor,* p. 639.
39. See the statement of Mangma the Genealogist, *ibid.,* at p. 218.

others are quite clear, and precisely what might be expected in view of the general organization of the society. It is especially to be remarked that in Alor "the two expressions of superego formation, religion and the technique of maintaining social cohesion, are not strong."[40] A strong sense of guilt can hardly develop, since that depends on "the internalization of the good parental imago, the tonicity of which is maintained by the hope of being reinstated into parental grace," and we learn that the disciplines of the society make reward for obedience an extremely uncertain matter, so that "the threats of punishment cannot become very securely internalized." Shame, which is, however, "really an external agent," remains as an important sanction.[41]

Yet, in this society, with its slight cohesion, it is notably the case that individuals tend to be isolated, anxious and mistrustful. The (psychologically) perhaps strongest and most resourceful individual within it is described as having "ego resources above average, but still not very great."[42] The simultaneous occurrence of a but slightly coherent social structure, held together by relatively weak sanctions, and of individuals lacking in self-esteem, mastery techniques and independence, is of considerable theoretical importance. The analysis of Alor afforded by DuBois and Kardiner attests the significance of the superego as an instrument of socialization. But there is no reason at all for thinking that the complete absence of a superego, were that possible, would witness the emergence of human agents such as Freud postulated as existing "before culture,"—aggressively pleasure-seeking and predatory. This is not the result that might theoretically be inferred from a further weakening of the already weak superego of the Alorese. The analysis of Alor allows the inference that a different type of moral discipline and training would involve the development of different kinds of human beings, but obviously not the inference that the absence of all training would witness an untouched core of elements going to make up a distinctive human nature prior to all society. Nor, even if we assumed that this untouched core was

40. *Ibid.*, p. 185. 41. *Ibid.*, pp. 185–186; see also pp. 118 and 173.

42. See Kardiner's diagram of the ego structure of Fantan the Interpreter, *ibid.*, p. 395. *Cf.* also the whole account of Alor in *The Psychological Frontiers of Society*, pp. 101–258. It may be noted in passing that the meaning of "ego resources above average" is not entirely clear.

sufficiently large and definite to constitute a recognizable, rather fully developed human nature, would there be any reason to think that that nature would show in precise detail the characteristics of the Freudian presocial man.[43]

Veblen also did not afford an adequate solution to the problem of order.[44] Thus, in *The Engineers and the Price System* [45] his remedy for economic ills, a "soviet of technicians," points up his tendency to envision economic problems simply as matters of attaining technological efficiency. It appears rather incidental to the main theme when he notes, in the same volume, the need of "the working out of a common understanding and a solidarity of sentiment between the technicians and the working force engaged in transportation and in the greater underlying industries of the system." [46] The "trouble," Veblen says in effect, is the sabotage of industry by business. It can hardly be denied that this is a "trouble," but the problem of organization in industry is left entirely to take care of itself.

It scarcely needs elaboration that technological efficiency is a very limited goal, one, moreover, that cannot even answer the question of *what* specifically shall be produced. Yet Veblen never gave this serious consideration, and a position substantially similar to his is also taken by a contemporary Veblenian.[47] Clarence E. Ayres, after an eloquent criticism of price theory, comes out on the question of value precisely where Veblen did: productivity is somehow good in its own

43. The general phenomenon of internalization of norms, whereby socialization is achieved, is a familiar one to social psychology and sociology, and knowledge of it is scarcely contingent on Freud's contribution alone. In sociology, for example, Durkheim had insisted before the turn of the century that social phenomena were external and exercised constraint, with the implication that prescriptions, at first coming from the outside (*i.e.*, from others) were gradually incorporated to mold the individual's own normative organization, and, at first appearing coercive, came gradually to appear "natural." See *Les Règles de la méthode sociologique* (Paris: Alcan, 1895). But the distinctive Freudian contribution was an emphasis on the nature of the emotional factors that accompanied the development of the superego in the individual. See, *e.g.*, *New Introductory Lectures*, ch. iii.

44. See Arthur K. Davis, "Sociological Elements in Veblen's Economic Theory," *Journal of Political Economy* LIII (1945), 132–149.

45. (New York: Viking, 1940.)

46. *Ibid.*, p. 168.

47. Clarence E. Ayres in *The Theory of Economic Progress* (Chapel Hill: University of North Carolina, 1944).

right. Ayres, taking his inspiration from Veblen, distinguishes technology from ceremony and status, and definitely holds that what is not technological must impede technology. Technology is the "locus of value." Even if it is granted that "price" is merely "price" and a very dubious measure of "value," a norm of productivity is obviously still only one, requiring supplementation by, and integration with, others, if a community and a functioning economic system are to exist.

The instinct of workmanship and the parental bent, with the co-operative disposition that the latter involves, could presumably organize the work of industry without other help, in Veblen's view. But this has little to recommend it in the light of modern industrial research. Elton Mayo, on the basis of studies in the organization of industry, states:

Human collaboration in work, in primitive and developed societies, has always depended for its perpetuation upon the evolution of a non-logical social code which regulates the relations between persons and their attitudes to one another. Insistence upon a merely economic logic of production—especially if the logic is frequently changed—interferes with the development of such a code and consequently gives rise in the group to a sense of human defeat. This human defeat results in the formation of a social code at a lower level and in opposition to the economic logic. One of its symptoms is "restriction." [48]

The reference to a non-logical or non-rational social code reminds us that Veblen recognized only two "social" factors in the industrial process. One was the division of labor, understood in the sense of the interdependence of industrial processes. The machine technology means the existence of a delicate, complicated mechanism of interlocking processes. Veblen regards it mainly from an "engineering" or mechanical point of view.

As was noted . . . , each industrial unit, represented by a given industrial "plant," stands in close relations of interdependence with other industrial processes going forward elsewhere, near or far away, from which it receives supplies—materials, apparatus, and the like—and to which it turns over its output of products and waste, or on which it depends for auxiliary work, such as transportation. The resulting concatenation of

48. *The Human Problems of an Industrial Civilization* (New York: Macmillan, 1933), pp. 120–121.

industry has been noticed by most modern writers. It is commonly discussed under the head of the division of labor.[49]

The division of labor as a phenomenon of social organization, as a problem of the relationship of specialized groups of men, is neglected.[50] Veblen's own view of the division of labor was doubtless useful, and particularly so for the development of his theme that business enterprise steps in to exercise sabotage and inhibition at crucial points in the interlocking of industrial processes. But his failure or refusal to see the problems of the division of labor as problems of the social relationships of industrial groups is closely connected with his anarchism. There is no reason to think that industrious and co-operative workmen would be produced by the resiliency of ancient instincts if merely the "dead hand" of absentee ownership were removed.

The other "social" component in industry which Veblen saw clearly was the cultural character of technology. Technology is a matter of the community's knowledge. It is cumulative; and Veblen often argues that it is more important than the sheer material items with which it is brought into fruitful contact.[51] Technology is for him essentially a matter of "know-how." He is able to make brilliant use of this point. Marx had pointed out that the laborer is "free" in a double sense: he is the "free" owner of his labor-power, which he cannot sell, lock, stock and barrel, but can sell only for limited periods of time (for otherwise he would be converting the situation from one in which he has a commodity to sell to one in which he would himself be a commodity); and he is "free" in the ironic sense of being free of the means of production. Veblen carries this point further. He indicates how the ownership of the means of production enables an effective control of the community's technological knowledge. That knowledge cannot be put to work except by contact with the material means, and thereby (as in the case of large-scale unemployment) the members of the community are separated not only from the means

49. *The Theory of Business Enterprise*, p. 15. *Cf.* also *Absentee Ownership*, ch. x.

50. Compare, *e.g.*, ch. ii of *Business Enterprise*, and ch. x of *Absentee Ownership* with Durkheim's *Division of Labor* (tr. G. Simpson, New York: Macmillan, 1933).

51. *Cf. e.g.*, *The Place of Science*, pp. 324–386.

of production, but in consequence of *this* separation are also "separated" from their own technological knowledge (or the possibility of its effective utilization).[52]

These "social" components in industry have been mentioned to indicate Veblen's important insights into the nature of industry (and, incidentally, its connection with pecuniary forces), but they do not of themselves save him from holding to an anarchistic view. It should be quite plain, however, that the anarchistic strain comprises only one strand in Veblen's complex thought. We may continue to analyze his anarchism and yet notice some qualifications of it by other strands in his thought through a consideration of his views on one of the most important problems he set himself, namely, the assessment of the effects of the machine discipline.

On the question of the effects of the machine discipline on the workman, and on the related question of the general significance of the machine in the social order, Veblen's thought is rather complicated. At least three elements may be found in it: (1) a *psychological* theory of the effects of the machine on the workman; (2) the view that the effect of the machine discipline is to produce a state of anomie[53]; (3) the view that the machine discipline carries with it or implies or builds up a set of distinctive norms or institutions, distinctively set off from the norms bound up with the system of business enterprise or the national establishment and Dynastic State. The presumption that the machine discipline develops or increases the workman's rationality is of interest here as it fits in with Veblen's anarchism. In *Imperial Germany,* Veblen had stated that the "mechanistic, matter-of-fact drift" might be conceived as natively congenial.[54] This would tie in well with the content presumed for the instinct of workmanship. Given workmen made rational by the machine discipline, over and above their endowment in terms of the instinct of

52. *Cf. Absentee Ownership,* Part I. Veblen's emphasis is also often that the *community's* technological knowledge is put into the effective control of *special* groups strategically placed.

53. Arthur K. Davis clearly notes that Veblen saw a tendency toward anomie in contemporary society. *Thorstein Veblen's Social Theory,* p. 94.

54. He took a somewhat different position in the title essay of *The Place of Science.* His very inconsistencies necessitate the procedure of separating the components of his theoretical scheme.

workmanship, the presumption is raised that a large part of the problem of social organization under any conceivable new regime would be automatically solved. "Quantitative habituation" would presumably take care of the interlocking of industrial processes. "Engineering" habits of mind would presumably supply the necessary social cement, in the absence of "pecuniary" institutions and under the guidance of trustworthy "native bents."

There is sufficient empirical evidence today that industry presents very considerable problems of social organization that do not take care of themselves in virtue of some primitive endowment of the workman (or, for that matter, in virtue of some endowment of management) and cannot be solved by the methods of approach of the engineer. Elton Mayo has recently given the name of the "rabble hypothesis" to that type of postulation in economic theory by which the circumstances of social organization and group participation are left out of account and human groups are looked upon as collections of isolated individuals activated by self-interest. He summarizes the basic concepts of the "rabble hypothesis" as follows:

1. Natural society consists of a horde of unorganized individuals.
2. Every individual acts in a manner calculated to secure his self-preservation or self-interest.
3. Every individual thinks logically, to the best of his ability, in the service of this aim.[55]

Mayo is concerned to demonstrate that in a very important sense orthodox economic theory studies "abnormal" situations, that appear in social crisis or when the forces making for group organization are in abeyance, so that the rabble hypothesis becomes in a limited way a true one. But there is a very clear additional implication in Mayo's work, supported both by the theoretical considerations he adduces and the research of himself and his colleagues: rationality as a sheer human faculty is a very limited factor in producing social cohesion. Even Freud, as we have seen, in a limited portion of his theory, tried to exhibit the rational faculty as making for cohesion. The evidence of industrial research is that if traditional-institutional sources of cohesion lapse, non-rational elements in human relations must again

55. *The Social Problems of an Industrial Civilization* (Boston: Harvard University, 1945), p. 40; *cf.* the whole of ch. ii, *ibid.*

be tapped in order to re-create it.[56] No amount of training in the sheer mechanics of the industrial process, even if it made workmen rational, would provide the bases for social order. It may well have been some realization of this that made Veblen give so wide an extension to the term "matter-of-fact" that it becomes clear that he included in it more than would be implied simply in the view that technology makes rational workmen.

The development of the third distinguishable element in Veblen's views on the machine discipline need only be mentioned here. It would have carried him farthest from his anarchism, but though it is present, it is not sufficiently developed to extricate him from his difficulties.

In his chapter on "Civilization and the Machine Process" in *The Theory of Business Enterprise,* Veblen treated the effects of the machine in such a manner as to give some warrant to the view that he was showing the "dissolving" effects of the machine process, dissolving in the sense that its tendency was to undermine existing institutions. Thus, to the industrial or factory population, "the natural right of property no longer means so much . . . as it once did." [57] Trade-unionism itself is at variance with the natural-rights dogmas that form the essential props of the business system.[58] In its extreme (socialistic) development it takes on an attitude of positive hostility to property and free contract.

> Trade-unionism does not fit into the natural-rights scheme of right and honest living; but therein, in great part, lies its cultural significance. It is of the essence of the case that the new aims, ideals, and expedients do not fit into the received institutional structure; and that the classes who move in trade-unions are, however crudely and blindly, endeavoring, under the compulsion of the machine process, to construct an institutional scheme on the lines imposed by the new exigencies given by the machine process.[59]

The "exigencies given by the machine process" are alleged to account for the iconoclastic temper witnessed in the "socialistic disaf-

56. *Cf.* Mayo, *The Social Problems of an Industrial Civilization, passim,* and, further, F. J. Roethlisberger and W. J. Dickson, *Management and the Worker* (Cambridge: Harvard University, 1946) and T. North Whitehead, *Leadership in a Free Society* (Cambridge: Harvard University, 1936).

57. *Business Enterprise,* p. 327.

58. *Ibid.,* pp. 328–329.

59. *Ibid.,* pp. 335–336.

fection," with its opposition to the institutions of property and ownership, as well as its opposition to (or at least its inability to see the value of) the old-time domestic and religious institutions. The machine discipline, in short, undermines the "old order" *without* creating on the part of the socialistically inclined workmen a definite and positive set of new norms to replace the old.

This inevitably calls to mind Durkheim's notion of anomie, literally "absence of law," or absence of norms.[60] Veblen's description of the effects of the machine discipline is also interpretable in part as one of the lapse or disappearance of integrating norms. His emphasis, however, is on the lapse of integration with the non-industrial or pecuniary classes. Socialism is a "disaffection." Given his anarchism, Veblen could not plainly see the necessity of norms of some kind to hold any society together.[61] In one case where he very definitely recognized the normative character of institutions, *The Theory of the Leisure Class,* he significantly dealt with the integration of the classes in the community by means of pecuniary norms, which of course he regarded as wasteful, repressive, and sabotaging. In another such case, *Imperial Germany,* he dealt with the norms emanating from and supported by the Dynastic State, which of course worked to the actual detriment of the "underlying population." If he dealt with the "seamy side" (A. K. Davis) of institutions, his analysis sometimes led him to overlook their functions altogether. This, again, can only be attributed to his anarchism, with its underpinning of a psychological theory that gave vast content to instincts as such.

The anarchism of both Freud and Veblen is sufficiently evident. Both men were severe critics of modern civilization. Each tried to implement his criticisms by an appeal to human nature. Each made the appeal to the "facts" of human nature by assuming a very large endowment for the "natural man," larger, in either case, than anything warranted by present-day psychological knowledge. When the "natural man" was filled full, it was possible to "oppose" him, in each case, to an institutional order, which in Freud's analysis was uncongenial but inevitable, and in Veblen's contained large ("pecu-

60. See especially *Le Suicide* (Paris: Alcan, 1930), Bk. II, ch. v.
61. See Parsons, *Structure of Social Action, passim;* Davis, *Thorstein Veblen's Social Theory, passim.*

niary") elements that were positively oppressive and destructive. For both, the institutional order comes pretty near to being a barren wilderness and the source of sorrows. Freud qualifies by allowing that civilization effects an after all indispensable restraint of the impulses of the "natural man," and, in terms of social theory, eliminates the hopeless difficulties in the way of rationalistic presumptions that would otherwise be raised for his views on human nature by positing the development of the superego. Veblen "didn't like," so to put it, business enterprise, the price system, ceremonialization of status, status itself, luxuries, the national establishment, or religion; he "liked" very little besides technology or technological efficiency; most of the rest was likely to be of the nature of "waste." As Freud never adequately explained the cohesion or existence of any society, so Veblen failed to explain how a society could maintain itself or continue to exist on the basis of a mere avoidance of "waste."

Inevitably, in view of differences of interest and of the purposes for which each constructed his view of human nature, there are differences in concrete achievement. Thus, the concept of the superego played a vital role in Freud's theory and saved it from falling into greater difficulties than it did. Veblen could scarcely have been interested in developing such a concept, given the terms in which the discussion of modern economic problems was posed by him or by the men, like Marx and Sombart, who had an important influence on him. On the other hand, Freud could never conceptualize the problem of order in society in terms remotely approaching those of Veblen. He saw virtually no sources in social structure for the "discontents" of civilization. He could only radically posit the incompatibility of all society and "human nature." In this sense, his anarchism is of course more unqualified than that of Veblen. Freud's anarchism, too, is final. Having decided on the incompatibility of biology and culture, he implies that there is nothing further to be done, except, possibly, to enjoy the incidental gratifications that civilization does permit. A "soviet of technicians" would have seemed to him ludicrous, not so much because it implied a possible reconstitution of society on a technological basis alone, but because it implied a purely social solution to a problem made insoluble by the very nature of man. Veblen's anarchism is less final, in that the dissolution of institutions would make a more livable life, although, of course, such an outcome is purely fantastic.

It is a very common device for a critic of society to implement his criticism by describing human nature in such a way as to make it appear to give support to the ideals he holds. Then society can be made over to conform to the human nature posited, and the particular ideals will be realized. An element of this sort is undoubtedly present in Veblen's social theory, although it does not stand by itself. If the critic insists, as Veblen did, that a "scientific" description of human nature be *forced* to give support to his ideals, there is always a good chance that the view he gives of human nature will be subject to severe strictures. Actually, very little is achieved by this procedure: the facts about human nature are misread or edited, and a frank avowal of ideals is avoided. The critic's norms go underground only to reappear in the guise of "psychology."

In the case of Freud, it can hardly seem that the nature he attributes to the natural man is a device for the concealment of ideals. It is true that countless students and critics have seen in him a kind of champion of a freer sexuality and freer attitudes toward it than generally prevailed in his day. But Freud made his indictment of civilized sexual morality quite plain. He did not make it by roundabout ways. An explanation for his refusal to espouse certain activist solutions, such as proposed by Wilhelm Reich, on the line of community of goods and women, is suggested by Roland Dalbiez:

> A great realist such as Freud could not be taken in by such fancies. Therefore those who favoured Reich's views willingly let it be understood that Freud lacked courage, and shrank from the practical consequences of his ideas. This supposition does not at all fit in with Freud's character. He has never hesitated to challenge public opinion; his temperament impels him to seek trouble rather than to run away from it. It is not through timidity, we believe, that Freud has worked out no programme of sexual reform, but because he has grown progressively more aware that a modification of cultural sexual ethics would, *in the final balance,* show a loss. The diminution of suffering which it would bring about in certain instances would be more than offset by the damage that would be done to the formation of character in childhood by the greater instability of the family. Freud . . . is never more himself than when mercilessly criticizing those who promise man happiness, either in this life or the next.[62]

62. Dalbiez, *ibid.,* vol. II, p. 311. For an entirely different view from Dalbiez'

This explanation is at least consistent with certain aspects of Freud's views on the relation between human nature and society. Change will not affect the ultimate incompatibility between nature and culture. Any institutional arrangement of sexual matters will breed unavoidable "discontents." Freud might be right in such a contention, but the ground on which he rests it is that society will in any circumstances be the enemy of the natural man. The contrast between Freud and Veblen appears at this point to be rather analogous to that between Malthus and Godwin. Where Godwin anticipated marvellous results from the removal of "bad" institutions, Malthus saw a kind of trap for man, that would continually be laid by the inexorable working of his own incompatible instincts: the sexual urge with its consequences in reproduction would work at cross purposes with the universal need to eat.[63] But Freud has not afforded convincing proof of the details of his view of human nature, which has the inconsistencies and shortcomings we have noted. It is not necessary to doubt that Freud was, as Dalbiez says, a "great realist," at least by intention, and, from its very character, his view of human nature can scarcely be considered a disguised statement of ideals. But, to say nothing of his more or less purely speculative excursions on human nature, such as he undertook in *The Future of an Illusion* and *Civilization and Its Discontents,* it is doubtful whether he did justice to what he saw in the clinic.

The examination of anarchism in Freud and Veblen serves not only to pose the general problem of order, which it must do by definition, but also to sharpen the question of the place of values or norms in the relationship between clinical psychology and social theory. In any society, norms are of the essence of the institutional structure and represent values from the point of view of the agents holding to them. If the relationship of the individual to society is to be considered, obviously a large part of the consideration must give attention to the individual's status relative to the social norms. Freud handled this problem by postulating a general incompatibility between social

on Freud's position on sexuality, considering Freud a typical "bourgeois" reformer merely urging a somewhat more "indulgent" attitude toward sexuality and taking him to task for not holding more radical views, *cf.* Erich Fromm's "Die Gesellschaftliche Bedingtheit der Psychoanalytischen Therapie."

63. See Parsons, *Structure of Social Action,* pp. 102–107.

norms and the individual, a postulation possible only through seeing human nature as relatively pre-crystallized and modified by his work on the superego. He therefore saw the problem, but to a considerable extent adopted unacceptable devices to resolve it. There are points in Veblen's theory at which the character of norms is correctly grasped, and at these points there is no reason why there should not be a profitable intercourse between Veblen's social theory and Freud's psychology, provided that that psychology is modified in specific ways. To a considerable extent, the necessary modification has already been effected in Freud's psychology, most successfully by some of the neo-Freudians. At this point we wish only to be clear about a crucial aspect of the modification. This consists simply in the view, which will subsequently be drawn out from the relevant literature, that the individual, from the point of view of clinical psychology, is to be looked on as the locus of a more or less complex value system. From the point of view of social science, the individual has to be looked on as to an extent a bearer of values, insofar as social norms have their impact on him. The sociologist knows that norms are subject to private elaborations, but for many purposes he is content to rest with the proposition that norms bring about a general uniformity and predictability and does not pursue the precise nature of their private elaboration or their possible place in the total, personal value system that an individual may have. It is our thesis that clinical psychology has increasingly since Freud's day seen the individual in terms of the particular organization of values he represents, and, moreover, that to see the individual in this way is an indispensable condition for fruitful relationship between clinical psychology and social theory. It is an essential point that so-called "neurotic" behavior may to an important extent be interpreted in terms of values to which the individual holds.

If so, the relationship between clinical psychology and social theory is fairly indicated in the following terms. An institution represents by definition a normative system sustained by agents who are its carriers. Any particular normative system may be abstracted and treated for some purposes *as if* it had a kind of life independent of the agents sustaining it. Or, better, for some purposes, it is useful to study the institution while keeping in the background the fact that it is sustained by human agents who also sustain other values in a total personal normative scheme. When a particular institution has been thus abstracted, however, it is possible to examine its normative structure in relation to total private or individual normative schemes. Institutions are of course sustained by *consensus.* A private or individual normative scheme will contain some elements from various institutional sources, although no two individuals may understand or be affected by the social norms in exactly the same way. In addition, the private individual scheme may contain elements far removed from formal social consensus. The point here is simply that to study the relation of an institutional normative scheme to an individual normative scheme is to study a relation between things that are genuinely different: firstly because the individual will have been affected by more than one institutional scheme, and is already valuationally diverse, so to put it (in virtue of the impact upon him of various institutional schemes); secondly because institutional norms fall into the complex of a *total* individual valuational system, including important unconscious components, and not necessarily exhausted even when all purely institutional normative influences have been taken into account: there may still remain an "individual" (although not necessarily "unique") component.

When we consider the connection between Veblen's social theory at two of its strongest points—the analysis of the leisure class and the analysis of modern Germany—and clinical psychology in its modern modified form, the points just sketched will figure as important background. It will be profitable, meanwhile, to examine how some of the issues raised in this section have been treated in the major traditions of clinical psychology, other than the orthodox Freudian.

### IV. ADDENDUM ON STRUCTURAL IRRATIONALITY

It must be noted that such a concept as structural irrationality raises a question of "values" in social science. There is no question, we may grant, about the existence of incompatible goals, actual or potential, within the same social system. Veblen's thesis about imperial Germany is a good enough illustration. If Karl Polanyi's thesis is correct, the goals that must be realized in market economy, involving the treatment of land, labor and money purely as if they were commodities, are incompatible with various goals implicit in social organization, such as emphasize the "human" character of labor and the traditional and sentimental values centering around land. Analytically, descriptions of this sort support our concept. But just what would a "rational ordering" in the type of situation that Veblen describes or that Polanyi describes consist in? Thus, in the case of Veblen's thesis, is there any warrant for saying that rational ordering of the components he describes would involve the playing down of the imperialistic component? The two components cannot coexist in a stable social scheme. For stability, one or the other must be played down. Is it not a question of "personal tastes" *which* shall be played down? Why not attempt to achieve ordering of the type the Nazis sought, which would roughly involve the playing up of the imperialist component as "order" is achieved through an attempted elimination of value systems contradictory to the National Socialist norms?

The only way to answer this type of question adequately is to keep firmly in mind the clue afforded by the procedure of the clinical psychologist who addresses himself to the constitutional elements present in his patient. He is guided by what his patient "really wants." The test of his helping the patient to what he "really wants" is in therapeutic results: the test is *in principle* quite objective. An *analogous* procedure on the social plane would be to engage in as thoroughgoing an analysis as possible of what actual social structure and institutions are like. Given the norms actually present in a social or institutional scheme, what are the chances for the success or stability of any particular arrangement? The social scientist, like the psychologist, is constrained to deal with what is "constitutionally" present. There are obviously certain things which he will ascertain quite readily. Thus, given the standards of living and the associated expectations of people in the Western World, he will know that any project for the radical elimination of the modern technology is not feasible. Any possible reconstitution of the general social order seeking to reconcile elements from among which that technology is missing would therefore be very unlikely to be successful. This is of course a very simple case. But, theoretically, there is no bar to the grasp, on much deeper levels, of the actual normative constituents in a society. This would enable prediction that any proposed or prospective institutional re-arrangement would, let us say, last either a long time or a very short time because it would be seen to be in conflict with strong actual or potential constituents in the social structure. Obviously, also, the net may be flung wide or narrow, depending on our purposes, when we speak of the constituents or components in the social structure. We may conceive the social structure in international terms, for example, and attempt to show the incompatibility of the goals of one or several nations with those of others, or we may analyze a purely intra-national situation.

This type of analysis indicates a sense in which it is not purely a matter of taste to decide which elements, in a description like Veblen's, shall be emphasized in order to achieve rational ordering. Reason, it will be remembered, is a *form,* not itself a force or material or even a concrete existent value or norm (although it may be the object of values or sentiments). It is a type of relationship among elements already *present in relative strength or in a particular degree.* To attempt to achieve order or stability by resolution or legislation or force or propaganda may be quite futile as long as elements actually present are not given adequate place or are neglected. Theoretically, then, the social scientist, in consideration of elements actually present, should be able to assess the ordering-value or reconciliation-value or possible stability of any institutional rearrangement. He should be able to see that a particular rearrangement, say, simply serves to conceal old goal-conflicts. Everything depends on how deep his analysis of what is actually present can go. If it goes deep enough, he may be in a position to show that a rearrangement such as was represented, say, by National Socialism, involved an emphasis on a set of normative components that could not stably organize the German nation internationally or, more doubtfully, intra-nationally. If the elimination of goal conflicts that disrupt a society is not desired, there can of course be no quarrel at the points at which it is not desired. Goal conflict will simply remain. On the individual level, if an individual does not wish to get well, there is also no quarrel, except that he will continue to manifest objective signs of "unhappiness." If he does not *"want"* to get well, conclusively, that is the end of the matter. On the institutional level, the situation is analogous: it depends on what existent norms are and where conflicts exist, although it also depends on *who,* or what elements in the class structure, and with what strength, may be in conflict. But the procedures and results of clinical psychology provide us with a useful warning for the social plane: analysis of actual values can easily be superficial or beside the mark. But under contemporary (and, for that matter, numerous non-contemporary) social conditions no analysis of this type can dispense with implicit or explicit use of the concept of structural irrationality.[64]

64. *Cf.* Gunnar Myrdal, *An American Dilemma* (New York: Harper's, 1944), *passim,* but esp. Apps. 1 and 2.

# 5. *The Normative Component of the Psyche*

## I. THE CONTRIBUTION OF ADLER

THE PSYCHIATRIC THEORY of Alfred Adler has its main value for our purposes in the clarity with which Adler exhibits a peculiar normative component in the psyche.

The work of Adler on the relation of the individual to society shows continuity with that of Freud, even if it is only the continuity that derives from taking a consciously opposite position, for Adler's polemical orientation is almost invariably against the views of his one-time master. The opposition, so persistent in Freud, between human nature and the social order, is virtually absent in Adler. In only one of his important works, namely, his *Study of Organ Inferiority and Its Psychical Compensation,*[1] significantly a work written relatively early in his career, does he postulate an opposition of this sort. Adler makes use of Freud's concept of the pleasure-principle to explain the genesis of "neurosis" from constellations of organic inferiority. He thereby emphasizes the "wanton," pleasure-seeking functions of organs before a "moral"[2] or cultural influence sets in and the organs are domesticated. A strain on the part of organs to function uninhibitedly and "naturally" is thus postulated; a strain whose effect is opposite to that of the cultural constraint toward organ-domestication. When the organ is "inferior," its domestication may prove particularly difficult. In this formulation, there is the germ of a theory of "neurosis" whose main terms are constitutional inadequacy, on the one hand, and what Adler calls "the pressure of life and culture," on the other.

Adler usually assesses the significance even of organ inferiority in psychological, not physical, terms. The opposition between nature

1. (Tr. S. E. Jelliffe, New York: Nervous and Mental Disease Publishing Co., 1917.)

2. The word is Adler's own: ". . . let us call them the 'moral' activities—the final success of which ensures the child's cultural development." *Ibid.*, p. 59.

and culture, in the general tendency of his work, falls far into the background: "I came to the conclusion that inherited inferiorities of gland or organ, if they made themselves felt psychically, were inducive to a neurotic disposition. . . . The decisive factor in such a case would be the situation in which the child finds itself and its personal appraisement of this position."

Adler makes quite unequivocal references to "the secondary nature of constitutional organ-inferiority and the primary nature of psychogenic factors in the etiology of neurosis." [3] The great body of his work dispenses with nature-culture oppositions. No doubt there is some loss involved in this, since Freud's persistent work at the relationship between nature and culture, whatever its shortcomings, led to the fruitful theory of the superego. Adler never developed such a theory, and in his analysis of organ inferiority he leaned on Freud's distinction of the pleasure- and reality-principles to formulate his conception of the domestication or socialization of organs.

But Adler has his own view of socialization. In fact, his whole schema of "neurosis" is a theory of the relation of individual to society according to which covert, anti-social power impulses are developed in the individual because the process of socialization has failed at some point. He does not refer to mechanisms such as are involved in the development of the superego, but his view of socialization is nevertheless clear. Socialization is the process whereby the individual is incorporated into a moral community. One brief and simple statement goes to the heart of his view: "We find adaptation to the community is the most important function of the psychic organ." [4] In every failure of "adaptation to the community," Adler would find some lesion originating in the relationship of the individual to others who were important to him at crucial, probably early, points in his life-line. Such a lesion is especially likely to be occasioned in children who are "spoiled" or pampered, children who are neglected or hated, and children who are physically inferior. "Spoiled" children tend to

3. *The Practice and Theory of Individual Psychology,* pp. 79, 80. Several words in the first of the quotations above are italicized in Radin's translation. It should be noted that Adler agrees with Freud in contending for the existence of a "neurotic" diathesis, nevertheless. *Cf. ibid.,* p. 316.

4. *Understanding Human Nature* (tr. W. B. Wolfe, New York: Greenberg, 1927), p. 32.

develop impossible expectations of others and are resentful when they are disappointed. Children who are neglected or hated tend to conclude that all of society is inimical to them and may develop a pattern of thoroughly vengeful behavior. Children who are physically inferior and suffer psychic consequences will also tend to develop vengeful reactions or else build a world of high, utterly impossible fantasy.[5] The general effect in all these cases is what Adler is wont to call a "mistaken" view of life, one in which the individual is an "enemy" of the community. "Neurosis" itself is anti-social, although the category of the anti-social is larger than that of "neurosis." "I want to be a grave-digger; I want to be the person who digs graves for others," said a four-year-old boy to Adler,[6] and in Adler's view the type of sentiment indicated in this statement covertly underlies "neurotic" manifestations at large. As a kind of general motto for some basic "neurotic" trends, Adler quotes Horace's phrase: "I refuse to adapt myself to circumstances; circumstances must adapt themselves to me." [7]

There is scarcely a passage in Adler's work which indicates more clearly than the following his conception of the anti-social character of "neurotic" behavior:

The reason for the intolerance of the neurotics toward the constraints of society, as the history of their childhood shows, is to be sought in the continuous conflict-attitude that has been practiced for many years against the environment. This is forced upon the child, without there being any real justification for its expressing itself in just such a reaction, by the . . . position it occupies and from which the child receives either lasting or intensified feelings of inferiority. The object of the conflict-attitude is the conquest of power and importance, an ideal of superiority constructed with an infant's incapacity and over-evaluation and the fulfilment of which presents compensations and super-compensations of a most general kind, in the pursuit of which there always occurs a victory over the constraints of society and over the will of the environment. As soon as this conflict has taken on more acute forms it evolves, from within itself, an antagonism against compulsions of all kinds, whether they be education, reality, common interest, external force, personal weakness, as well as all the compulsions presented by such factors as work, cleanliness, acceptance of nourishment, normal urination and defecation, sleep, treatment of

5. See *What Life Should Mean to You, passim.*
6. *Practice and Theory of Individual Psychology,* p. 15. 7. *Ibid.,* p. 28.

disease, love, tenderness, friendship, loneliness and its opposite, sociability. In toto we get the picture of a man who does not want to play the game, a dog in the manger.[8]

Refusal to conform to the standards of the community, rebelliousness, the substitution of a private system of constraints for the constraints involved in communal norms—these are the essence of the "neurotic" way of life, in Adler's view. Adler's emphasis on the *relation* of the individual to others (with an associated emphasis on the relation of the individual's private normative scheme to a communal normative scheme) occasions the statement: "We claim that the neurosis is an illness of *position* and not of disposition." [9] Even the explanation that Adler affords of unconsciousness is affected by his conception of opposition to communal norms. He implies that there would be no "need" for the unconsciousness of "neurotic" trends if they were not so definitely anti-social that the "neurotic" is constrained to hide their nature from himself or from others: "The unconscious nature of the power-goal is conditioned by its unbridgeable contradiction with the real demands of the community feeling." [10] Again, Adler notes that a certain patient's tendency to depreciate his brother operated unconsciously, and remarks: "Nevertheless it accomplished more than it would were it consciously realized, because the influence of the community feeling is made impossible." [11] Even the diseased psyche cannot altogether escape "the voice of the community." [12] The view that Adler takes of compulsion-"neurosis" is quite in accordance with these more general views: he states that this form of illness ". . . discloses the unconscious purpose of the patient to unburden and free himself by means of a diseased compulsion from the compulsion due to the necessary demands made by society. . . ." [13]

Adler has thus in a certain sense maintained the opposition between the pleasure-impulse of organs and the requirements of domestication. But he does not by any means state or imply that man is *natu-*

8. *Ibid.*, pp. 26–27.

9. *The Case of Miss R* (tr. E. & F. Jensen, New York: Greenberg, 1929), p. 175; *cf.* also, *ibid.*, pp. 176 and 275.

10. *The Practice and Theory of Individual Psychology*, p. 77; *cf.* also, *ibid.*, pp. 227–234.

11. *Ibid.*, p. 233. Italicized in Radin's translation.

12. *Ibid.*, p. 196.

13. *Ibid.*, p. 207. Part of this statement is italicized in Radin's translation.

*rally* anti-social. Rather, he may be made anti-social through specific experiences (of being pampered or hated or made to feel inferior because of organic defect), and the general implication of Adler's theory is that human beings at birth represent potentialities that may be realized in a variety of ways. There is nothing remotely resembling a "complete man" at birth. Adler thus avoids Freud's anarchism.

It must be noted that the discrimination of the anti-social element does not merely have the significance of a statement of Adler's personal values. If Adler has shown the pathological effects or associations of unconscious personal opposition to certain typical demands of a moral community, there can be no question about the scientific value of discriminating the element he did. Our criterion of what is actually *present* in the individual again comes to the fore. If, *for him,* "anti-social" behavior produces pathological effects, then "anti-social" does not simply signify what Adler or others may dislike because of a personal scheme of values.[14] In fact, the anti-social element Adler uncovered is, implicitly or explicitly, widely recognized in clinical psychology. There may be disagreement on the precise significance of this element or on the role it plays in the total dynamics of the mind, but it is almost invariably observed or inferred, no matter what place it may then be assigned in a theoretical interpretation.[15]

Adler's theory of social structure is too rudimentary to warrant treatment. More important than this is his recognition of the influence of cultural circumstances upon the individual. Thus, he definitely connects the "masculine protest" with current cultural conditions. It is the "obvious advantages of being a man" that have produced "severe disturbances in the psychic development of women as a consequence of which there is an almost universal dissatisfaction with the feminine role."[16] But Adler fails to systematize his views on culture. The net result is that the body of his work represents no

14. This is not to deny that Adler's psychology is sometimes homiletic rather than scientific nor does it save him from the criticism that he shows no adequate understanding of the power of unconscious forces in the psyche.

15. An excellent instance of implicit recognition of this element in "neurosis" is afforded by Stekel's paper on "The Final Results of Psychoanalytical Treatment," in J. S. van Teslaar, ed., *An Outline of Psychoanalysis* (New York: Modern Library, 1925), pp. 319–360.

16. *Understanding Human Nature,* p. 133. See also *Practice and Theory . . . ,* pp. 16–22 and 109–143 and *The Neurotic Constitution, passim.*

genuine attempt to relate the data of clinical psychology to those of social theory. Freud unquestionably made many errors in the attempt to bridge the gap between the fields, but he did present a relevant theory. Finally, on the scientific level, Adler has a minimal contribution of his own to make to the problems of rationality and social cohesion.

### II. THE CONTRIBUTION OF JUNG

As with Adler, our interest in Jung attaches primarily to his exhibition and distinctive treatment of a normative component in the psyche.

Jung's polemical orientation is also against the doctrine of Freud, although he does not spare criticism of Adler. While this orientation is not in doubt, a noteworthy strain in his criticism is the fact that he regards the views of Freud and Adler as not so much positively incorrect as one-sided, in accordance with the conception that there are as many psychologies as there are human psychological types and that therefore what one "sees" in the psychic realm depends upon "who" one is.[17] We may at once indicate the character of Jung's orientation against Freud and approach what is in effect his contention for the existence of a normative component in the psyche by considering the distinction between "signs" and "symbols."

Jung asserts that "what Freud terms symbols are no more than *signs* for elementary instinctive processes." [18] But when Freud speaks of "symptomatic" rather than "symbolical" actions, his terminology is quite justified, given his standpoint.[19] Signs or symptoms are reducible to phenomena of which they are the mere indicators or marks, but symbols refer to a reality irreducible to those ultimate components which figure as crucial in the Freudian (or Adlerian) scheme of theory. Jung's intent is not to deny that there are signs or symptoms of repressed sexual wishes or of covert power drives. He objects, however, to the extremely large scope allowed to reductive procedures, more especially in strict Freudianism. In "neurotic" phenomena there do occur the manifestations that Freud and Adler professed to see, but also, Jung contends, a residuum not reducible to sexual wish or

17. See *Psychological Types*, pp. 618–628.
18. *Ibid.*, p. 82, footnote.
19. *Ibid.*, p. 606.

power drive. The irreducible residuum is for Jung the field of the symbolic. This is made comprehensible by Jung's view that psychological phenomena involve serious questions of values, especially when we deal with persons seeking new orientations. The discrimination of a value component that cannot be eliminated or reduced, logically, lies behind the distinction of symptom and symbol.[20]

The distinction of symptom and symbol is persistent. Well before the writing of *Psychological Types,* Jung had made an essentially similar distinction of "concrete content" and "symbolic content," and had contended that "to understand the psyche causally means to understand but half of it." [21] The latter statement is closely connected with Jung's distinction, and he develops it elsewhere as follows:

According to Freud's causal conception, there exists only [the] same immutable material, the sexual component, to whose activity every interpretation is led back with a monotonous regularity. . . . To the idea of final development, of such paramount importance in psychology, the spirit of a *reductio ad causam* can never do justice, because each change in the conditions is seen as nothing but a "sublimation" of the fundamental factors, and therefore only an inept expression for the same old thing.[22]

The entire context of Jung's work makes it clear that his position is that the psyche as a whole is incomprehensible unless we postulate that the psychological agent has goals or purposes cherished as values. Freud had either overlooked or vainly attempted to reduce irreducible moral data. Jung plainly avers that "behind the confused deceptive intricacies of neurotic phantasies, there stands a *conflict,* which

20. Dalbiez (*ibid.,* vol. I, p. 108) appears to think that Jung's view involves the danger that clinical psychology, while avoiding the hazards of reductionism, may become unscientific. Of course, if there are no *symptoms,* there can be no medical psychology. But Jung has not denied symptoms, but, rather, has claimed that they are intimately compounded with symbols, which does not negate medical psychology. An analogous situation prevails in general medicine. If there were no illness, there would be no medicine, but the physician does not cease to be treating illness, nor is medicine denied, if in illness there are also signs of health. In Jung's scheme, "symbols" point to the "healthy" content that may be used to alleviate symptoms.

21. *Collected Papers on Analytical Psychology* (tr. C. E. Long, London: Baillière, Tindall & Cox, 1916), pp. 221–222 and 341.

22. *Contributions to Analytical Psychology* (tr. H. G. and C. F. Baynes, New York: Harcourt, Brace, 1928), pp. 22–23.

may best be described as a *moral* one." [23] It is especially *symbols* that mark the presence of moral conflict and at the same time point to a solution of mental difficulties. Although both Adler and Jung see a normative component in the psyche, and their views are in many respects closer than Jung seems to think, the normative component the latter discriminates is distinctive. Jung's characteristic emphasis is on a struggle for "freedom" or "individuation."

"Freedom," for Jung, is opposed to "convention." Thus, with the division of labor many collectively or socially useful functions have been developed, and convention attends to and emphasizes these, but at the same time the "individual" has "declined." It is no longer "man that counts, but his one differentiated function." [24] This one differentiated function is developed at the expense of "individuality." Other *possible* or *potential* human functions ("inferior functions") do not attain development or differentiation, and yet "the time will come when 'the cleavage in the inner man must again be resolved,' that the undeveloped may be granted an opportunity to live." [25] If a culture selects for emphasis and encourages certain particular functions, it is yet possible that "far higher individual values lie hidden among the neglected functions." [26] Jung's emphasis in the opposition of "freedom" and "convention" is upon the realm of our own unrealized potentialities when regarded as a source from which protest against cultural prescriptions may originate. Jung makes no room for social or cultural influences in this realm. He prefers to speak somewhat obscurely and arbitrarily, and with more than a hint of biologism, of the "archaic man." But this need not prevent us from seeing that a most essential part of his interest is in the genesis and development of latent norms or values which are in opposition to the established and socially accepted. Relevant sociological and psychological issues are very much confused by Jung. But, again, a clear and distinctive conception of "neurosis" emerges. What Jung peculiarly sees in "neurosis" is the development, unsuccessful in terms of the health

23. *Collected Papers . . .* , p. 242. See also *ibid.*, pp. 206–277, *Modern Man in Search of a Soul* (tr. W. S. Dell and C. F. Baynes, New York: Harcourt, Brace, 1936), pp. 132–142 and *The Integration of the Personality* (tr. S. M. Dell, New York: Farrar & Rinehart, 1939).

24. *Psychological Types*, p. 94.

25. See *ibid.*, pp. 95–96.

26. See *ibid.*, p. 97.

of the individual, but quite real, of standards of value representing an original and ideal moral standpoint, opposed to traditional norms. The health of the individual may be established or regained if the strength to hold to his individual value scheme in opposition to traditional norms is supplied. His disease arose from the suffocation of his originality or "freedom." "The genuine neurotic," says Jung's translator, "is typically a man who cannot reconcile the claims of traditional forms and values with those of the obscure, but unbending law, within." [27]

Jung's explicit distinction between "the service of the collective conscience" and "the service of freedom" [28] never falters, and he returns to some of the questions it raises in his work on *The Integration of the Personality*. In this volume, he makes some sharp and characteristic comments on "institutions," which function, of course, in the interest of the "collective conscience":

> That old proverb, *extra ecclesiam nulla salus*—outside the church there is no welfare—rests on the knowledge that an institution is an assured, passable way . . . whereas outside of it no ways and no aims are to be discovered. We must not underestimate the fact that to be . . . lost in chaos means a bitter shock when we know that it is the indispensable prerequisite of every renewal of the spirit.[29]

Jung speaks also of the "effective protection . . . offered by dogma," and states that "excommunication is . . . necessary and useful . . . from the social standpoint." [30] In the latter statement, it may be inferred from his context, he is referring to the utility to a society of the suggestion of new norms.[31] Religion is for Jung only the institutional form *par excellence,* and his religious terms are to be taken in a general institutional sense. His analysis again peculiarly opposes traditional form to new, vivifying and creative (moral) insight. The interesting question of "freedom" for the *many,* so often hinted at by Jung, is now given an unequivocal answer. Convention is "a collective necessity." It is true that "it is a make-shift and not

27. *Psychological Types,* p. xvi. 28. *Ibid.,* pp. 226 and 227–234.
29. *The Integration of the Personality,* p. 116. 30. *Ibid.,* p. 115.
31. Jung does not intend by this kind of statement what Durkheim might have intended by it, namely, that "excommunication" is useful since it functions to reinforce the existing sentiments and representations of a mass of "believers."

an ideal," but the mass of mankind is held unconscious by routine and presumably always will be, even if this means "repudiation of wholeness and a flight from the final consequences of one's own being."[32]

It is entirely possible that the necessary existence of culture and social organization may make "freedom" for the many an unlikely eventuality, but here questions of degree and quantity would be of extreme importance. Instead of entering upon these questions, however, Jung indulges himself in statements to the general effect that masses are "blind beasts."[33]

Analysis of the relationship of the individual to the group supports Jung's view that there is a distinctive normative component in the psyche of the type he indicates. We know, generally, the kind of problem that is posed when the individual defies the mores, and we must agree that the defiance is not necessarily always of the sort that a particular culture's legal code will define as "criminal" (although it is not implied that no kinds of "criminal" action or orientation can afford suggestions for a new normative organization). We know also that under contemporary conditions, in which conflicting moral codes are present rather than an unquestioned single code, a lapse of the influence of any particular scheme of mores on the individual is rather likely to occur. The analysis of the case of the "marginal man" particularly suggests that an individual faced by, or influenced by, say, two alternative cultural schemes is apt to achieve a certain detachment from both and a keen insight into the "limitations" of each.[34] But we are likewise aware that childhood training runs deep. It is readily conceivable, then, that in many situations there would be a keen awareness on an individual's part of the "limitations" of one or more cultural schemes by which he had been influenced or in the values of which he had been trained, and yet at the same time a failure to achieve emotional independence.

These are general socio-psychological considerations that may be supported by life-history materials, and do not need any particular clinical demonstration. But there is every reason to think that, if such

32. See *The Integration of the Personality*, pp. 289–290, 295.
33. See *ibid.*, pp. 274, 281.
34. Everett V. Stonequist, *The Marginal Man* (New York: Scribners, 1937).

elements of a conflict between an individual's urge away from certain cultural compulsions and an urge toward obeying strongly sanctioned ways are present, they would manifest themselves in the clinic in countless forms, and the clinician should be able to refer manifestations of one kind and another to the urges that lie behind them. Moreover, if an individual has by canny comparison and reflection seen the "limitations" from his point of view of certain alternative cultural schemes, again assuming him to be a "marginal man," it is easily conceived that under clinical analysis the form of re-organization of personal life that would most appeal to or motivate him would involve "independence." Even if he is not fully aware of this himself, skilled clinical work should indicate signs or manifestations of it. *Such* signs or manifestations Jung would have called "symbols"; signs or manifestations of a tendency still to be "frightened" in later life by sanctions applied in childhood he would have called "symptoms."

The use of the case of the "marginal man" is only illustrative. The problem Jung has posed is actually universal. The theme of the individual seeking "liberation" from the mores, as Jung himself has recognized, occurs time and again as a central theme in literature and religion. Evidently, the problem is involved with the very circumstances of human living in any society. It shows itself even in primitive Trobriand society, in which a man may defy the incest taboo until he is driven to suicide by public mention of the defiance.[35] The likelihood that a "mores versus individual" problem would not crop up in the clinic is minimal. And it is crucial to observe that Jung's theoretical handling of the problem (granting that polemic will exaggerate differences) is different from Freud's. Freud holds to the presumption that biological impulse must involve man in conflict with any cultural scheme. Jung, by putting questions of normative organization to the fore (at least in one vital part of his system) gains this much: he avoids many criticisms of the type we have already levelled against the anarchism of Freud and opens the way to a significant integration of the theory of clinical psychology and that of social psychology or sociology. The latter disciplines find human

35. *Cf.* Bronislaw Malinowski, *Crime and Custom in Savage Society* (New York: Harcourt, Brace, 1926).

normative organization to be a considerable part of their subject-matter and if in their "downward" urge toward understanding the individual they abruptly found no trace of problems of values (despite their expectations)—which would be the case in an extreme Freudian view (probably more extreme than Freud's)—the inevitable impression would be that of a discontinuity of disciplines.[36]

A final consideration may be adduced. We have previously in this study made use of the device of demonstrating convergence of independent strains of thought in order to reinforce the probability of a point of view. In the present case, we may give a single obvious instance. Erich Fromm's analysis of the contemporary "escape from freedom" is in virtually all relevant respects exactly the same as Jung's analysis of the opposition between "freedom" and "convention." Fromm is, of course, a neo-Freudian, and consequently this is another instance either of convergence of independent strains of thought or of an important agreement within the context of otherwise divergent strains.

It is now clear also what the main difference is between Adler and Jung in respect of the type of normative component in the psyche that each distinguished. Adler, as it were, sees a more "elementary" normative component. His emphasis is on alienation from the community. The preservation or creation of "relatedness" (to others), which was Adler's major problem, is recognized by Jung. But Jung might put his point of view by urging that "relatedness" is only a first step, in the moral-clinical perspective rendered by the "freedom-convention" opposition. He might say that it is elementary that man must be a member of society (and be rid of "neurotically" grounded anti-social impulses) but that for certain individuals it is morally vital (from *their* point of view: otherwise, the clinician in this respect has nothing significant to say to them) to go beyond this and achieve an "independent" personal organization, or "individuality."

It is not the purpose of this study to assess the clinical merits of the respective contributions of Freud, Adler and Jung. But since our

36. One reason we have introduced parenthetically, the phrase, "probably more extreme than Freud's," is that the notion of the superego, had Freud developed it and allowed it to qualify his anarchism more seriously, might have made him give as much stress to normative components in the psyche as Jung.

treatment unavoidably suggests certain characteristic differences in perspective, these may be made explicit. Freud as clinical psychologist is the unsurpassed analyst of the *mechanisms* of mental illness: his strength lies in the indefatigable scrutiny of each twist and turn in diseased mental process. The most complicated, remote and refined emotional processes are brought back to dynamic origins by the dissolvent power of his clinical intelligence. Adler is the spokesman of the moral community and its ineluctable claims, recalling undomesticated and untamed natures to a sense of obligation and of ultimate relatedness to others. He seeks to penetrate the secret sources of an anti-social sentiment that even increases its effectiveness by being relatively unaware of itself. "Neurosis" appears to him like nothing so much as a form of diabolism, a mobilization of resource and energy "against the community and against the gods." Jung is the advocate of the independent spirit: for him a "neurosis" is the life-pattern of an individual who has been unwilling to be a mere creature of culture and take the imprint of the conventions of his time and place, but who has somehow failed to bring off his "revolt." It is Jung's avowed purpose to remove the hindrances to his realization of himself as a distinct and peculiar individuality.

Jung's polemic, in lumping Freud and Adler together, obscures certain resemblances of Adler's work to his own. Thus, there is small justification for regarding Adler, with Freud, as an exponent of a "causal" rather than a "final" view. If anything, Adler is much closer to Jung in this respect. His emphasis on the highly purposive character of the psyche was strong and persistent. On the other hand, Jung's polemic also conceals some important resemblances of his own work to Freud's. This brings us to Jung's general treatment of culture and social organization.

Jung sharply repudiates certain aspects of Freud's reductionism. Thus: "Even if there can be no doubt about the sexual origin of music, still it would be a poor, unaesthetic generalization if one were to include music in the category of sexuality. A similar nomenclature would then lead us to classify the cathedral of Cologne as mineralogy because it is built of stones." [37]

37. *The Psychology of the Unconscious* (tr. Beatrice M. Hinkle, New York: Dodd, Mead & Co., 1937), p. 145.

This type of statement might lead us to think that Jung would have quite a different perspective from Freud's on the nature of culture. Jung even, not ineptly, characterizes the Freudian theory as one in which "the whole edifice of culture becomes a mere surrogate due to the impossibility of incest," and makes reference to the "well-known Freudian absurdity" that "art and religion are nothing but substitutes for repressed infantile sexuality." [38] But Jung's views on culture and matters relevant to the analysis of culture are, generally, not one whit sounder than Freud's, and abound in as many "absurdities" as the latter's. Thus, Jung takes the view that there is an equivalence between the psychic structure of "primitive man" (in the anthropological sense) and the psychic structure which is "at the bottom" of the mind of modern man.[39] But the "primitive man" (of anthropology) is also the "natural man" or "archaic man." The implication is that primitive man is without culture, and this is reinforced by Jung's manner of relating primitive mentality to the "infantile psyche." Primitive man, the "natural man," the infant or child—these are all more or less the same for him. He does not afford much help on the matter of the mentality of the child when he tells us, with characteristic obscurity when he verges on these premises, that "in childhood . . . those retrospective intuitions first arise, which extend far beyond the limits of childhood experience into the life of the ancestors." [40] Confusion and obscurity are bound to occur in relating psychological factors or forces to factors on the social or cultural level when, as is the case with Jung's treatment, there is no clear separation of the psychological problems centering around the new-born human and his potentialities, the human in the early days of his training in a particular group and culture, and the present-day primitive.

The failure of Jung's analysis of culture is perhaps nowhere better illustrated than in his work, *The Psychology of the Unconscious.* In this work, Jung tells us that "the secret of the development of culture lies in the *mobility of the libido,* and in its capacity for transference." [41] Since "libido" is more or less synonymous with "life energy,"

38. *Contributions to Analytical Psychology,* pp. 24 and 364.
39. *Ibid.,* pp. 55–61.
40. *Ibid.,* p. 59.
41. *The Psychology of the Unconscious,* p. 20.

we may put this in other words by saying that "the secret of the development of culture lies in the fluidity of life energy," which statement does not reveal much about any "secret." Jung's point, however, is that the development of culture is to be understood on the analogy of the vicissitudes and "travels" (or, as Jung says, *"Wandlungen"*) of the libido in the phenomena of psychopathology. Jung's translator thus renders the point in psychopathology which affords the motif for Jung's analysis of mythological products, ritual practices and related phenomena:

> Instead of . . . employing the libido in the real world . . . certain people never relinquish the seeking for satisfaction in the shadowy world of fantasy and even though they make certain attempts at adaptation they are halted and discouraged by every difficulty and obstacle in the path of life and are easily pulled back into their inner psychic world. This condition is called a state of *introversion*.[42]

This statement points to Jung's theory of energy-distribution and, although it indicates only one of the simpler processes of energy distribution in psychopathology, it affords us a good notion of the method by which Jung proceeds to analyze culture. Another comment made by Dr. Hinkle brings us even closer to the presuppositions of Jung's method. She notes that the Freudians, in observing and describing dream expressions and the substitutive figures of repressed ideas and feelings, concluded that there was "a similar mechanism at work in myths and fairy tales." She remarks, accordingly, that Karl Abraham "could say that the myth is a fragment of the infantile soul life of the race and the dream is the myth of the individual." [43] The view thus imputed to Abraham is quite close to that adopted by Jung in *The Psychology of the Unconscious.* Jung raises the analogy between "the myth of the individual" and that of the "race" to a sheer identity. This is really his basic presupposition. Cultural development and change are assumed to occur in the history of society by the same processes by which development and change occur in the individual psyche. Let us follow the paths of, and transformations of, the libido, more especially in the diseased mind, says Jung, in effect, and we shall

42. Beatrice M. Hinkle, in "An Introduction to Psychoanalysis and Analytic Psychology," in *The Psychology of the Unconscious,* p. xxx.
43. Hinkle, *ibid.,* pp. xix–xx.

have an infallible clue to the paths and transformations of the human cultural process. More generally, underlying Jung's theory of culture is the quite gratuitous assumption that the psychological motors of human history are to be ascertained or found by assuming that cultural development occurs by the production of "objective" results from historical libido stages which are precisely like the libido stages in the psyche of contemporary man. The psyche of contemporary man, the basic point of reference, is taken usually in the forms or phases of mental illness, though it may also be taken in mental health: it depends on what analogy fits the cultural facts that Jung is at any point attempting to force into a purely, exclusively psychological framework.

We may clarify what Jung means by "objective" results from historical libido stages. To take one of his numerous arbitrary examples, he suggests that "the generation of fire originally occurred as . . . an act of quasi-onanistic activity, objectively expressed." [44] He wishes to convey by the phrase, "objectively expressed," what he calls the "realistic destination" of the libido when it functions in human history. The libido in history has results beyond those which are evident in the mere play of energy in, say, a sick mind. In the play of energy in a sick mind, the phenomena present do not produce substantive extra-psychological results, like the generation of fire. The libido in history has an "actual material" to work upon. But, aside from the production of extra-psychological results, the historical libido stages are for other theoretical purposes just like any libido stages in psychopathological states.[45]

Despite Jung's erudition and psychological insight, his work at the level of analysis of culture not only rests on untenable presuppositions but contains numerous specific shortcomings that reduce its value even further. Thus, his excursions into the psychological foundations of mythology are often ingenious. Nevertheless, they illustrate well the deficiencies of the "comparative method," as that was used in nineteenth-century anthropology. Jung may often be right in his assumption that there are common and universal meanings for certain mythical forms, but his method is "comparative" in the worst sense, in that he undertakes no intensive check on the specific cul-

44. *Ibid.*, p. 174.

45. See *ibid.*, pp. 157–174.

tural contexts of the mythical forms emergent in one culture and another. His assumptions about common and universal meanings for various mythical forms must therefore at best be regarded as merely "suggestive." [46]

We may recall once more the three questions we continually pose for any psychology purporting to be relevant to analysis of the social order. Inevitably, as was the case with Freud, Jung, insofar as he tries to make a psychology perform also the functions of a sociology (which he does in *The Psychology of the Unconscious* by the technique of understanding cultural phenomena on the analogy of the fortunes of the libido) fails seriously in regard to the third question. *The Psychology of the Unconscious* and all of Jung's similar work fail to bridge the gap between the data of clinical psychology and those of social theory. The technique of arbitrary assimilation of the data of one discipline into those of another hardly serves to bridge that gap: it simply makes the task of doing so impossible by assuming that no gap exists. In such work, Jung does not even satisfactorily answer the second of our questions since he shows no particular relevance of libido transformations to events at the social or cultural level. But the beginnings of a genuine and relevant contribution, affording more satisfactory answers to our three questions, are present in Jung's discrimination of a peculiar normative component in the psyche and in his analysis of "freedom" and "convention." It is perhaps well at this point to note again that such a component was not altogether lacking in Freud's system, especially when we have regard to the implications of the concept of the superego. There is no doubt, however, that Freud inevitably missed any such component when he exclusively emphasized the transformations of primary sexual substance.

It is clear by now that normative components in the psyche have received a good deal of emphasis in the history of clinical psychology.

The normative components discriminated by Adler and Jung carry obvious implications for the psychic constitution of "normal" or "usual" persons. Adler's analysis implies that "normal" persons have a more or less non-rebellious co-operative outlook in their inmost na-

46. See, *e.g.*, *ibid.*, pp. 341–427, with special reference to the myth of the hero battling the dragon.

tures. Jung's, generally, implies that the "usual" psyche, at least, is morally determined by the nature of whatever conventions are flourishing.[47]

### III. THE NEO-FREUDIAN CONTRIBUTION

Having reviewed the character of the normative component in two clinical theories that, at least, actually exhibit it clearly, we may ascertain its status more definitely. The normative component in the psyche, in our sense, does not have reference directly and simply to the value systems current in a culture (as these are incorporated by the individual).

Kardiner has taken value systems simply in the sense of consciously accepted normative schemes. This is a legitimate enough starting point:

> A value system can be defined as a generally accepted appraisal of patterns of interpersonal relations (*e.g.*, honesty); achievement (*e.g.*, heroism); goals (*e.g.*, salvation, success); approved types of gratification (*e.g.*, aesthetic, those pertaining to order, systematization, efficiency); and pertaining to social ideals (respectability, status, strength, skill). . . . All value systems are conscious directives and by implication also involve avoidances. They contain all aspirations, ideals, and morality which are publicly sanctioned. The value systems of a culture are among its most conspicuous features. . . .
>
> Whereas all value systems are conscious, they are end results of a complex of constellations deeply rooted in unconscious factors.[48]

Value systems as systems of social norms may be sustained or reinforced by unconscious factors or, in degree, they may not receive support from unconscious factors. But value systems in the sense of institutional normative systems are not simply or exclusively produced by unconscious forces. The latter point has been made quite clear by Cora DuBois:

> Individual childhood experiences in respect to hunger and discipline may find modes of expression in institutionalized fields, and certain institutions are reinforced because of the personal emotional content that can be

47. This treatment of Adler and Jung has by no means been intended to be comprehensive, but has been conditioned by special interests. No special reference has been made to the status of reason in Jung's theoretical work because he does not carry the problem beyond where Freud left it.

48. *The Psychological Frontiers of Society*, pp. 234–235.

directed into them. One must be careful not to use such nexi as sacrifice and childhood experiences as exclusive causal sequences. It would be ludicrously antihistorical to say that childhood feeding habits gave rise to a system of sacrifice in Atimelang. They have merely reinforced and made significant to many individuals that widespread Indonesian custom.[49]

Social norms, then, the value systems of a culture, have a certain independent status. They are not merely emergents from unconscious factors operative in various individuals (even if those unconscious factors have themselves already been molded by what Kardiner has called primary institutions).[50] But, granting the legitimacy for Kardiner's purposes, of looking upon all value systems as social norms, are any advantages to be gained from defining an unconscious or not necessarily conscious normative component in the psyche? To define such a component does not, of course, involve a denial that any culture, being a culture, will show a range of relatively conscious norms or systems of norms. In fact, the sociologist has a great deal of interest in the values or norms held, by consensus, by numbers of individuals who are members of groups with which he seeks to deal. Numerous sociological researches demonstrate preoccupation with social norms as the essential phenomena in the data under consideration. Thus, typically, the sociologist may connect the decline in the birth rate in the modern Occident with the phenomenon of "individualism," or with a "striving spirit" conceived to be derived from the effects of certain capitalist institutions. He may contend that the institution of marriage, especially when there are children, builds or encourages a system of values that has the effect of depressing the death rate; or that the family builds values protective against suicide. He may contend that the circumstances of urban life induce normative systems that result in a significantly higher rate of mental disease for urban than for rural areas.[51]

49. *The People of Alor,* p. 162.

50. These are the institutions through which the child receives his initial disciplines and gets his "basic personality." These institutions do not necessarily, perhaps do not even characteristically, take their effect through direct learning processes.

51. See Warren S. Thompson, *Population Problems* (New York: McGraw-Hill, 1935), esp. ch. xi; Roderich von Ungern-Sternberg, *The Causes of the Decline in Birth Rate* (Cold Spring Harbor, N.Y.: Eugenics Research Association, 1931), esp. pp. 86–131 and 201–202; Ernest Groves and William F. Og-

These, and cognate hypotheses or contentions, have a statistical flavor. A certain probability of occurrence of a characteristic normative pattern is dealt with. When we turn to the kind of data with which the clinical psychologist deals, still bearing in mind the typical approach of the social scientist, a methodological issue is suggested which has been well stated by Karl Mannheim:

> Turning to the psychologist or psychiatrist who has the opportunity while at work in his consulting room of probing into hidden motives by sympathetic intuition, or sounding the depths of the unconscious, one senses a new kind of self-satisfaction, which regards the proud methods of the archivists and field-workers as superficial dabbling. In his opinion these men touch only the institutional surface of human history, a mere façade which hides the living spirit. For psychologists and psychiatrists only the personal aspect of experience matters; the hidden motives of individuals are the mainspring of events.
>
> But all these students . . . have to face the opposition of the theorists, who sometimes as economists, sometimes as sociologists, raise the methodological objection that all these forms of approach give us nothing but fragments, unnaturally torn out of their context, and that their real meaning can only be revealed by imagining a kind of working model of society, designed to include every aspect of its functions.[52]

In the point of view that Mannheim thus states, and further defends, it is not the case that political science without biography is mere "taxidermy" (Lasswell) or that our descriptions of social life are all simply "formal" even if "valuable" (Dollard), since institutions are dead, massive things and the "true reality" lies beneath them.[53] But it is obviously not the case, either, that one can neglect the kind of data that the psychiatrist or sociological psychoanalyst may afford. Even the (institutional) value systems which the social scientist is concerned to analyze are not necessarily entirely conscious.

---

burn, *American Marriage and Family Relationships* (New York: Holt, 1928), Pt. II, ch. x; Durkheim, *Le Suicide,* Bk. II, ch. iii; Maurice Halbwachs, *Les Causes du Suicide* (Paris: Alcan, 1930), ch. viii; Benjamin Malzberg, *Social and Biological Aspects of Mental Disease* (New York: State Hospitals Press, 1940), ch. iii; Pitirim A. Sorokin and Carle C. Zimmerman, *Principles of Rural-Urban Sociology* (New York: Holt, 1929), ch. xii; Louis Wirth, "Urbanism As a Way of Life," *American Journal of Sociology* XLIV (1938), 1–24.

52. *Man and Society in an Age of Reconstruction,* p. 28.

53. See Lasswell, *Psychopathology and Politics* (Chicago: University of Chicago Press, 1930), p. 1; Dollard, *Criteria for the Life History,* p. 1.

If the appearance of women's dress is importantly influenced by pecuniary criteria, or if business men are influenced in their dealings by a preconception regarding the "putative stability of the monetary unit," it does not follow that the agents involved are fully aware of these things. It is clear that a normative system can flourish in a culture without anything like full consciousness of it. In fact, when it is in considerable degree unconscious, it tends to function more automatically and surely. "Full" consciousness, if we may so put it, is therefore not a necessary concomitant of a normative system.

On the other hand, psychoanalysis in general makes it clear that when, as in the phenomena of "neurosis," it is contended that individuals are "unconscious" of certain forces or factors, the meaning of "unconscious" is not absolute. The individual is not "aware," yet, paradoxically, he is also not "unaware." It is as if certain recesses of the personality did have an "awareness" of what is usually said to be "unconscious," or as if there were still a "dim" consciousness. Thus, Karen Horney has noted that "there is no strict alternative between conscious and unconscious, but . . . there are, as H. S. Sullivan has pointed out in a lecture, several levels of consciousness." She continues this line of thought as follows:

> Not only is the repressed impulse still effective . . . but also in a deeper level of consciousness the individual knows about its presence. . . . This means that fundamentally we cannot fool ourselves, that actually we observe ourselves better than we are aware of doing . . . but we may have stringent reasons for not taking cognizance of our observations. . . . I shall use the term "register" when I mean that we know what is going on within us without our being aware of it.[54]

This statement is not adduced in an attempt to destroy the distinction between consciousness and unconsciousness. Nor do we wish to deny that the human data with which the psychoanalyst may deal run "deeper," in the sense of involving a more intensive analysis of personality, than the data with which the sociologist deals. But what our account thus far suggests is a gradient of consciousness. If we adopt this conception, it is perfectly plain that there is in principle no reason to object to the notion of an unconscious normative compo-

54. *The Neurotic Personality*, p. 69.

nent in the psyche. However, is it useful to speak of a *normative* component? It is useful to do so for obvious sociological and psychological purposes, as when we note that individuals are influenced by the social norms of which they receive the impact and which they subsequently sustain. There is every reason to think that this kind of normative component, derivative from the influence of an institutional system upon individuals, is not a superficial matter. Normative components in this sense, also, are not necessarily conveyed through a direct learning process: in fact, insofar as they are unconscious or a degree of unconsciousness attaches to them, they would tend to be implicitly rather than explicitly transmitted or incorporated anew by a new generation. But this does not quite get at what we have intended by a normative component in the psyche. The individual is influenced by various, and perhaps conflicting, normative systems. Moreover, while it is true that he is a locus for the impingement of social norms, we cannot assume that he is the lifeless stamp of those norms. The social norms, rather, would appear to hit on a field that, in degree possesses its own dynamic, its own principle. What the culture provides is sifted in a sensitive mental and emotional process. The final emergent is not the mere imprint of the culture. Some of the facts of individual variation and creative response would be impossible to explain on such an assumption. The hypothesis is inevitably suggested that to remain on the level of abstract analysis of social norms [55] will afford incomplete insight into individual normative systems. When we say "individual" in this context, however, the reference is not necessarily to the "unique." Rather, it is to what we might call the "private." "Private" or "intimate" value constellations may show many points of resemblance from one individual to another and may well afford data for the construction of typologies.

However, there is still a question whether we may legitimately speak of a peculiarly "private" *normative* component. It may be granted that the individual sustains various cultural values and is thereby a value-impregnated agent. But the real question is not only whether this is true but whether it is also true that we may sector out and usefully speak of normative factors in that complex of phenomena that psychiatrists usually discuss under the heading of "uncon-

55. The term "abstract" of course carries no implication of unreality.

scious forces." Granted that social norms may influence the individual deeply (and unconsciously, for that matter) the question remains whether anything *of the essence* of the "unconscious" may be defined as normative. Adler and Jung unequivocally thought that this was the case. Can such a view be defended in the light of the neo-Freudian contribution?

To leave out of consideration *all* normative components (including those that come by way of the individual's incorporation or assimilation of social norms) would put the clinical psychologist in the impossible anarchistic position in which the early Freud was involved. Freud, it is true, did introduce, finally, the concept of the superego. The treatment of the superego involved the treatment of moral components in the personality. But it did so in a strictly limited way. Morality was involved in the sense that the young human being under constraint adopted certain cultural values held by his parents. Since, however, he was still an "animal" underneath, these were superimposed and he achieved a poor and insecure compromise of humanity and animality. If there are no other normative components in the psyche than those Freud pointed to in his analysis of the superego, a strong anarchistic strain cannot be eliminated from the theory of clinical psychology. Adler and Jung, as has been noted, recognized other normative components. In Freud's view, there is a tendency to claim that man becomes ill because he maintains a precarious balance between humanity and animality easily upset in particular individuals. In Adler's view, man becomes ill because he is ill taught by emotional experiences which fail to enforce a discipline of accepting human limitations and living with others. Tension between the animal and human poles cannot ultimately be resolved in Freud's view: The "ferine" strain is always present and represents a lurking threat to the stability of human culture and social organization. It is unnecessary to repeat our previous criticisms of this view. In Adler's view, tension exists, not between humanity and animality, but between the moral community and certain "rebellious" individuals. It is true that such individuals may be produced time and again, but if they can be humanized or domesticated, there is no rift left at any point within the nature of man itself. By this means, an anarchistic outlook is avoided by Adler. Jung sees a tension at a new level, between the conventional and the ideal, but this also does not involve anarchism. Jung insists rather on the general human need for convention.[56]

Some of the work of the neo-Freudians, or at least of students who are reasonably well acquainted with sociological disciplines and at the same time seek to apply the methods and results of psychoanalysis, suggests that the strain in Freud above referred to has not quite been eliminated. This may be illustrated in a statement of John Dollard's, who says that the psychoanalytical point of view

> gives a solid sense of man as an animal and tends to stress the biological driving forces of human action. Culture is seen as a device for modeling and remodeling a recalcitrant animal and as performing the remarkable feat of his socialization. We learn from this view, for example, that while animals may be made docile in social life by reducing drive forces . . . , men are made tractable by culture (*i.e.,* by internalizing social prohibitions).[57]

There is perhaps not very much to be directly gainsaid in this formulation, but if it is too strongly emphasized and carried much further in presuming the recalcitrancy of the animal man while at the same time great definiteness is assumed for his pre-cultural endowment (as by Freud)—then one may forget that man must first grow up in a specific culture in order to be human, in order to be able to sympathize with an individual's defiance of the mores, in fact even in order to invent psychoanalytical technique or be a psychoanalyst. Much of the neo-Freudian literature, however, need not be subjected to such strictures. We may adduce the work of two of the most significant of the neo-Freudians: Kardiner and Fromm.

We may approach Kardiner's work advantageously from the point of view of asking *who,* or *what kind* of person, is seen in relation to culture or social structure. There is a very important difference in this respect between the work of Kardiner and that of Freud. One of Kardiner's primary tasks is to examine for each particular culture the relationships that exist between the psychological make-up or structure of the individuals participant in it and the prevalent institutional forms. Ostensibly, there is a resemblance between this and the task

56. The fascistic strain of contempt for the masses in Jung's later work is connected with his insistence on the general need for convention.

57. *Caste and Class,* p. 39.

Freud set himself in his sociological works. But a crucial difference arises from Kardiner's use of the concept of basic personality type. Kardiner derives the basic personality from the "primary" institutions that involve established modes of rearing the child within the earliest kin group, where there are put into practice thorough-going disciplines with respect to feeding, weaning, anal training, etc. The emotional life of the child is formed in these daily disciplinary experiences and in the associated expectations he comes to have of parents or other relatives. A particular kind of human being will be formed or turned out in a particular culture, and the various individuals participant in a culture will have personalities that tend to range around a basic mode or type. This does not preclude the emergence of highly individual traits serving to distinguish one personality from another (which Kardiner defines as "character"), but the emphasis is on certain fundamental and shared features of personality. Aside from the institutions that carry through the primary disciplines, there are secondary institutions, including many facets of religion and the economic culture, which the individual is likely to encounter in their more important and developed forms only after the primary institutions have done their work. Two points are crucial. The first is that from the point of view of the psychologist there is little to be gained, at least at first, from a direct examination of the relationships between primary and secondary institutions, such as the sociologist might be tempted to undertake. In the life of the culture as it is actually lived, there intervenes, so to put it, between primary and secondary institutions, the basic personality structure. The question of congruity or lack of congruity between different types of institutions is mediated by the psychologist through an analysis of the nature of the personality institutionally precipitated up to a certain point in the career line.

More important for the matter under consideration is a second point, the point, simply, that by the time participation in the secondary institutions is ready to be undertaken it is a definite, particular type of personality that will undertake it. There are three relevant steps in the history of clinical psychology from the work of Freud to that of Kardiner. The first step was taken by Freud in the postulation that it is a purely animal and liberally (and pre-culturally) endowed man that faces culture. The second step was also taken by Freud in the postulation of the development of the superego, whereby man internalizes social prescriptions that still shift uneasily on an unregenerate animal base. The third step, taken by Kardiner, is to treat a very considerable part of the problem of the relation of the individual to culture by postulating that *the one who* faces culture is already thoroughly molded by some of the disciplines of the particular culture he faces. In the third step, man's animality has been thoroughly "mixed" with his training, and there is no necessary reservation that he may somehow still withdraw to the base of an animality apart from the social and cultural process. Anarchism is thus quite definitely avoided. But the implied thoroughness of the process of socialization means that social and cultural training penetrates deeper than Freud had indicated. The individual must therefore the more thoroughly be looked upon as a locus for the impact of cultural training and prescriptions or norms. He does not simply acquire, relatively late in the career-line, a superego generically the same for individuals in different societies. By the same token by which anarchism is avoided we are constrained to regard the formation of a private, intimate normative scheme as very deeply influenced by social norms. It is noteworthy in this connection that the normative component that Adler discriminated was in reality anti-normative: it was a normative component the character of which was rendered precisely by its opposition to general social norms. It is *against actually prevalent* norms. The normative component that Jung discriminated likewise could not exist or would be meaningless except in relation to actually prevalent norms. "Ideal" ways are "ideal" only in relation to and by contrast with conventional ways.

If normative influences run deeper than Freud had thought, this had, nevertheless, been anticipated. If they influence the individual deeply enough, and penetrate into his "unconscious," it may seem idle to carry the question further. It would seem to have to be admitted that normative factors *participate* in the essence of "the unconscious." But it is worth indicating one further methodological point. Let us consider Kardiner's analysis of the question of congruity (or relative lack of it) between basic personality and what he calls secondary institutions. Actually, that analysis is in part implicitly an analysis of normative components. To examine basic personality in relation to secondary institutions is to engage in one phase of the examination of individuals in relation to social norms, since the latter are as much involved in secondary as in other institutions. If the level of institutions requires a normative analysis, then a significant portion of the task of analysis of individuals must consist (in the context of discussion of congruity between institutions and individuals) in an analysis of their moral nature or of *some functional equivalent.* Congruity between the "rules" that institutions involve and "something else" can only be ascertained if the "something else" also involves "rules," either because its nature is immediately and essentially describable as involving "rules" or because at some point that nature contains a component relevant to "rules" in the sense of denying or affirming them. It is clear that the new-born human being, which is simply a set of potentialities, cannot be conceived as "opposed" to the institutional order. When it has assumed definiteness through social training, and therefore has a specific moral constitution, it may or may not be opposed to all sorts of institutional prescriptions. This general view is not incompatible with Kardiner's.

In the case of Fromm, we have already noted an important resemblance to Jung. Fromm unequivocally distinguishes a peculiar normative component in the psyche, although he does not call it that. In detail, his analysis of course differs from Jung's and is directed toward different ends. Thus, Jung implied the existence of a psychological élite, and in his late work tended to depreciate the masses outside it. Fromm's analysis implies that what he calls "freedom from," while it may be difficult, is nevertheless very widely possible. It is irrelevant to our purpose to pursue other differences. This one is noted incidentally because it raises an issue once more with regard to anarchism. Is it possible, as Fromm's analysis implies, to have an entire society composed of individuals "free" in his sense, for whom the essential "moral law" is not of the nature of convention? Could such a society function and continue? We already know what Jung's answers to these questions would be, in view of his insistence on the necessity of convention. There is some evidence in favor of Jung's position on this necessity, although his position does not answer certain questions with regard to the "amounts" of "freedom" and "convention" that may be combined in a functioning society, with regard to how "freedom" and "convention" may be distributed among different groups in a still functioning society, etc.[58] But in any case, with differences of detail, Fromm sees substantially the normative component that Jung did.

Another contribution of Fromm's is also quite important for our analysis. Although it bears on the latter somewhat indirectly, it does so none the less effectively. In a paper on the socially conditioned nature of psychoanalytical therapy,[59] Fromm undertakes to criticize the assumptions of Freud's therapy (and the personality of Freud insofar as it bears on therapeutic questions). He contends that Freud rather radically underestimates the significance of the reality or total character of the analyst himself.[60] What Freud had to say about the relation of analyst to patient, Fromm reminds us, seldom went beyond a very limited technical-medical mode of discourse. Freud recommended to the analyst an attitude like that of the surgeon, and, withal, emotional coolness and indifference. Beyond this, he urged analysis for the analyst and not *valuing* what the patient presented. The recommended attitude is one of not "judging," of neutrality and tolerance.

In the course of an attack upon Freud's own professed "freedom from values," Fromm explicitly states that "there are neurotic conflicts that are to a certain degree moral conflicts."[61] This *explicit* statement is obviously a *limited* one. But Fromm implicitly concedes a considerable significance to normative elements in psychological problems as seen by the analyst when he treats of the factors that in his view are essential to genuinely successful use of the therapy initiated by Freud. Fromm first lists—and this primacy is quite in accordance with the tenor of his paper—the unconditional affirmation (unconscious as well as conscious) by the analyst of the patient's claim to happiness. Immediately after this he lists "the freeing of morality from its taboo-like character." He had previously repeatedly stressed the need for the analyst to be genuinely free of the moral

58. Some aspects of these and related questions are treated in Mannheim, *Diagnosis of Our Time*.

59. "Die Gesellschaftliche Bedingtheit der Psychoanalytischen Therapie."

60. *Cf. ibid.*, pp. 367–368.

61. *Ibid.*, p. 392.

judgments of "bourgeois" society. He had contended that if the analyst is not thus free, he is very likely to be, or inevitably is, a failure in his work. More specifically, the contention is that if the patient, however dimly, senses that the analyst takes the same condemnatory attitude toward the violation of cultural prescriptions and taboos that has already been encountered in childhood and later, then his original "resistance" will not only be transferred but reinforced. As soon as it is claimed that the analyst's (not necessarily conscious) value system has a vital influence upon the patient at all times, normative elements in the psychic make-up of both analyst and patient are by implication assigned a very important role—a role, in fact, that cannot be eliminated, since Fromm tirelessly insists that the analyst, to be successful, must give up "the unconscious affirmation of the taboos of bourgeois society." [62] His mind, in other words, must have a certain moral constitution if he is to achieve authentic therapeutic effects. And there is no reason why the moral constitution of the analyst's mind should be of importance to the patient unless moral problems are of importance in the make-up of the latter's mind.

When we speak of a peculiar normative component in the psyche we refer to certain basic values and attitudes of the personality. The reference is not restricted to "conscious" or professed values, or to rationalizations, or to purely secondary psychic products (secondary, that is, from the point of view of psychoanalysis). To give a place to a normative *component* in our sense is not to deny that man has a biological endowment, nor to deny certain crucial dynamisms and mental mechanisms, nor, in general, to gainsay the significance of emotional forces. In fact, a normative component in our sense has importance just because it has important emotional bases. It is present in that range of psychic phenomena with which the psychoanalyst most typically or most characteristically deals. It intrudes into the sphere which Roland Dalbiez calls the "lower psychism." If, as has been contended, it is deeply influenced by social norms, even an intensive analysis of norms on the "abstract," institutional level will only afford some conceptions as to the "materials" that go into the making of a very intimate, private organization of life (even if that organization of life is sufficiently widespread or common to enable

62. *Ibid.*, pp. 395, 369, 396.

the view that a single basic personality type exists in a particular culture). Professed, conscious values may or may not be in accordance with the values implicit in any particular character structure. Professed values may be superficial, in that they do not inform behavior or are not effective in motivation, but such a statement would be untrue of the normative component in our sense. A major reason for pursuing the point that a distinctive normative component is actually exhibited and dealt with by clinical psychology is just the fact that the examination of interplay between various normative levels (institutional and individual) must be of considerable interest to both the social scientist and the psychologist.

It is noteworthy that the neo-Freudians are ever more clearly departing from Freudian anarchism. Kardiner's work, for example, in one sense consists in an exhibition of the emotional forces that serve to hold a society together. His accounts of Comanche and Alorese personality and social structure are especially distinguished for the exhibition of the operation of cohesive forces.[63] It remains true that there are still shortcomings in the neo-Freudian literature directly connected with the problem of order in society. One of the most conspicuous relates to the conception of the term "social" or "collective." Thus, scrutiny of Dollard's useful work on caste and class reveals repeatedly that the "social" is used to refer to a coincidence of individual behaviors and reactions. The element of consensus, of the common, is left out, and there is a corresponding impoverishment of the "social." This may help to obscure the fact that the task of analysis, for example in the type of work Dollard has undertaken, is not complete when tensions and aggressions that may be presumed to threaten existing social structure have been defined. To stop at this point is to leave one phase of the endeavor to connect social and individual levels of analysis in a somewhat rudimentary state. While circumstances of culture and social structure may help to produce characteristic tensions in one individual and another within a defined social group, the tensions produced may simply function as private discomforts irrelevant to the institutional structure as long as they do not achieve some form of group recognition and organization. The

63. See below, chap. 6, section 1.

stability of a social order is not seriously threatened when there is only private dissatisfaction with it, just as it is not sustained except by a consensus that goes beyond private satisfaction with it.[64]

64. This lacuna in neo-Freudian literature is also quite evident in Fromm's *Escape From Freedom.* No mention has been made in the above of the neo-Freudian analysis of the limitations upon rationality as a faculty. The neo-Freudians have of course taken over Freud's essential insights with regard to this point. Insofar as they have made a relevant contribution of their own, it has consisted in making the analysis of rationality somewhat more concrete by connecting it intimately with the analysis of cultural circumstances.

## *PART THREE*

# *Toward Integration*

# 6. *Psychoanalysis and the Leisure Class*

## I. MODES OF RELATING INSTITUTIONAL AND INDIVIDUAL LEVELS

IF NORMATIVE COMPONENTS are of crucial importance at both institutional and individual or clinical levels of analysis, that still does not provide systematic modes for relating the two levels. It is the design of this chapter to outline such modes and to make concrete applications in a study of connections between Veblen's analysis of the leisure class and some significant psychoanalytical propositions.

We may first raise once more the questions that have been posed throughout for any psychology purporting to be relevant to sociological analysis. The scientific value of the Freudian psychology was treated in our second chapter. It has been quite clear that the attempts of Freud and others, such as Jung, to bridge the gap between the analysis of the individual and the analysis of society, ended in failure. The second of our questions—Is the psychology applicable to social analysis?—has thus far therefore had to be answered in the negative. But an analysis of more recent work indicates that it may be answered positively, and there are also beginning to emerge some well conceived answers to the third question: If the psychology is applicable to social analysis, how may the application be worked out? Several points are in order.

The first point refers to the sheer matter of the connection of the levels of individual and social analysis. The original Freudian failure in bridging a gap between the levels has not discouraged subsequent inquirers. We refer to inquiries with a new orientation, not to mere reassertions of Freud's sociological dogmas. Recent investigation strongly suggests that the institutional and individual levels may be meaningfully and validly related. The manner in which the relatively overt institutional level and the covert, private level may be related is suggested, for example, in Dollard's work on caste and class. To take a concrete instance of Dollard's analysis, in discussing the very common submissiveness of the Negro, he states:

From the standpoint of the Negro one can see two possible motives in his submissive behavior. The first is based on the familiar formula that repressed antagonism is often replaced and concealed by servile behavior. The repressed antagonism itself is presumably an answer to the initial demand for self-abnegation. A second motive will probably be that of identification with the socially powerful white person accompanied by idealization, pride in the white man, permissiveness, and a wish to serve him. Eventually, this second motive gives rise to a wish to be like the white man.[1]

Dollard speaks of an "affect-conscious social science," and his aim in his study of caste and class may be described as an analysis of the emotional underpinnings (*i.e.*, the sustaining emotional forces) that hold up the caste structure of "Southerntown." He seeks also to analyze the emotional lines of force that imperil the caste structure, which, from the point of view of the emotional lives of the various individuals from various strata who carry it on, is in a somewhat unsure equilibrium. In the passage just quoted, Dollard indicates two different types of emotional reactions on the part of the Negro, one of which would represent a threat to existing social structure (at least potentially) and the other of which would serve to sustain that structure. The connection between the levels of individual and social analysis is, by implication, emphasized repeatedly and exhibited concretely. The following is a cogent statement on this line:

It can be assumed that human beings never give up possibilities for gratification just for fun; self-restraint is difficult and there must be an adequate social premium on it. The general formula seems to be that the middle-class Negroes sacrifice the direct impulse gains of the lower-class group and expect to have in return the gratifications of prestige and mastery. They *expect* to get them, but the fact is that they are not always paid out according to their cultural model.[2]

The implication is clear that there occurs an accumulation of resentments and tensions that threaten the maintenance of important features of the caste-class system. More directly still, Dollard notes that since there are lacking among Negroes in Southerntown various

1. *Caste and Class in a Southern Town*, p. 174. 2. *Ibid.*, p. 424.

"outlets for aggression available to a minority group," especially in the way of political organization, "a common result is to drive hostile protest under ground, to keep it a lurking and latent force in the social order." He comments further that "it is doubtless the failure to describe this fact and to see in proper perspective the aggressive tensions within societies that makes so many social developments and movements surprising to social scientists." [3]

The method of Dollard's approach, taken as an example of neo-Freudian approaches, absolves it of many of the criticisms that have had to be made of Freud's sociology. An inquiry like that of Dollard establishes a scientifically valid mode of relating two levels. A major factor in making such inquiry scientifically valid is the simple fact that the non-identity of the institutional and individual levels is at least implicitly recognized. It thereby becomes meaningful to attempt to connect them, since "connection" is not conceived as a process whereby one level swallows the other by purely verbal techniques or by analogy. This point holds also for the work of others of the neo-Freudians. However, this is merely a start. To establish that there is a connection between the two levels, and to state it correctly, is a beginning beyond which sociological psychoanalysis has already gone.

This brings us to a second point, namely, that one important type of connection between the institutional and individual levels is the connection of interdependence. Dollard's work had already implied such a connection, but other work has made it clearer. Thus, Karl Mannheim has, in posing "the problem of transforming man," made some sharp and pertinent observations. He remarks that "no economic order can be brought into existence as long as the corresponding human type does not also emerge," and accordingly observes further that even capitalism could function "only when it simultaneously created the corresponding human type which in the earning of money is dominated by the principle of 'more and more.'" [4] An institutional structure can, then, only function and go on as it receives support in the character and value-orientation of the human agents carrying it on. On the other hand, these agents are molded by the institutional structure. Revolutionary changes made in the objective

3. *Ibid.*, p. 286.
4. *Man and Society in an Age of Reconstruction*, p. 201 and footnote, p. 201.

institutional structure of a society would have to be balanced against the inner states of individuals accommodated to older or different social forms. Manipulations on the objective level would have to take account of the psychological heritage from previous institutional forms. If, on the other hand, a start is made by subjective transformation of certain selected individuals, these must face an institutional structure not accommodated to their value-orientations or emotional dispositions. An analysis of this kind does not imply a psychologico-political impasse, and appears to allow of no resolution only because thus abstractly stated. Mannheim notes that "the danger of the external method of transformation consists in the fact that it only outwardly changes society without really transforming man." On the other hand, in assessing the danger of the "internal method," he comments that the selected "transformed" individuals may "break without resistance as soon as the special surroundings in which they move are destroyed by a sudden social upheaval." [5] Further:

> Here we can be helped only by interdependent action and thought which make use of both the internal and the external approaches in the sense that they combine at every step the transformation of society with the transformation of individual personality. Moreover, as with most theoretical paradoxes, the problem is insoluble on the level of abstract thinking. The exaggerated consistency of one-sided logical systems of thought tears out of their context things which, if reconciled in action, can be gradually united into a more and more appropriate pattern of conduct.[6]

No one, perhaps, has more clearly seen the interdependence of the institutional and psychological levels than Kardiner, in certain aspects of his work on widely different societies. The Comanche, in the late phase of their development, were a most warlike people. Their male children were reared to be effective fighters and fearless of death. One of the main emphases of Kardiner's psychology has been upon "executive capacity" and the development of "action systems." Given the training an individual receives, what can we expect him to be able to do? How will he live up to expectations or necessities in performance and execution? "Neurotic" behavior is marked by ex-

5. *Ibid.*, p. 227.
6. *Ibid.*, pp. 227–228; *cf.* the whole of the treatment of "the problem of transforming man," *ibid.*, pp. 199–236, and *Diagnosis of Our Time, passim.*

ecutive incapacity, by failure in those performances that usually lead to the realization of the aims set forth in a culture. Comanche society left open and developed all the psychic channels to the production of an effective set of action systems in the individual. He was turned out unimpaired, unblocked, a freely executive man. These "free" individuals, however, were organized in a society whose major goal was that of aggression and predation against other societies.

Comanche society seems almost like a robber band, except that the forces making for cohesion go much deeper. It is, after all, a distinctive society and peculiar culture that are involved. Under what conditions, however, did it hold together? And hold together it did, until the development of surrounding cultures put a stop to the predatory activities of the Comanche. It was a democratic society. Men were equal within it, although especially able men could become chiefs. A chief's status, nevertheless, was not hereditary, and an old man recounting the prowess and strength of his youth was likely to be laughed at. Individual possessions seldom amounted to much, and everyone had to make his own way. Competition was possible, but kept within limits as far as its possible results were concerned, since certain minima of subsistence and social regard were secure for everyone. Men were united in the goal of war against other societies. Comanche society could continue to exist on its own terms only as long as this goal was paramount. The analogy with a robber band has a certain usefulness if not pushed too far. It is easily imagined what might happen in a robber band if, say, a leader accumulated such spoils and power that others became dissatisfied and envious; or what might happen if factious and mutually suspicious sub-groups developed. Comanche society was organized to play down possibilities of this sort. There were comparatively few tension points to constitute threats to the democratic union of predatory, warlike men. Characteristically, the practice of sorcery, a good indication of envy of others and inability to get results in the usual ways, was an activity of old men who had lost their powers and were accorded little prestige.

Evidently, the development of certain types of personalities in any considerable number would have been disastrous to Comanche society as it was actually constituted. The type of personality developed at certain points in other cultures, which is generally "passive" and dependent on the technique of strict obedience to gain the favor of a wealthy and powerful parent who controls all boons, could it have developed on a large scale in Comanche society, would have threatened its destruction. A certain freedom and audacity on the part of its individuals were indispensable to its continued existence. Of course, in the first place the primary institutions were such that the passive type of personality scarcely had a chance to develop despite some inevitable and unavoidable variations from one Comanche family to another.[7]

The inspection of cultures gives the strong impression that in any particular culture certain goals are achieved by sacrificing other latent or possible goals. Comanche culture affords an excellent instance. The fine personal organization of its individuals coincides with their pursuit of the goal of predation. The two sets of phenomena—the peculiar personal organization and the peculiar character of the goal—are most intimately linked. Kardiner indicates how little "neurotic" is the Comanche reaction to the prospect of death. If death in battle is accepted as destiny and goal, the individual Comanche's emotional orientation to it cannot be improved, from the point of view of maintaining a frictionless society. What this single well described case already forcibly implies is the following: Given a culture that projects certain specific goals, there cannot simply be *any* kind of individuals. An indispensable condition for the retention and maintenance of those goals is that individuals have a psychological equipment that will sustain them and make them appear more or less worth-while. On the other hand, given certain types of individuals, there cannot simply be *any* kind of goals. Some goals will appear meaningless, others will arouse resentment, and a certain few may enlist enthusiasm and evoke pleasure. In every culture ever known, there have been *specific* goals and *specific* kinds of individuals. Cultural goals and the psychological make-up of individuals are involved in a mutually conditioning interplay that no social order can avoid. There are two noteworthy features in this type of formulation. One is the explicit way in which the interdependence of individual and culture, long since known in a general way, can be stated. The other is the

7. See *The Psychological Frontiers of Society*, pp. 47–100, 422, 428.

depth of the investigation of individual personality which can be carried on by the sociologically oriented psychoanalysts.

In Kardiner's analysis, similar points may be seen to emerge from the study of cultures quite different from Comanche. We take a single aspect of his discussion of Western culture, namely, the Protestant Reformation, in its relation to the peculiar development of personality in the Protestant community. The importance of the change wrought by the Reformation in the relationship of the individual to his Church, in the departure from Catholicism, is a familiar historical theme. The individual under the Catholic dispensation always could feel that he had in back of him an organization to which he could bring his deepest personal problems and his sense of sin: the Church had prescribed, authoritative ways of dealing with these problems. Under Protestantism, the relation of the individual to the Church became much looser. He was thrown much more on his own, and had to discover his own way to God. Thus, the cumulation of private tensions which Catholicism had allowed release in institutions like the confession had to be handled alone. Kardiner aptly describes this development from the point of view of interest to him by noting that under Catholicism there existed a kind of "externalization of conscience." The external Church was present to give periodic reassurance as an authoritative tribunal, and, after reassurance from outside, one could start a new cycle of behavior with a clean slate. It has long since been suggested that intense worldly activity directed toward economic success provided a mode of release for the almost unbearable doubts and tortures suffered by the Protestant individual. A set of unresolved emotional problems centering, in consciousness, on the question of salvation, makes the individual restless and uneasy; but the channel of intense worldly activity crowned by success compensates for private doubts. Since there was a marked tendency to reckon the possession of wealth as a sign of salvation, the psychological technique of the Protestant individual was, as it were, to run hard, in order not to have to stop and look, and since there was applause from the bystanders it was plausible for the runner to think that he was winning a race.

Our interest is in the interplay between the institutional and individual levels. The change in the relationship of the individual to the

Church marked an institutional transformation that was accompanied by significant psychological phenomena in the way of increased feelings of anxiety and defencelessness. On the other hand, individuals hard-pressed by a sense of sin and guilt and unconsciously seeking some alleviation, if only through fanatical activity that would mitigate preoccupation with the problem of salvation, would find strenuous economic enterprise quite congenial. Since it was Calvinist dogma that some would be saved and some not, a strong element of competitive striving in economic activity would also be in accordance with important personality trends.[8]

A correct conception of connection between the institutional and the individual levels, grounded in the recognition of the non-identity of the levels, is only a starting-point in relating them. The exhibition of interdependence carries us somewhat further. Interdependence, however, has been, by implication, further broken down. The third point we wish to emphasize, then, is the aspect of relationship between the levels that refers to congruity or lack of congruity and to the associated conception of reinforcement or lack of reinforcement. Congruity has reference to the fact of accord between institutional

8. *Cf. The Psychological Frontiers of Society,* ch. xiv. The above brief summary has been slanted toward bringing out interdependence between the institutional and individual levels. Kardiner's account has a context which the above has not rendered. It may be noted that Kardiner expresses some disagreement with Max Weber (*ibid.*, p. 437) but in important respects his psychological views are not inconsistent with Weber's analysis of the Protestant ethic. We would add one item to the above account, suggested by the following statement by Kardiner: "In the angry God of Calvin we recognize the old angry Hebrew God, with all his cruelty but without his sense of fair play, and completely lacking the mercy and forgiveness of Jesus. So there is not much use trying to achieve salvation; the best one can do is to prove by one's works that he is saved. Success in worldly life is one of the ways of establishing the fact that one is saved, hence industry is exalted to a high position, operating now with the sanction of the new church and in harmony with new social goals." (*Ibid.*, p. 439.) The implication is plain that gnawing doubt about salvation existed, as in fact Weber also contended. It may be suggested that this factor is connected with, and accords with, a removal of limitations upon the striving to accumulate money. A direct "causal" link is of course out of the question, but the psychological impossibility of achieving personal certainty about salvation, despite repeated and unceasing efforts, might be *accordant* with an endless and insatiable striving to obtain money. This would indicate one line of accordance between the "compulsive" type of character and certain capitalist economic activities.

structure and individual tendency. The description of Comanche society and psychology, again, affords an excellent illustration of congruity: the lines of affect accord well with the goals set out by institutions. It is clear, also, that if incongruity goes beyond a certain point the existing structure of a society will be endangered.[9] The basic tendencies of the subjective personality may also be such as to make especially congenial and reinforce the norms implicit in the going institutional structure, or they may have the opposite effect. The levels, however, are not reduced to identity. In Kardiner's type of analysis, the ultimate sources of congruity or lack of it and reinforcement or lack of it are to be sought in the so-called primary institutions. The conception of congruity, however, is a valuable one whether or not we operate with that of primary and secondary institutions (although Kardiner has thus far used this latter conception with considerable effect). Congruity and reinforcement may, theoretically, work both ways in an interplay between institutional and individual levels as institutional norms reinforce individual trends and *vice versa*. As long as cohesion is to be preserved, each level imposes limitations on the other. Insofar as individual trends reinforce or weaken specific institutional norms, they at least *function* as if they were themselves normative or involved important normative components. It is worth noting that the neo-Freudian analysis enables us to discriminate normative components peculiar to individuals in peculiar social structures, whereas the normative components described by Adler and Jung could run through a variety of social structures and possibly be universal.[10]

Our methodological treatment has emphasized the *connection* (and *non-identity*) of the institutional and individual levels; it has indicated that the levels are connected in a relation of *interdepend-*

9. *Cf.* the account of the changed institutional situation that had to be met by the modal Tanala individual with personal resources adapted to the circumstances of an economy of dry rice cultivation, when wet rice cultivation was taken up, in Kardiner, *The Individual and His Society*, pp. 329–337.

10. For an analysis that implies the great utility of distinguishing peculiar normative components in connection with investigation of different social structures, *cf.* Karl Mannheim's treatment of *principia media,* in *Man and Society in an Age of Reconstruction*, p. 177, *sqq. Principia media* serve to bridge a gap between absolutely general and absolutely unique conceptions of social structure.

*ence;* it has specified *congruity* or the lack of it and *reinforcement* or the lack of it as important features of the connection of the levels. With the clues thus provided, we are in a position to work out the integration of Veblen's social theory with the Freudian type of psychology in a concrete instance.

## II. THE THEORY OF THE LEISURE CLASS

Veblen, in *The Theory of the Leisure Class,* afforded a notable exposition of the norms of that class. The exposition occurs in a framework that Veblen makes only partially explicit. We noted in Chapter 3 that money is for Veblen an institutional phenomenon and that the theoretical analysis he made in certain of his papers implied a two-way institutional action of money justifying our reference to the first and second pecuniary dimensions. *The Leisure Class,* however, if it is a study in the second pecuniary dimension, rests on a further distinction of which Veblen was undoubtedly aware. This is the originally Aristotelian distinction between "economics" and "chrematistics." Very briefly, "economics" refers to the "law of the household" and "chrematistics" to the "art of finance." Adapting and extending this distinction somewhat to modern sociological uses, we may say that under the "law of the household" we deal with an economic system or situation wherein definite limitations are placed upon the accumulation of money because of the existence of a (limited) set of culturally defined needs. As long as the uses and purposes of money are defined by these needs, money appears as entirely instrumental and its accumulation is necessarily limited. Its indefinite accumulation then appears senseless. Chrematistics may be taken to refer to an economic system or situation in which activity directed to the acquisition of money is not bound or limited by the constant keeping in view, or definition as ultimate goals, of a limited set of traditional needs. Once money ceases to be referred to a limited set of specifically and culturally prescribed needs, there are, in principle, no limitations upon the striving to obtain it. It can be accumulated indefinitely for its own sake.[11]

11. *Cf.* Aristotle, *Politics* (tr. Jowett, Oxford, 1885), Book I; Marx, *Capital,* vol. I, *passim* and p. 170, footnote; Max Weber, *The Protestant Ethic* (tr. T. Parsons, London: Allen & Unwin, 1930), ch. ii; Polanyi, *The Great Transformation, passim.*

In *The Theory of the Leisure Class,* Veblen undertook to describe cultural activities of a type contingent on the existence of a chrematistic system. He understood clearly that in the institutional system he was studying "the desire for wealth can scarcely be satiated in any individual instance, and evidently a satiation of the average or general desire for wealth is out of the question." He continues this argument:

> However widely, or equally, or "fairly," it may be distributed no general increase of the community's wealth can make any approach to this need, the ground of which is the desire of every one to excel every one else in the accumulation of goods. If, as is sometimes assumed, the incentive to accumulation were the want of subsistence or of physical comfort, then the aggregate economic wants of a community might conceivably be satisfied at some point in the advance of industrial efficiency; but since the struggle is substantially a race for reputability on the basis of an invidious comparison, no approach to a definitive attainment is possible.[12]

Historically, the freeing of the accumulation of money from the limitations imposed by the postulation, as goals, of specific traditional needs, did not at once and through all social strata produce in Western society cultural activities of the type Veblen described in *The Leisure Class.* Rather, before these activities supervened, as Max Weber among others has pointed out, the Protestant ethic enjoined, and there actually prevailed, a characteristically different orientation toward money. Traditionalism indeed broke down, and the bounds to the theoretically indefinite accumulation of money were thereby removed, but this did not at once imply that anything like ostentatious use was to be made of money.[13] By the time that Veblen, how-

12. *The Theory of the Leisure Class,* p. 32.

13. By John Wesley's time, tension had very definitely appeared between frugality and ostentation or its like. Wesley noted that industry and frugality went with "religion," but inevitably produced riches, and, with riches, "pride" and "anger" and "love of the world" and "the desire of the flesh" and "the desire of the eyes." This clearly indicates that Wesley was aware that it was not easy to maintain effectively restrictions upon the uses of money acquired. *Cf.* Weber, *ibid.,* p. 175. According to Weber, Wesley gives the advice that "those who gain all they can and save all they can should also give all they can, so that they will grow in grace and lay up a treasure in heaven." *Ibid.,* p. 176. The implications of Wesley's statement for schism in Protestantism are plain, as there occurs re-affirmation of the old religious virtues of industry and frugality (in revolt against those who have grown rich and lax on the basis of those very virtues) which, re-affirmed and followed, will again lead to wealth, etc.

ever, took up the fortunes of money in society, the historical Protestant limitations on the uses of money once accumulated had long since lost their original scope and vigor.[14] There are three historical steps, from pre-capitalist traditionalism (an "economic" type of economy), through a non-traditionalistic economy wherein there are still limitations on the cultural uses of money with abstention recommended or insisted upon, to a non-traditionalistic economy wherein restrictions on the cultural uses of money no longer have powerful effect. Veblen's classical description of the institutions encountered in the third of these historical steps has certain high points which we will review, seeking to make sharper some associated points that he merely implied.

*The Theory of the Leisure Class,* although especially distinguished for its analysis of the role of money (as a peculiar sign of belonging to a special class) in the social structure, to some extent deals with the leisure class at large. The leisure class is taken as a very common phenomenon in the history of societies, and, in the absence of developed pecuniary institutions, its residual distinguishing characteristic is the exemption of its members from industrially or materially productive or serviceable work. Cultural emphasis is put upon this peculiar exemption, and it has its conventional signs, such as the physically unnecessary constriction of women's feet or bodies or the putative physical impotence of members of the leisure class in the performance of menial tasks. When money comes upon the institutional scene and replaces other means of marking off the industrially exempt leisure class, it also breeds conventional signs. Money is used as means in the phenomenon of ostentatious or conspicuous consumption or display. This is perhaps the most familiar of Veblen's themes in *The Leisure Class.* The emphasis on conspicuous consumption is sharp and insistent. In women's and men's dress, houses, public buildings, articles of daily consumption, the holding of reactionary opinions, proficiency in recondite or obsolescent branches of learning—in these and many other phenomena Veblen finds evidence of the intrusion of the motive of making manifest, or creating a presumption of, pecuniary

14. For an interesting and relevant perspective on the relation of Veblen's *The Leisure Class* to Weber's *Protestant Ethic,* see Arthur K. Davis, "Veblen on the Decline of the Protestant Ethic," *Social Forces* XXII (1944), 282–286.

prowess. Virtually no cultural activity escapes the pervasion of pecuniary norms. What is made "conspicuous" in conspicuous consumption is the pecuniary solvency of the conspicuous consumer. Conspicuous consumption, moreover, is "invidious." Pecuniary standards frequently take subtle forms, and Veblen's analysis indicates that aesthetic judgments, for example, may be, consciously, removed from any consideration of money but actually influenced precisely by criteria in the last analysis pecuniary.[15]

In Veblen's analysis, some emphasis is also placed by implication on the mobility of money. Money, in the circumstances of our economy and society—although of course within limits in fact, whatever cultural presumptions may be—shifts rapidly from hand to hand. It is an eminently detachable possession or appurtenance. By comparison, say, with heritable land in the circumstances of a society of more or less feudal complexion, it manifests a really extreme mobility. This implies a certain turnover in the membership of the moneyed or leisure class, but the mere fact of detachability is more important for our purposes. Closely associated with this is the mobility of present-day society itself. We recall at this point how Veblen indicated that even men and women have come to be judged in pecuniary terms. Quick movement from place to place and the frequency of superficial contacts are favorable to the judgment of men by criteria which cannot fail to impress quickly, by external and easily identifiable signs. Money, or the marks of its possession, can be simple and crude enough not to fail to leave an impression on everyone: it may be externally displayed, and its possession may be quickly inferred by others in a large variety of ways, in clothing, in comportment suggesting a moneyed background, in casual consumption of expensive goods.

A further point may be set out more definitely and given a wider context. Money, Veblen indicates, casts upon its possessor an imputation of general excellence and superiority. The norm that the moneyed person is a "worthy" person has great force. *Beati possidentes,*

15. See *The Leisure Class,* esp. ch. vi. It may be suggested that pecuniary norms may directly or indirectly pervade even psychiatric practice. See Fromm, "Die Gesellschaftliche Bedingtheit der Psychoanalytischen Therapie," and Kingsley Davis, "Mental Hygiene and Class Structure," in *Psychiatry* I (1938), 55–65.

as Veblen is frequently fond of saying—not only "blessed" in virtue of the benefits accruing from possession but also in virtue of the judgment passed upon them because of the fact of possession itself. That the possession of money should imply worth appears to Veblen to call for special explanation. He considers this point not only in *The Leisure Class,* but again, in a way that merits special attention, in *The Theory of Business Enterprise:*

> Under this current, business régime, business gains are the basis of individual wealth, and the (pseudo) notion of joint acquisition has taken the place of the manorial notion of joint work. The institutional animus of ownership, as it took shape under the discipline of early modern handicraft, awards the ownership of property to the workman who has produced it. By a dialectical conversion of the terms, this metaphysical dictum is made to fit the circumstances of later competitive business by construing acquisition of property to mean production of wealth; so that a business man is looked upon as the putative producer of whatever wealth he acquires. By force of this sophistication the acquisition of property by any person is held to be, not only expedient for the owner, but meritorious as an action serving the common good.[16]

In this passage, as may be gathered from reading it in connection with other portions of his work,[17] Veblen is in effect suggesting, if we may restate his theme for our purposes, that acquisition was once the hallmark of productive and co-operative endeavor. The possession of money or tangible equivalents thereof implied such prior endeavor and could only have such endeavor as an antecedent. In the course of time and of the modern business situation, however, the connection between the possession of money and prior productive and co-operative endeavor becomes more and more remote and insecure. Finally (for Veblen, characteristically) there tends to be a sharp separation between productive and co-operative endeavor in any reasonably unequivocal sense and the possession of money. But acquisition once had the unfailing antecedent of work for the common good, and the presumption persists that it still has this antecedent long after it has been severed from it. "Both in his own estimation and in the eyes of his fellows, the man who gains much does well; he is conceived to

16. *The Theory of Business Enterprise,* pp. 290–291. *Cf.* also the further course of the argument, *ibid.,* p. 291.

17. See especially *Absentee Ownership,* Pt. I.

do well both as a matter of personal efficiency and in point of serviceability to the common good."[18]

In *The Theory of Business Enterprise,* Veblen was content simply to note the persistence of the "sophistication" that acquisition implied work for the common good, so that thereby acquisition itself became good. Why should this "sophistication," however, persist? Although "survivals" may exist in a culture, as nineteenth-century anthropologists almost tiresomely pointed out, merely to adduce them explains nothing. Some cultural elements survive and others do not, and the point is to explain why this is so. In this case, however, the explanation is implicit in *The Leisure Class.* Veblen in effect here points again and again to the important functional adaptation of such a "sophistication" as the one that the wealthy man is "worthy" to a society in which business activity directed toward the making of profits has in fact become of tremendous scope and importance; in which money is very closely connected with power; in which there still exists (as there does in every society) the need to evaluate or judge men by *some* criteria, but under circumstances of great mobility and frequent superficiality of contact where judgment must be made with extraordinary rapidity. In view of these circumstances, the "sophistication" spoken of has a high functional adaptation.[19]

A further point in connection with the evaluation of men in terms of money is utterly clear from *The Leisure Class,* and consists in the tendency toward the exclusion or playing down of other means of evaluation. The pecuniary norm is supereminent, and its supereminence implies a double hierarchy. Other norms are taken as less important, less definitive grounds for the assignment of merit, and thereby fall into place in a ranking in which it is at least clear that the pecuniary norm is at the top. Secondly, the pecuniary norm itself involves a gradation. Thus, moneyed persons are the most worthy,

18. *The Instinct of Workmanship,* p. 349.

19. It may be noted, incidentally, in view of the argument just presented, in how much better a methodological state certain aspects of Veblen's thought are than they would at times appear to be from his own presentation. Veblen had a tendency to present "survivals" as if they were self-explanatory, but we have just seen a concrete instance in which his own analysis supplies the understanding of why a particular "survival" has occurred, in view of the *continuing* functions of the "sophistication" referred to.

those to whom there attaches an aura of contact with the moneyed next most worthy, down the line to persons neither moneyed nor in contact with the moneyed whose worth is therefore minimal.

Not only men, but also "things"—commodities, objects of art, etc. —tend to be evaluated in terms of the pecuniary norm. Such evaluation is also understandable in the sense of a functional adaptation to the peculiar circumstances of our economy and society. Under a system of highly developed division of labor, the consumer's ability to judge by "intrinsic" features of worth or merit is obviously reduced in virtue of the limitations of his knowledge and experience and of the proliferation of goods and services. In a highly mobile society, where the establishment of taste and judgment on traditional bases by specifically recognized leading groups has tended to lapse, and where the atmosphere is full of vague, shifting and competing norms, it may be suggested that the relative simplicity and definiteness of the pecuniary norm make a strong appeal. (This factor would also be of some importance in the evaluation of men). It is easy, and in a sense economical, to equate the "expensive" and the "good." That a potential conflict between the two has a tendency to be resolved in favor of the former is suggested by an able contemporary student of a field that afforded Veblen some of his best materials, namely, that of women's dress.[20]

A final point of interest, never directly set forth by Veblen, but intimately associated with and implied by his thesis in *The Leisure Class*, is that money reveals nothing about the circumstances of its accumulation. It does not bear on the face of it any marks that might give a clue whether it was accumulated by approved or disapproved methods, through operations of *haute finance* or through unspectacular diligence, through means involving mainly direct or mainly indirect contacts with others in the course of enterprise. Money is "abstract," *i.e.*, drawn away from the concrete circumstances of its origin or accumulation. On the market "money talks," as the popular phrase has it, and no one inquires too closely how its possessor arrogated to himself its gift of speech. This severance of possession from its concrete antecedents is undoubtedly a factor in the "sophistication" noted by

20. Helen E. Meiklejohn, in Walton H. Hamilton *et al, Price and Price Policies* (New York: McGraw-Hill, 1938), Section VI, p. 337.

Veblen that the wealthy man is the "good" man, who has done hard and productive work in the interests of the community. It is also a factor in the common phenomenon that the specific sources of accumulated money even if, say, they at first carry an implication of "vulgarity," do not necessarily for long prevent the entrée of the accumulators into "elevated circles." Since money can function in the same ways no matter how it was accumulated, it achieves a functional anonymity that may be presumed to have a kind of retroactive effect.

To emphasize the abstract and anonymous character of money is also, by the same token, to emphasize its impersonal character. The "ability to pay" or "pecuniary prowess" is self-sufficient, and further inquiry about the solvent individual is irrelevant. The impersonal character of money is one phase or instance of a more general feature of contemporary social structure, namely, the large scope and force of impersonal relations within it. For our purposes, impersonal relations may be defined briefly as relations in which the exclusive predominance of one goal (or perhaps several, but in any case a strictly limited number) effects exclusive regard to a single aspect or function of other persons (or in any case to a limited number of aspects or functions). In specific types of impersonal relations, the functional totality, or the sum and integration of the various aspects of the being of an individual, is irrelevant.

### III. SOME PSYCHOANALYTICAL PROPOSITIONS

We turn from *The Theory of the Leisure Class* to some of the important concrete findings about the individual made in clinical psychology, especially in psychoanalysis. The individuals who are observed and treated in the clinic are the products of our specific culture, and contemporary psychoanalytical thought bears excellent evidences that the character trends or traits they manifest are, even if with "exaggeration," trends and traits likely to be widespread in the population at large.[21] The significance of modern psychiatry would be very limited if it dealt with absolutely peculiar or rare personality types, but the whole of that psychiatry denies that this is the case. That the "neurotic" individual bears a fundamental resemblance to others was

21. *Cf.* in general, the works of the neo-Freudians already referred to, and ch. 2 of this study.

a contention definitely involved even in Freud's work. The character trends and traits we will review, then, possess a far larger significance than would attach to a rehearsal of the features of a mere uniqueness.

The first trend that may be mentioned is the striving for power. This was a feature of character structure very much emphasized by Adler. A striving for power in the interest of overcoming a sense of inferiority was of central interest in his psychology, and could take a variety of forms in his analysis, such as conquering, subduing and dominating, and could appear in a variety of fields of activity—economic, intellectual, etc. Adler is scarcely alone in this emphasis. Thus, Wilhelm Stekel testifies:

> The deeper I penetrate into the nature of psychoanalysis, the stronger is my conviction that the analysis really means a continuous struggle with the reluctant patient, who is, at heart, unwilling to get well, even though he pathetically avers the contrary. The illness is generated expressly for the purpose of enabling the patient to dominate his environment and to carry out his will, though at great cost to himself. The patient is therefore antagonistically disposed towards the analyst from the very beginning. His own fate comes to be a secondary consideration. For the time being, the physician stands as a symbol for the whole world. The patient aims at winning a victory over his father and over his teacher and over his whole environment by defeating his analyst.[22]

Among contemporaries, Karen Horney has perhaps given the most emphasis to "the quest for power, prestige and possession." [23] Horney analyzes the "neurotic personality *of our time*," and in that connection it is easy enough to see why there is so much emphasis on power, prestige and possession. But it is important to notice that in the psychologies of both Adler and Horney there is an attempt to fit the striving for power into the context of a theory of the character structure. The striving for power is an important trend, but it is very clearly derived from other basic features of the personality, with which it is seen to mesh. This does not mean that basic features of the personality are necessarily *not* connected with the nature of contemporary society and culture—far from it—but the point is that the quest for power, prestige and possession is not naïvely taken as a mere datum of our

22. Stekel, in van Teslaar (ed.), *ibid.*, pp. 324–325.

23. *The Neurotic Personality*, ch. x. On competitive striving, *cf. ibid.*, chs. xi and xii.

society or of particular individuals within it. Whatever the origins of the emphasis on the quest for power, etc., Horney's psychological theory integrates it with important general character trends, which she connects with "basic anxiety," and which Adler connected with the sense of inferiority. Now neither "basic anxiety" nor the sense of inferiority, both of which concord well with and may even develop a striving for power, originate *directly* within the larger society or within the market-place. The locus of origin of each of them is the more immediate family group. Therefore the individual emerging from the family group, *before* he is enmeshed in the activities of the larger society, has a determinate psychological equipment that may be analytically [24] examined apart from the specific features of the institutional scheme.[25] The examination of that psychological equipment in relation to going institutions may be quite fruitful, but that is something else. This same point will hold for other traits or trends to be mentioned.

The so-called "neurotic" personality frequently, if we may draw out certain elements both implicit and explicit in the relevant (especially neo-Freudian) literature, shows a trait closely allied with the striving for power, namely, manifesting superiority. The "neurotic" wishes to put in evidence superior knowledge, superior morals, superior cleanliness and superiority generally, even in the most trivial details. This striving to show superiority is apparently endless and insatiable. Associated with it is an apparent incapability of tolerating any signs of excellence in others, which have the effect of immediately suggesting a comparison that provokes feelings of ill-will and envy. This is in turn associated with competitive striving. The "neurotic" wishes his superiority to be manifest on his sleeve, as it were, and would like all to admire and to acknowledge at once his strength, wisdom, beauty and goodness. The driving forces for traits of this type are conceived to come from a basic insecurity, and if no type of endeavor of which the individual is capable will finally give him a peaceful sense of worth in his own eyes it is understandable that there should be ceaseless activity designed either to convince himself that

24. Not in the sense, "psychoanalytically," but "by scientific abstraction."

25. This of course is not to say that the individual has literally not been in any way influenced by the institutions of his society.

he is worthy or to elicit acknowledgments of worth from others that may bring at least a temporary glow or sense of satisfaction. This of course presumes that there is a fundamental need for a secure sense of being worthy. If that need never ceases to operate and yet is never genuinely satisfied, it is evident why there should be unending striving of the type indicated. The exaggerated forms taken by the attempt to prove one's self worthy are also associated with the power impulse.

The "neurotic," it is fully attested, is "not himself." He is a "stowaway" (Horney). He chases after "false gods." He is described as being quite unclear about what his own basic values and wants are. He constantly expends energy on activities and projects that net him but little in the way of satisfaction. The neo-Freudians, especially, have placed emphasis on the development of the potentialities of the personality. Such development has reference to the cultivation of activities that give "intrinsic" satisfaction, to achievements that do not merely leave a sense of having rushed after the wind. Security, in their view, is of the essence of the character structure, and is not bound up with appurtenances easily detached or lost. But the "neurotic" engages in activities that stem from and lead to insecurity. He is frequently typically engaged in a quest for detachable appurtenances, especially for appurtenances that will seem to him to enhance prestige or merit in the eyes of others. Hence he may concentrate all energy on being regarded as a "grand fellow" (though not on actually being one) or, if a woman, on being regarded as a perfect wife or mother. This fundamental trait of not being "one's self" binds in a good many others. A thorough confusion about one's basic values and a really deep-going lack of understanding of one's self help to explain a good many characteristics of the "neurotic personality."

It must be remembered that the analysis of the neo-Freudians with respect to the points under review is *empirical*. If, *in fact,* they find modern personalities so constituted morally that the striving to obtain certain concrete things or to attain certain concrete goals demonstrably (clinically) brings no "satisfaction" *to the individuals involved* and from their point of view, there can be no question about the scientific character of their analytical enterprise. This point is important enough to bear repetition. The confusion and lack of self-understanding spoken of, then, make it comprehensible that the individual should be readily influenced by all sorts of competing valuations. If he is deeply uncertain of himself, how can he be sure of what is "good"? Perhaps the next person possesses superior wisdom.[26] If community consensus runs to the effect that certain external signs are the best signs of merit or excellence, this affords an easy resting-point for an individual full of unease and may even afford a measure of relief as an outlet is found in the form of an activity whose results may bring high social approval but which at the same time does not require any considerable self-searching—which last, *enfin,* it may be the desire to avoid at all costs.

Furthermore, if one is not "one's self," some of the traits previously mentioned also become understandable from a new point of view. Uncertainty about the value of one's qualities or possessions may easily provoke envy of others. Also, a deeper source for envy is indicated. An uncertain individual, driven by emotional forces of which he has little or no understanding, and repeatedly defeated in the attempt to secure "satisfactions" or attain "happiness," would have to be very remarkably constructed indeed if he did not generally envy others who, he suspected, were more fortunate than he; or if he did not unconsciously engage in activities of a "sadistic" type.[27] From this point of view, too, there may be afforded explanation of the attempt to put superiority in evidence, as when it is indicated that this may arise from a kind of desperate denial that one has fundamentally disappointed one's self.

The "neurotic," it has been indicated, is not "himself." The phenomenon of "self-alienation" has in fact come in for some special attention. For our purposes, it is sufficient to point to only a single aspect of the process of self-alienation, namely, projection. By this convenient device, which of course operates automatically, it is possible to attribute to others all sorts of motives and characteristics that appertain to one's self. It is as if the "neurotic" sectioned off a part of himself and then threw it away, to rediscover it as a part of the per-

26. This is of course not psychologically incompatible with the tendency to manifest superiority, which may in fact be bound up with the suspicion or fear that others are really superior.

27. See Horney, *The Neurotic Personality* and *Our Inner Conflicts* (New York: Norton, 1945), *passim.*

sonality of other individuals. It is himself that he rediscovers, but, if that self is given the guise of another, it is possible to criticize it mercilessly while preserving a certain precarious peace of mind about one's self. This functions to hide from the individual all sorts of traits that might otherwise be susceptible of change (or cause him great alarm: the function of projection may partly be to conceal what it would be disorganizing to see clearly). The personal status quo is thus preserved,[28] at the same time as bitterness and hatred are felt toward others because of their "evil" traits.

This serves to suggest a final trait, namely, hostility. Some of the traits previously mentioned frequently make a pattern or constellation. Envy and the desire to manifest superiority as well as the impulse to power and domination have been noted. These already to some extent imply hostility. The pattern, however, may be added to by the mention of an aloofness or haughtiness that has the effect of suggesting that others are beneath contempt. It was Jung who, though in a somewhat different context, noted in a telling phrase the "Godalmightiness" of modern man.[29] The *noli me tangere* attitude has been remarked by numerous investigators.

### IV. PSYCHOANALYSIS AND THE LEISURE CLASS

We may summarize certain of the prominent features of Veblen's analysis in *The Theory of the Leisure Class* and related work, including some features that were not altogether explicit but were nevertheless implicit or that may be seen to be intimately connected with his analysis, and set these features beside those character traits and trends we have selected from psychoanalytical literature. Firstly, then, in the case of Veblen's work, our review has stressed the following:

1. The phenomenon of conspicuous consumption, bringing out the consumer's pecuniary prowess and provoking the ill-will or rivalry of others;

2. The mobility or detachability of money, which occurs in the context of a society which is itself highly mobile in the sense that

28. On self-alienation, with an interesting attempt to fit projection under the more general concept of "externalization," see Horney, *Our Inner Conflicts*, esp. chs. vi and vii.

29. *The Integration of the Personality*, p. 274.

its members shift quickly from place to place (or from one social stratum to another, although within limits);

3. The fact that money casts an imputation of excellence or worth on men and things;

4. The playing down of other than pecuniary norms. A double hierarchy is involved here, such that ranking is made according to the amount of possession (for men) or degree of expensiveness (for "things") and such that the pecuniary norm tends to rank above others;

5. The abstract character, the anonymity and impersonality of money, which is an important instance of a generally prevailing impersonality in social relationships.

Further, there has been noted the functional adaptation of the "sophistication" that the wealthy man is the "good" man to the circumstances of a society in which the scale and scope of enterprise for a profit are in fact very large, in which money is intimately associated with power, and in which the persistent need to evaluate men by *some* criteria easily takes the path of evaluation in pecuniary terms because of great mobility involving superficiality of contact. Similarly, the evaluation of "things" in pecuniary terms has some functional adaptation to the circumstances of a highly developed division of labor and to the situation of a society mobile in the sense that its standards are vague, unsettled and competitive.

In the case of the review of characterological traits and trends, the following main features have emerged:

1. The striving for power (which must, of course, be power over others);

2. The striving to make superiority manifest, associated with incapability of making a generous appraisal of others and envy of their qualities or possessions or appurtenances;

3. The basic insecurity and doubt about one's worth that make it understandable that the "neurotic" should ceaselessly strive to manifest superiority. Since the doubt can never be put to rest, and there nevertheless persists a need to allay doubt, the consequence is an endless attempt to show one's self to be worthy, and even worthier than others (the power impulse being associated with this);

4. The fundamental characteristic of not being "one's self" or of being "self-alienated." A widely observed tendency or trait consists in an uncertainty about one's basic values, an uneasy shifting from one type of valuation or one point of view to another, which can easily lead to the adoption, with a certain sense of relief, of a goal that sets out purely "external" objects. An aspect of the process of self-alienation is the mechanism of projection, which enables a transfer of self-hatred as others are presumed to have "objectionable" traits;

5. The common feature of hostility or a generally inimical attitude, which is to an extent implied by, and also tends to form a constellation with, the striving for power, envy and the striving to manifest superiority. Aloofness and "Godalmightiness" tend to accompany these phenomena.

The characterological features thus summarized have of course been selected, but the relevant literature amply attests that they are widely observed and widely regarded as very important.

It is now profitable to revert to the *connection* but *non-identity* of the institutional and individual levels; their relationship of *interdependence;* the question whether the levels are *congruous* and whether there occurs what we have called *reinforcement.*

The pecuniary and leisure class phenomena Veblen analyzed are going institutional forms today. Veblen may have erred in claiming, at various points, an amount of intrusion of pecuniary norms into ostensibly non-pecuniary activities that other students might not allow, but the essentials of his characterization remain valid today. He undoubtedly set off a most important *strain* in modern and contemporary institutional structure. Are the elements he set off the same as those found in the investigation, for example, of the power impulse in individuals? Obviously not; but, equally obviously, there is a connection between the two sets of phenomena. If the striving for power and domination is an important element in the personality, it may find an excellent outlet in the striving for acquisition. On the level at which Veblen pursued his observations and studies, he noted a striving toward acquisition which was definitely "invidious," designed to put others "in the shade" by comparison. The character of the activity or behavior that he remarked is in important respects utterly *congruous* with the characteristics of individuals that have been uncovered in the clinic.

The connection of the power impulse and the motive of manifesting superiority with the complex of institutional phenomena Veblen exhibited is patent. The acquisition of money easily confers power and unquestionably enables the manifestation of "superiority" over others. The high evaluation of wealthy men and expensive things may well channel the power impulse into the line of pecuniary activity. It is important to emphasize that it will *channel* the power impulse. A different institutional structure, emphasizing other than pecuniary norms, might well channel the same impulse into other fields of activity. However, the matter does not rest here. Veblen wrote under circumstances in which the acquisition of money became liberated and theoretically unlimited, and, as was noted, by the time of his analysis cultural restrictions upon the expenditure of money had tended to lapse. The modern situation regarding acquisition and expenditure allows a special and peculiar scope to the power impulse and the striving to manifest superiority. In theory, there is no limit to acquisition: power may extend itself indefinitely; the limits to conspicuous consumption are, likewise, loose and wide. It is true that the two characterological traits mentioned might also find scope within, and be congruous with, a cultural system that emphasized certain other norms than the pecuniary. There are even other institutional structures within our own society for which this statement would hold. Thus, the highly hierarchized structure of modern bureaucracies and armies would give ample scope to the two associated traits mentioned, and would present many features congruous with them. But there are perhaps few, if any fields, in which the "lid is off" to the extent to which it is in the field of pecuniary striving. Also, there has at least been a cultural presumption that the pecuniary field is a peculiarly "democratic" one. It is open to anyone to accumulate indefinitely, while advancement in a governmental bureaucracy, say, is frequently and avowedly contingent on special qualifications such as education, and movement upward within the hierarchy is somewhat notoriously slow, hedged and difficult.

The theoretical absence of limits to accumulation ties in with another of the traits or trends reviewed. This is the basic trend in character that has been described as a doubt about one's worth, that cannot, yet, somehow, desperately, must be allayed, and which leads to the ceaseless striving to manifest superiority. Again there would appear to be high congruity with the institutional system described by Veblen. In theory, that system allows constant renewal of acquisitive activity and an indefinite pursuit of the goal of manifesting superiority. The institutional system provides the individual with a scope that corresponds very well with this basic trend. Outlets are provided such that the going institutional forms allow an endless symbolic repetition of the endeavor to prove essential worthiness. It has already been suggested that there might be "accordance" between the "compulsive" type of character and certain capitalist economic activities.[30] The connection between the *appetitus divitiarum infinitus* and the insatiable desire to obtain a sense of being worthy certainly merits further exploration. It is clear, however, that neither the striving for power nor the impulse to manifest superiority nor basic doubts about being worthy nor any of the other characterological traits or trends reviewed may be looked upon as *creating* the institutional structure. That structure has a history and background of its own.

It has been noted how the "neurotic" wishes his superiority to be manifest on his sleeve, as it were. Veblen's analysis indicates how admirably money can perform this function. He stressed *conspicuous* consumption, and the marks of the possession of money are plain and external, so that he who runs may read. The fact that money casts an imputation of excellence or worth on men and things fits in very well here. The opportunity is created to bear quickly identifiable marks of excellence. The mobility and detachability of money in a society itself mobile are also of importance in this connection. The functional adaptation of evaluation in pecuniary terms to the circumstances, among others, of quick, superficial contact wherein the need for evaluation in *some* terms still persists has been remarked. Money and its uses are admirably adapted to making an "impression" quickly. There would seem to be a positive encouragement or *reinforcement* from institutional circumstances of the "neurotic" desire to have superiority at once recognized and admired. On the other hand, the "neurotic" trait in question may easily be presumed to re-

30. See, above, footnote 8, this chapter.

inforce the institutional modes. The fact that money is mobile or detachable, again, gives "democratic" scope to the trait. As it moves rapidly from hand to hand, everyone, in theory, is given an opportunity to show superiority or at least remove the stigmata of inferiority. It would be difficult if not impossible to find a system of institutional arrangements that "fits" better with the trait indicated. There has already emerged more than a casual congruity between certain basic value-attitudes of the "neurotic" personality and the system of pecuniary norms.

On the institutional level, there was noted the functional adaptation of the evaluation of men and "things" in pecuniary terms to the peculiarities of the social structure, with special stress on the vagueness and shifting character of other (than pecuniary) norms when traditional values have lost their traditional significance. We would suggest a connection between the phenomena thus indicated on the institutional level and the characteristic of self-alienation. In connection with the latter, the basic confusion and uncertainty about his own values that haunt the individual and his potential readiness to succumb to the temptation of pursuing "extrinsic" goals were remarked. With an insecure personal anchoring, lack of a self-knowledge that would better indicate goals ensuring some sort of "satisfaction," a tendency to self-doubt when one's neighbor is doing something else that may be more highly "approved" and some temptation to engage in activity that will win certain obvious social gains and social approval and at the same time not call for a self-examination to be avoided at all costs—with this complement of attributes, it is suggested, the individual may easily be drawn into the orbit of those who evaluate in pecuniary terms. It is patent that, *to some extent,* these traits could equally well "fit" into another cultural system emphasizing other than pecuniary norms. A basic uncertainty about one's values may generally make the path of taking certain socially approved norms, whatever they may be, the (ostensibly) simplest "way out." However, even here we may suggest that there is a rather special "fit": the pursuit of money as such meets rather well the qualifications for an activity that may be highly preoccupying and afford "an answer" (to a fundamental confusion) that seems, at least, to call for no further questioning.

The playing down of other than pecuniary norms perhaps calls for no special comment. It fits in well enough with what has already been noticed. Thus, for example, more highly "intrinsic" marks or criteria than pecuniary ones would fit in much less well with the desire to manifest a superiority that shall at once be evident. On the other hand, a feature such as the abstract character, anonymity and impersonality of money (within a society itself marked by the scope and force of impersonal relations) calls for special notice. The abstract character of money enables it to perform the function of casting an imputation of superiority without further inquiry. The pecuniary norm tends to be final: there is no recondite appeal beyond it. The possession of money argues excellence or power, and of course means "ability to pay." This, too, seems to be admirably adapted to certain of the traits noticed. No inquiry need be set going about manner of acquisition, characteristics of the possessor, individual peculiarities, etc. Money is self-validating and functionally anonymous. It will buy commodities or bring prestige with a generous disregard of *who* is buying or *to whom* prestige is accruing. The inquiry about personal worth and the haunting doubt about such worth may obtain some lightening from this circumstance. The institutional system, putting an abrupt period to inquiries about worth, avers unequivocally that wealthy men are worthy and expensive goods excellent. Also, the abstract character and anonymity of money, it must be argued from the very manner in which money functions, cater well to the striving for power. All sorts of services and goods may at once be commanded by someone from "nowhere" as long as he is pecuniarily solvent. With no inquiry about his characteristics or background, without question about "who" he is, he is enabled to initiate accommodating behavior on the part of others. The abstract character of money here gives rare opportunity for the expression of certain well known character trends. Financial manipulations, moreover, may affect profoundly the lives of countless persons whom the financial manipulators never see: power is thus peculiarly able to dispense with all forms of direct contact, and the sense of power can thereby be enhanced.

At this point, too, room is made for the expression of traits of aloofness or haughtiness. In virtue of power conferred or prestige accruing—and the system of pecuniary norms is well geared to conferring power and assigning prestige—and in virtue of the large gradations of power and prestige, it becomes possible to assume an enormous "distance" from the commonalty of men. However, here quite clearly, other institutional systems may "fit" with or cater well to the indicated traits. That the pecuniary institutional system and the social structure associated with it give great scope to impersonal relations, in our sense, means that they give *opportunity* to the expression of hostile impulses. They do not necessarily directly create such impulses, although it might be urged that the effect of daily routines of dealing exclusively with single aspects or functions of men is at any rate to create a certain indifference toward, or forgetfulness of, the total nature of human beings.[31] To the extent that this is true,we may infer that there takes place here also some reinforcement. Aloof and hostile individuals would find congenial a mechanical or impersonal dealing with men and tend to hold to and "exaggerate" it beyond strict necessity, while the social structure encouraged at least indifference.[32]

The mechanism of projection calls for some special comment. It is readily conceived to act as a kind of "diabolical" agent in the whole leisure class framework. Competitive pecuniary activity inevitably spurs on, and involves, the desire to prevail over others or be more solvent. In the more unmitigated phases and derivatives (such as conspicuous consumption) of such activity, this mechanism could easily work out in the form of the attribution to others of a savage and unqualified will to superiority. In the "neurotic" character, the inevitable reaction to this would be an attempt to meet, and defeat, this imputed will to superiority. But, in turn, the assertion of a will to superiority would tend to generate another "superiority" response, and so on, in theoretically indefinite intensification. Projection and

31. This view is a strong underlying strain in the works of Elton Mayo previously referred to, *The Human Problems of an Industrial Civilization* and *The Social Problems of an Industrial Civilization.*

32. We are not of course broaching the question of the extent to which impersonality is a valuable or even indispensable mode of carrying on relations, at least in certain spheres and phases of social activity, in the interests of "efficiency." A problem of reconciling "efficiency" and "humanity" is beyond our scope here.

allied phenomena as such have no direct connection with the leisure class framework, but given the characteristics of the latter, projection has a field of rare suitability in which to work.[33]

If it has been stressed that Veblen sectored out an important *strain* in modern institutional forms, the enterprise here undertaken should be similarly understood: *i.e.*, it is clear, for example, that no such proposition has been advanced as that money is invariably pursued for reasons of obtaining power over others or that the existence of pecuniary norms is invariably seized upon as an opportunity to manifest superiority. Perhaps the best way to indicate the emphasis intended is to revert once more to the modes of relationship of the institutional and individual levels. The fact of connection is quite clear. At certain points congruity has also been witnessed. And there has been reason to argue that the process of reinforcement is at work. We also see interdependence, which is more general than reinforcement. As has been noted, given certain types of individuals only certain cultural goals will seem congenial and worth-while; on the other hand, given certain cultural goals, only certain types of individuals will find them desirable. The system of pecuniary norms is seen to afford highly attractive goals to individuals possessing the traits that have been reviewed, goals more attractive than many other possible ones. On the other hand, individuals endowed with the traits reviewed, rather than others, will find pecuniary goals very congenial. But in order for these goals to be preserved, they obviously do not need the full support of all individuals. We may infer a margin of indifference within which cultural goals may be preserved provided they obtain a certain amount of support and provided

33. It is worth noting that in his theory of the "fetishism of commodities" (*cf. Capital*, vol. I, pp. 81–96 and *ibid.*, vol. III, pp. 962–968) Marx emphasized a peculiarity of consciousness whereby the actions of men in society (*i.e.*, the genuinely effective forces in the creation of value and in the relations of commodities to one another on the market) appeared to them rather to be the action of "objects," of things external to men. Marx thereby noted a phenomenon of "attribution" to "commodities" or to "nature" of what originated in human society. This peculiar externalization forms an interesting parallel to the phenomena of projection and self-alienation remarked by the psychoanalysts. However, it is only a parallel or analogy, at least when stated in this form. Unless analysis of this parallel can be carried much further it may be misleading in the sense of suggesting a much more immediate affinity between "Freud and Marx" than actually exists.

antagonism toward them stays within certain limits. The goals also need not have precisely the same type of support from all individuals. Some may find in them excellent outlets for the traits we have reviewed and support them strongly; others less characterized by these traits may give them slighter support; others still may possibly support them for quite different reasons.

The types of inquiry launched by Veblen, on the one hand, and by the psychoanalysts on the other are of course independent. Their congruities and convergences are such as might emerge from the discoveries of two explorers, who, unknown to each other, were exploring opposite ends of the same general terrain. Thus, it is a certainty that the essential work of Adler, Stekel, Horney and others was done independently of Veblen's if for no other reason than that the work of these psychologists grew out of the heritage of problems that had been left by Freud and is entirely explainable within the framework of the history of the problems of clinical psychology.[34]

The limitations of the analysis thus far should be explicitly stated:

Firstly, the analysis is far from being exhaustive, in that not all possible connections between phenomena of the type that drew Veblen's attention and those on which the analysts have worked have been explored. Only certain high points of connection have been stressed. As an example of a possible connection that has been left out of account, it might be suggested that a world in which pecuniary norms, activities and institutions are strong and pervasive may be peculiarly attractive and understandable from the "neurotic" point of view in a special sense. The mobility or detachability of money, the possibility of losing or acquiring it over night, may make a particular appeal to a personality in whose mental make-up an element of magic and an element of highly unrealistic fantasy are important features.

Secondly, the analysis has implied the working of a principle of limited possibilities, which itself indicates a limitation. Thus, individuals in whom a power impulse is important might find a certain *number* and *variety* of institutional goal-systems congenial. Not only

34. Horney apparently is acquainted with *The Theory of the Leisure Class* (*cf. The Neurotic Personality,* p. 213) but from the point of view stated this is quite incidental.

the system of pecuniary norms need seem attractive. Any other system of goals allowing scope to the power impulse might seem attractive. As long as analysis shows only that a *range* of goals may satisfy or be congruous with a trait or trend, the ideal of scientific analysis is far from being reached. Ideally, refinement of analysis of both the institutional and individual levels would enable more exact statements, such that we could say, for example, that such and such a specific trait or character trend could find satisfaction only in such and such an institutional goal or form, or that a specific institutional goal or form would prove attractive to a specific trait or trend. The analysis has, however, at some points suggested more than a merely casual or permissive type of connection between the two levels. Thus, it has been noted that the pecuniary system gives a rather unique scope to the impulses of power and of manifesting superiority in that the possibilites of attainment within the system are, at least in theory, indefinite and "democratically" open to all.

Thirdly, there are considerations of social class that have not been remarked. Veblen's analysis proceeded on the notion that pecuniary norms had some tendency to seep downward through the strata of the community, but he saw some resistance on the "lower" strata, and the operation of counter-norms. Psychoanalysis does not afford us much help here. Its work has been largely with so-called "middle-class" individuals, and we have no accounts of the psychological constitutions of "lower-class" individuals at all comparable with the accounts we have been afforded of members of the "middle class." The whole range of the work of Freud, Adler and Jung affords extremely little on this line, and that of the neo-Freudians not much more.

A useful framework for further dealing with this third item is provided by a consideration of some of the main points of one of the few psychoanalytical studies that gives explicit and serious attention to social class in relation to character structure, namely, Erich Fromm's paper on psychoanalytical characterology and its significance for social psychology.[35] Fromm reviews the major traits of the so-called "anal" character, which are found to consist in a passion for order amounting to pedantry; self-willed obstinancy; frugality

35. "Die Psychoanalytische Charakterologie . . ."

and thrift; a pathological tendency to hold apart, intact, safe from alien "intrusion," everything in any sense interpretable as "private"; a pervasive tendency to "hold on" and "give nothing"; a tendency to expend energy in unproductive envy of the work and possessions of others. Fromm takes the field given by the problem of the "spirit" of capitalism to exemplify the application of psychoanalytical characterology to sociological problems. The "spirit" of capitalism involves concentration on duty rather than happiness as the goal of life and a major value; emphasis on frugality and on a "private sphere" that must remain inviolate; restriction and devaluation of sexuality; stress on "rational" considerations rather than love as affording prototypes for the organization of human relationships; a "rationality" that is itself peculiarly arid and approximates rather to the nature of "orderliness" (in the sense of a precise and compulsive regulation of one's life, related by Fromm to Karl Abraham's description of the "orderliness" of the "anal" type[36]). "The main character traits of the bourgeois spirit" are compared with the typical "anal" character traits, and it is argued that if the correspondences pointed to are real the typical libidinal structure of man in "bourgeois" society is characterized by a strengthening of the "anal-libido" disposition.

It is of special interest to note Fromm's contention that the typical traits of the anal character are today to be found in the "lower middle class."[37] This suggests that the lower middle class is a kind of special outpost wherein there are still maintained cultural restrictions upon consumption which had to a large extent lapsed by the time that Veblen undertook his analysis of the leisure class. Fromm speaks unequivocally of "frugality" and "thrift."[38] At first blush, there is nothing in particular in Veblen's analysis to indicate the truth of this

36. *Ibid.,* pp. 272–274.

37. *Ibid.,* p. 275, and footnotes, pp. 275–276. There are certain obvious differences between Fromm's approach and ours. It is sufficient to mention that Fromm has attempted to establish a direct correspondence of character traits found by clinical study and character traits found or inferred by certain historians and sociologists in the investigation of the development of capitalism. (It is important *not* to confound the "spirit" of capitalism as such with traits of personal character.) We have rather examined a set of connections between character traits and institutional forms.

38. *Cf.* also *Escape From Freedom, passim.*

implication of Fromm's study. Rather, Veblen's work would lead us to expect a certain seepage downward through the social strata of leisure class norms. This would be qualified by the simultaneous existence of some counter-norms for the classes doing the industrial work of the community. And it would also be qualified by the non-participation in the system of pecuniary norms of the very poorest elements in the community, whose poverty sapped all disposable energies for taking thought of anything but of what was indispensable in the daily struggle for existence, and whom Veblen found characterized by a peculiar conservatism,[39] which may be called the "conservatism of necessitous condition."[40] The implication of Fromm's study is nevertheless compatible with Veblen's views. The lower middle class may be simultaneously subject to the pressure of important cultural restrictions upon the use of money and to the pressure of pecuniary norms enforcing show or ostentation. This would have the effect of multiplying tensions for the members of this class, who would, in virtue of being subject to distinctive tensions, have somewhat distinctive personality structures by comparison with members of other classes. (If the child does not directly face tensions or "contradictions" involved in any social situation, his parents do, and consequently, from the beginning of life, he takes the indirect but none the less very real psychological impact of frustrations his parents have suffered.)

The way has certainly not been closed to the discrimination of different personality types in different strata or classes within the same society.[41]

Along with Kardiner, Professor Linton speaks of a basic personality type for a society as a whole.[42] But he also distinguishes "status personalities," contending, however, that "the status personalities recognized by any society are superimposed upon its basic personality

39. *The Leisure Class,* ch. viii.

40. This phrase is taken from Albert B. Wolfe, *Conservatism, Radicalism* and *Scientific Method* (New York: Macmillan, 1923), p. 62.

41. Kardiner's dubious (if qualified) contention for the existence of a single "basic personality type" under all variants of "Western" culture is made in *The Psychological Frontiers* (esp. pp. 337–339); see also Kardiner in Linton (ed.), *The Science of Man in the World Crisis,* pp. 107–122.

42. *The Cultural Background of Personality* (New York: Appleton-Century, 1945), p. 129.

type and are thoroughly integrated with the latter." [43] Linton nevertheless does allow a significant distinction between knowledge of a particular value-attitude system and participation in it. Thus, he suggests that free men may be aware of and reckon with the attitudes of slaves without, however, sharing them. A relatively mobile society, wherein members of all classes are presumed to pursue much the same goals—say, wealth, prestige, influence—is likely to show a certain amount of cohesion based on the circumstance that persons from all classes have like goals and agree that those goals are "good," even if the equipment for their attainment varies and the chances to attain them are unequal from the inception of endeavor. But a society with a more rigid class system, in which important "goods" are definitely recognized as inaccessible to certain groups and in which there are even prescriptions for the "lowly" to order themselves "humbly," may also have a sufficiency of elements making for cohesion in view of *common* acceptance of a differentiating structure. The attitudes of those "looking down" may be complemented by the attitudes of those "looking up." There are shared values: all men, both masters and slaves, may think masters properly the elect and slaves properly the lowly: if there is not some substantial agreement on this, the social structure is endangered.

But are basic personality types really the same in the latter situation? From the fact that masters' and slaves' attitudes may be complementary, it scarcely follows that they are the same or have the same psychological significance. Of course, one may still elect to say the basic personalities are the same, since the differentiation of basic personality types is dependent on one's purpose. But one's purpose is very easily such as to make it important to distinguish between basic personalities of master and slave, lord and serf, prince of the church and lowly parishioner. And it is easily of importance to make such distinctions in contemporary society. We have remarked the "conservatism of necessitous condition" which Veblen claimed existed among the very poor. Here there is no "radicalism," apparently because—to put it in Veblen's terms—the preoccupation with the sheer necessity of making a living is so demanding and the results of endeavor directed to this end are so uncertain that little energy or

43. *Ibid.*, p. 131.

inclination is available for "taking thought" of general social circumstances in a way that might lead to a "radical" conclusion. These are Veblen's terms. In other terms, it may be put forward as a tentative hypothesis that the personality emerging under conditions where there is a sheer, bitter fight for subsistence and a place of residence, in an atmosphere where frequent defeat is taken for granted and where there may be older-sibling and parental desertion, turns out either "crushed" or peculiarly "limited." [44] It is at any rate plausible that superego development should be different here from what it is in the middle class layers. The goals of achievement and success that pervade the general society may also penetrate here, but the inhibitions on various (say, "criminal") techniques for attaining the goals may be mitigated.[45]

44. An excellent instance of what is meant by a "crushed" personality is seen in Kardiner's vivid analysis of Lomani of Alor (*The Psychological Frontiers of Society,* pp. 206–211). See also DuBois, *The People of Alor,* esp. p. 639. It is significant that the utterly resigned Lomani grew up amid death, poverty, high mobility of residence and loneliness. (This should not, of course, be taken to imply that membership in "lowest" classes would unqualifiedly involve resemblances across cultures.) The reference to a peculiarly "limited" personality is intended to suggest that certain "moral" elements present in middle class personalities may be played down, *i.e.,* elements especially connected with the superego, "conscience" and the faculty of ideal imagination of the sufferings of others.

45. On this point, R. K. Merton's paper, "Social Structure and Anomie," is highly pertinent. It may be noted, incidentally, that the hypothesis suggested would forcibly bring to the fore again the question of the normative component of the psyche.

# 7. *The Case of Modern Germany: A Critical Approach* *

## I. IMPERIAL GERMANY

ANOTHER of Veblen's notable contributions to modern social science is his analysis of *Imperial Germany and the Industrial Revolution,* with which his *The Nature of Peace and the Terms of its Perpetuation* is closely associated. We will review Veblen's essential thesis in *Imperial Germany,* and attempt to relate certain significant portions of that thesis to modern psychoanalytical and psychiatric work. However, in the case of this analysis, it is indispensable, in order to do justice to fact, to introduce intermediate terms. The psychoanalytical contribution to the specific analysis of German institutions and German character structure is only in its incipient phases. It would be scientifically unsafe to rely solely upon it in treating socio-psychological aspects of Veblen's theme in *Imperial Germany* and in *The Nature of Peace.* As a check on what the psychoanalysts or psychiatrists have thus far had to say on the subject of Germany, we shall refer to a type of study that approaches it without particular regard to psychoanalysis, in order to see whether there is or is not essential correspondence between non-psychoanalytical and psychoanalytical treatment. There have been some important studies of modern Germany which treat what we here call *overt* norms. We already know that overt norms have important connections with those covert normative systems to which the psychoanalysts have more particularly given attention. If the analysis of certain German norms afforded by historians, sociologists and essayists cannot possibly bear the interpretations of German character structure which psychoanalysts have suggested, doubt is thrown upon the latter. If, on the other hand, an essential congruence emerges, the psychoanalytical interpretations tend to be reinforced. Given the uncertainty and novelty

* This chapter is allowed to stand as written in early 1946.

of psychoanalytical endeavors in this whole field, these must certainly be rejected as unlikely constructions if they fail to harmonize with the implications of well known historical facts or with legitimate inferences drawn therefrom. The literature actually drawn upon in this chapter is relatively small, and the aim of the chapter limited. We are here in a very complex field, and all that is attempted is a first approximation to the statement of an important problem. Our previous study in Chapter 6 encourages us in the view that a fruitful integration of Freudian and Veblenian themes is feasible, and the present chapter is embarked upon as a preliminary to further integration.

An exhaustive study of Germany would undoubtedly have to give consideration to important aspects of the modern German economy, but we are primarily interested in a methodological analysis, and economic facts will be considered only as this is unavoidable for our theme. It may be stated at once that we assume there is a *limited* truth in the view that Nazism is a kind of "last stage of capitalism," a set of institutionalized expedients to ensure the survival and continuation of a large-scale profit system endangered by proletarian masses "below." Even those who come nearest to this view qualify it. Thus, Robert Brady, who has held that Nazism represents organized and self-conscious monopoly capitalism, states at one point in a recent analysis:

> Problems of monopoly controls, becoming politicized as an incidence to the wielding of coercive authority, are necessarily handled with a view to many factors other than mere price and marketing advantage. Only the historically untutored, or politically and philosophically naïve could suppose that the power phase of coordinated monopoly controls would be handled in terms of "duopoly," "oligopoly," imperfect competition and the like. The proper terms of reference are those associated with what Weber refers to as *Buerokratie, Patrimonialismus, Patriarchalismus,* and *Feudalismus.*[1]

The implication is plain that in the modern German economy

1. *Business as a System of Power* (New York: Columbia University Press, 1943), pp. 45–46. *Cf.* also the same author's *Spirit and Structure of German Fascism* (New York: Viking, 1937), and Franz Neumann, *Behemoth* (New York: Oxford University Press, 1942).

sociological factors have become inextricably interwoven with economic forces. The "politicizing" to which Brady refers has indeed been characteristic for the whole of modern German economic history, in which the State and its forms have played a peculiarly important role. The inevitable compounding of sociological and political with economic analysis is especially clear in one of the best studies of National Socialism, Franz Neumann's *Behemoth.* At this date, it may seem almost idle to indicate that even if one assumes the validity of Marxian propositions about the inherently "self-contradictory" or "self-destructive" tendencies of the modern capitalist economy, these point to but a single strain, however important it may be, in the vast social, economic and psychological complex of modern societies. Thus, for instance, if one assumes the essential validity of the view that the capitalist economy is "self-contradictory" and liable to periodic and worsening "breakdowns," there still remains the complicated task of analysis of human reaction to these phenomena. Organized anti-capitalist reaction on the part of the "lower classes" is only one possibility, that exists side by side with possibilities of reactions of a nihilistic character [2] or on the line of simply embracing the system to which the proletariat is presumed to be opposed. In the history of the German Social Democracy there has even been a strain of "social imperialism." Thus, one wing of the Social Democratic Party in 1907

> was definitely "social imperialistic," and we use here the term in its original meaning, of an imperialistic policy desired by and for the working classes. This group despised the left liberals and the petty bourgeoisie, and sought an alliance with the captains of industry. It fully accepted colonial expansion as a boon for the working classes, expecting rising wages and a quickening of the natural life of capitalism, which would hasten the coming of socialism.[3]

2. For this type of reaction, *cf.* Konrad Heiden, *Der Fuehrer: Hitler's Rise to Power* (tr. Ralph Manheim, Boston: Houghton Mifflin, 1944), *passim,* but esp. pp. 310–328 and 350–352; also, Hans E. Fried, *The Guilt of the German Army* (New York: Macmillan, 1942).

3. Neumann, *ibid.,* p. 212. It is true that Neumann soon comments: "There is no doubt that the huge majority of the party remained uncontaminated by social imperialism, and never accepted the fallacious reasoning that class interests can best be served by warfare against imperialist competitors." *Ibid.,* p. 213. But our point here is simply to emphasize the complexity and variety of possible responses to the challenge of the Marxian view of capitalism.

Moreover, Neumann makes room for socio-psychoanalytical interpretations of important phases of the phenomenon of Nazism. Thus, in connection with a discussion of National Socialist bureaucracy, he indicates that, with the operation of this bureaucracy,

> the natural structure of society is dissolved and replaced by an abstract "people's community," which hides the complete depersonalization of human relations and the isolation of man from man. In terms of modern analytical social psychology, one could say that National Socialism is out to create a uniformly sado-masochistic character, a type of man determined by his isolation and insignificance, who is driven by this very fact into a collective body where he shares in the power and glory of the medium of which he has become a part.[4]

To return to the question of the possibility of variant reactions that was raised just above: one writer has stated that "those who were unemployed for three years turned Communist; those on the other hand, who were unemployed for five years, turned Nazi."[5] Allowing for the "literary" quality of this statement, it undoubtedly expresses a relative truth. Thus, if we follow Konrad Heiden's analysis, it is clear that, with the German inflation, increasing numbers began to listen to Hitler; that, generally, Hitler's adherents increased in times of economic distress and decreased in times of relative prosperity; that countless German workers, demoralized by post-war inflation and unemployment, reacted, not by turning to radical solutions, but by clinging desperately to the jobs that millions of others wanted and that seemed virtually the sole stable factors in a chaotic social system.[6] Julius Braunthal, a Socialist of Austrian background writing in England in 1943 summarizes a significant aspect of the experience of himself and his socialist friends when he states:

> Socialism without freedom was simply inconceivable to us. Never did the thought enter our minds that the working class, that struggled for Socialism as the gateway to economic security as well as that of freedom would be prepared to submit to a social order providing economic security without freedom. We were not aware that the psychological revolution had

4. *Ibid.*, p. 402. For substantially similar types of interpretation on Neumann's part, *cf. ibid.*, pp. 430, 439.

5. Valentin Giterman, *Die Historische Tragoedie der Sozialistischen Idee*, as quoted by Julius Braunthal, *Need Germany Survive?* (London: Gollancz, 1943), p. 139.

6. Heiden, *ibid.*, pp. 125–150, 350–351, 401.

profoundly changed the scale of values. Once the cry was "Rather death than slavery!"; it is now: "Rather slavery than starvation!" [7]

The above perhaps gives a sufficient indication of the fact that even if a more or less Marxian *economic* analysis of modern German capitalism is accepted, there remains a residue of political, sociological and psychological factors which make up an indispensable addendum to purely economic analysis and without which the development of Nazism cannot be explained. There is certainly no straight line from "increasing misery" to proletarian revolution, and "capitalist" support is scarcely directly creative of National Socialism.[8] It is our purpose to give to sociological and psychological factors a major share of attention.

Already in 1904, in *The Theory of Business Enterprise,* Veblen broached some of the essential issues that he was later to set forth in a broader perspective in *Imperial Germany* and in *The Nature of Peace.* One of the important features of the earlier analysis was its insistence that the machine technology formed the material base of business enterprise, without which the latter could not get along. But if business enterprise could not get along without the machine technology neither could it, in the long run, get along with it, since the latter bred a frame of mind on the part of the industrial population unfavorable to the maintenance of business institutions. Business interests would for this, among other reasons, look to military ventures and associated institutional forms as a way out of their difficulties:

> In this direction, evidently, lies the hope of a corrective for "social unrest" and similar disorders of civilized life. There can, indeed, be no serious question but that a consistent return to the ancient virtues of allegiance, piety, servility, graded dignity, class prerogative, and prescriptive authority would greatly conduce to popular content and to the facile management of affairs. Such is the promise held out by a strenuous national policy.[9]

7. Braunthal, *ibid.,* pp. 162–163. Thus Braunthal on the working class. An able psychological analysis of the lower middle class in relation to Nazism is given by H. D. Lasswell in "The Psychology of Hitlerism," *Political Quarterly* IV (1933), 373–384.

8. *Cf.* Heiden, *ibid.,* pp. 113–114, 445.

9. *The Theory of Business Enterprise,* p. 393.

The motivation behind the adoption of a "strenuous national policy" would thus be to provide a "corrective" for a population chafing under the business régime, but in this direction Veblen saw the possibility of a certain mitigation of the scope and discretion of business men. He states:

> When once the policy of warlike enterprise has been entered upon for business ends . . . loyal affections gradually shift from the business interests to the warlike and dynastic interests. . . . The eventual outcome should be a rehabilitation of the ancient patriotic animosity and dynastic loyalty, to the relative neglect of business interests. This may easily be carried so far as to sacrifice the profits of the business men to the exigencies of the higher politics.[10]

Veblen thus discriminates a *profit* element and a *power* element in the complex of modern industrial societies, and tends to regard the two as ultimately incompatible. In fact, he called the last chapter of *The Theory of Business Enterprise* "The Natural Decay of Business Enterprise." Three main institutional systems figured in his analysis in this chapter: the machine technology and the norms cohering around it and around applied science; the system of business enterprise; the military establishment and associated state forms. The dominance of the system of business enterprise was seen as threatened by the possible ascendance of either the machine technology as an institutional complex or of the military establishment as an institutional complex. However, Veblen concluded in a somewhat qualified vein by stating: "It seems possible to say this much, that the *full* dominion of business enterprise is necessarily a transitory dominion."[11] This clearly leaves open the possibility of an unstable combination of all three elements, although it implies that in any such combination there would be important restrictions on the "dominion of business enterprise." This analysis is of particular interest in view of modern German history, in which laissez-faire principles never attained the popularity or scope they have enjoyed among English-speaking peoples, and in which the "dominion of business enterprise" has always been importantly qualified by the intermingling of state and "pure" or private economic enterprise.

10. *Ibid.*, p. 395.
11. *Ibid.*, p. 400; our emphasis.

Running through *Imperial Germany* is a contrast between England and Germany, crucial for our analysis, which contrast will not be lost in the brief review that follows.

England long enjoyed an isolation from the Continent that prevented her embroilment in wars and enabled her to go ahead with the development of her technology. She went through a period of "borrowing" in the early 16th to early 17th centuries, getting technological "know-how" from the Continental countries. From the later 17th century to the historical present she has been engaged in a work of technological creativity, as distinguished from the earlier period of borrowing.[12] This technological history put England, in the industrial respect, well ahead of her Continental neighbors. But in the course of time she has paid the "penalty of taking the lead." The machine technology developed in modern England does not stand isolated. Two encrusting features of great importance have grown up around it. One is the institution(s) of conspicuous waste, which has a doubly inhibitive effect from the point of view of sheer technological productivity and efficiency. The scheme of conspicuous waste directly encourages the expenditure of industrial effort in the making of industrially useless items. (Closely associated with this are the "wasteful" activities of leisure-class elements, typically cluttering with race-tracks and with supernumerary houses land that might otherwise be devoted to agricultural uses). In addition, certain distinctive "wasteful" activities, such as sports, create and encourage on the part of the working population a bent of mind that reduces industrial efficiency. The "virtues" that preoccupation with sport inculcates are worse than useless from an industrial point of view.[13]

12. This is given by Veblen as a rough but serviceable generalization. *Cf. Imperial Germany,* pp. 92–93.

13. Sport may in a sense be useless from an "industrial point of view." So are a great many other things, a conclusion from which Veblen never shrank. He tends to regard all human activities not undertaken in the interest of industrial efficiency or procreation as pathological aberrations. In his paper on "Industrial and Pecuniary Employments," he said of a "modern industrial community" that it is one "where the margin of admissible waste probably always exceeds fifty per cent of the output of goods." (*The Place of Science,* p. 306.) He does not indicate how he arrived at such a figure. To argue that what is waste "in the economic respect" is not necessarily "waste" in other respects (*cf.* the critique of Cummings in *Essays in Our Changing Order,* pp. 16–31) does not clarify the general concept of waste. *Cf.* T. W. Adorno, *ibid.*

On the other side, as an additional encrustation or parasitic growth upon the machine technology, is the system of business enterprise. Business enterprise is interested essentially in the making of money, not in the making of goods or the improvement of industrial equipment. The making of money is frequently and radically incompatible with the making of goods. A common device of business enterprise is the curtailment of production with the object of maintaining prices. As corporation debts accumulate, and there are ever larger fixed charges to meet, the pressure to make money increases and there is corresponding curtailment of technological enterprise. The phenomenon of technological obsolescence is particularly noteworthy, and it is difficult to find a remedy for it, more especially one "that will approve itself as a sound business proposition to a community of conservative business men who have a pecuniary interest in the continued working of the received system, and who will (commonly) not be endowed with much insight into technological matters anyway." [14] As long as obsolescence entails no pecuniary difficulties, *i.e.*, as long as it gives no single group of business men a large differential advantage over others, a remedy is not likely to be seriously sought: Veblen instances as typical the narrow gauge and general inadequacies of Great Britain's railways.[15] Thus, the productivity of the machine technology is once more obstructed and limited.

The effect of the machine technology is to breed a scientific habit of mind, and a somewhat "subversive" one, not inclined to a profound reverence for powers that declare their sources to be mysterious but divine. England has had long experience of such a technology, and the English State is *relatively* non-coercive and not given to an undue "disciplining" of its underlying population.

In 1870, Germany came on to the industrial scene on a large and important scale. She "borrowed" the machine technology from England, [16] and in a period of a few decades developed an industrial

For a quite different conception of the significance of sport in English life, see Hermann Kantorowicz, *The Spirit of British Policy and the Myth of the Encirclement of Germany* (English edition revised by the author and translated by W. H. Johnston, London: Allen and Unwin, 1931), ch. i.

14. *Imperial Germany*, p. 130.

15. *Ibid.*, pp. 130–131.

16. See William H. Dawson, *The Evolution of Modern Germany* (New York: Chas. Scribner's Sons, n.d.), p. 75.

system that, in England, had been maturing since the late 17th century. Germany was far in arrears to begin with [17] but her development after 1870 was phenomenal. The essential reason is that Germany took over England's technology without taking over in any considerable degree the institutional encrustations that had grown up around it in its home. Germany had an ample supply of frugal, industrious workers content with relatively low wages, as well as a supply of well-educated men not accustomed to large pecuniary rewards. German frugality was a general phenomenon. At first, therefore, the institutions of conspicuous waste took little hold, and to that extent the borrowed German technology remained free of inhibiting forces. The same was true for the system of business enterprise and corporation finance. It achieved a relatively slight initial development in Germany, which was able to do well in the sale of cheaply priced goods, produced by workmen with comparatively low wages. Latterly,[18] Germany shows signs of going in the direction taken by the English, but there was, initially, sufficiently slight emphasis on the two encrusting, inhibitive systems to allow Germany to spurt forward rapidly and enable her to challenge England to a test of relative technological power in war.[19]

The machine technology, therefore, in the case of Germany, came late, and its "subversive" effects have not yet had time to take effect. The machine technology is a great solvent of old institutions, a great source of change, but it takes time to achieve its effects. Most important of all, it has not succeeded in the case of Germany in undermining the foundations of the Dynastic State. A crucial political and social contrast between England and Germany thereby appears:

> It is as difficult for the commonplace Englishman to understand what the German means by the "State" as it is for the German to comprehend the English conception of a "commonwealth," or very nearly so. . . .

17. Before 1848, Germany hardly even had anything approaching a modern class system, in the sense of an opposition between bourgeoisie and proletariat. Her main social classes were the landowners and their tenantry and the handicraftsmen and their helpers. *Cf.* Werner Sombart, *Die Deutsche Volkwirtschaft im Neunzehnten Jahrhundert* (seventh ed., Berlin: G. Bondi, 1927), ch. xvii.

18. Veblen writes in 1915.

19. Veblen is inclined to think that Germany in 1914 may have struck "too late" when her differential advantage of a late-comer who had avoided the "penalty of taking the lead" was dissipated. *Imperial Germany,* p. 262.

The State is a matter not easily to be expounded in English. It is neither the territorial area, nor the population, nor the body of citizens or subjects, nor the aggregate wealth or traffic, nor the public administration, nor the government, nor the crown, nor the sovereign; yet in some sense it is all these matters, or rather all these are organs of the State. In some potent sense, the State is a personal entity, with rights and duties superior and anterior to those of the subjects, whether these latter be taken severally or collectively, in detail or in the aggregate or average.

Plainly, government by consent of the governed is not a State. The sovereignty is not in the people, but it is in the State. Failure to understand this conundrum is perhaps the most detestable trait of unreason that taints the English-speaking peoples, in the apprehension of intelligent Germans.[20]

The Dynastic State, to carry on war effectively, needs the modern technology. But that technology breeds an industrial proletariat tending not to fall in with the consensus that supports the Dynastic State, but rather opposed to it. Therefore, just as, in Veblen's earlier analysis in *The Theory of Business Enterprise,* business enterprise could not get along either with or without the machine technology, so now it appears that the Dynastic State also cannot get along with or without that technology. But now that attention centers on the Dynastic State, Veblen's emphasis has shifted somewhat. It is not that the tension between business enterprise and the machine technology has lapsed, and it should still be present in both the English and German cases, but a contrast is now stressed in that the tension between Dynastic State and modern technology rather distinctively sets off the case of Germany from that of England. As long as, in the midst of tensions, a certain institutional equilibrium and stability may yet be maintained, a peculiar situation in respect of the waging of war appears for Germany, which, like Japan, manifests the "unique combination of a high-wrought spirit of feudalistic fealty and chivalric honor with the material efficiency given by the machine technology."[21]

20. *Ibid.,* pp. 160, 161, 162. Veblen, incidentally, realized very well that the Dynastic State was not simply a coercive political form maintaining its power on the basis of sheer imposition upon a recalcitrant population. *Cf.* his treatment of the high degree of community acquiescence in the State's ends and claims in the case of Prussia: *ibid.,* pp. 164–165; *cf.* also Davis, *Thorstein Veblen's Social Theory,* pp. 277–278.

21. *Essays in Our Changing Order,* p. 251. This point, so clearly made in *Imperial Germany,* is reiterated in *The Nature of Peace,* p. 201.

The contrast between England and Germany is maintained and repeatedly insisted upon in Veblen's allied study of *The Nature of Peace*. He here distinguishes powers that may "safely be counted on spontaneously to take the offensive" and powers that "will fight on provocation," placing Germany and Japan in the class of the former and England and France in the class of the latter.[22] Veblen's context shows that the contrast between France as a "national commonwealth" and Germany as a Dynastic State would also be maintained for England and Germany.[23] For our purposes, the analysis afforded in the two studies is substantially the same. The differences between England and Germany are not taken as absolute. There is a discernible nationalistic-imperialistic strain in the cases of both England and Germany, and the contrast is therefore relative.

Of the general validity of Veblen's theme in *Imperial Germany*, there can be no doubt. He is not only supported, as might be expected, by his main authorities, Dawson and Sombart, but by a host of others. We may briefly indicate some of the evidences that favor Veblen's view.

The argument regarding Germany's economic advantage in being a latecomer is well exemplified in the history of railway development in England and Germany. Veblen, as has been noted, had remarked the narrow gauge and generally poor state of the English railways in 1915. To Germany, railways were typically a British invention, one that was indeed originally taken over with the policy associated with it in its homeland, namely, that the State should not interfere in business pursuits. But this association, strongly ingrained in England, was much looser in Germany. About a decade before the World War, more than nine-tenths of the German railways were owned, managed and directed by the German government, while in England the railways were in private ownership. Up to the eighteen-seventies, German railway enterprise was haphazard and unco-ordinated. The principle of charging what the traffic would bear was widely observed; rates were uncertain; freights were dear. In the late seventies, Bismark remarked needlessly high working expenses

22. *The Nature of Peace*, p. 79.

23. Davis, *ibid.*, ch. vi, takes Veblen's essential work in *Imperial Germany* as an attempt to contrast ideal types of States: constitutional (England) and autocratic (Germany).

and charges, needless duplication of materials and lines, a confusing multiplicity of freight charges and the hampering of transport of passengers and goods for reasons of competitive business. He noted that railways, by instituting discriminating tariffs, in effect developed industries in some areas and inhibited their development in others; that they reduced rates in the interest of getting large masses of goods to transport, and thereby often favored foreign producers at the expense of home industries: something entirely out of accord with the policy of protection for which Bismark stood. In 1879 was begun the German system of state railways. Between 1879 and 1885, Prussia trebled its railway property, and the figure for 1885 almost doubled again between that date and 1913. In the thirty years that followed the initiation of state railways, Germany's railway rolling-stock virtually trebled, at the same time as vast general improvements occurred. J. Ellis Barker commented in 1919: "The German goods trains . . . are . . . much more economical than are English toy trains pulled by toy engines, and composed of insufficiently loaded toy trucks." [24] Technologically, before the World War, the German railways were far ahead of the British. They afforded cheaper service and were more convenient and more predictable in their uniform arrangements of traffic and stable freight charges. Moreover, capitalization per mile of road was a great deal higher for English than for German railways, and inflated capitalization was a major factor in creating high English freights and fares.

The general phenomenon of German thrift, industry and frugality was often insisted upon by the English themselves. The debate over free trade versus protection initiated about the time that Lord Salisbury came into office in 1885 produced many conflicting opinions, but the fact stood out that England's trade supremacy was not so secure as it once had been. In official reports, consideration was given to German rivalry, and while one report concluded that Germany had not been gaining in recent years at the expense of English trade in markets common to the two countries,[25] in another official source

24. In *Modern Germany* (sixth ed., New York: Dutton, 1919), p. 226. The account given closely follows that of Barker, *ibid.,* pp. 214–234.

25. The report went on to say: "Its [Germany's] gains have been special and in certain directions. Our preponderance remains substantially what it was ten years ago." Quoted from House of Commons Sessional Papers, 1888, XCIII, 10,

there are found the following significant sentences: "The average English commercial man of the present day is unfit to compete with the thrifty and industrious Germans. The former is bent on the pursuit of pleasure, whilst the latter gives himself no leisure until his future is assured." [26]

The fact is thus emphasized that that phase of the capitalist ethos which enjoins unremitting devotion to work enjoyed, at this time, less general effect in England, the home of modern industrialism, than in Germany, which showed no significant industrial development of the modern type until roughly some hundred years after the English industrial revolution. The institutional heritage of modern England contains too many features, on the lines of a kind of "human" self-cultivation and of generous use of leisure time for purposes removed from daily work, to have allowed the type of devotion to the latter that has been remarked in the case of Germany.[27]

The combination of the modern machine technology with dynasticism and strong feudalistic holdovers which Veblen remarked is now almost a matter of common sense about Germany. One succinct confirming statement, made by its author in a review of the history of the Second Reich, will suffice: "In Germany classes which were elsewhere obsolescent were in control of techniques and resources vastly in advance of anything previously conceived of." [28] Similarly, the character of the Dynastic State, as an organ designed to achieve power and acting independently of all "moral" considerations, is a matter so familiar that it needs no special emphasis. There has even been a great deal of self-congratulation in Germany both because of the specific character of the Dynastic State (or of a variant thereof, such as the Nazi State) and because of the historically established leadership of Prussia in setting the patterns and standards of German statesmanship.

---

by Raymond J. Sontag, *Germany and England: Background of Conflict* (New York: Appleton-Century, 1938), p. 217. Sontag's comment on this conclusion is: "Probably the conclusion erred on the side of optimism, but not grossly." *Ibid.*, p. 217.

26. Quoted by Sontag, *ibid.*, p. 218, from House of Commons Sessional Papers, 1888, LX, Commercial No. 16.

27. *Cf.* Kantorowicz, *The Spirit of British Policy, passim.*

28. Rohan Butler, *The Roots of National Socialism* (New York: Dutton and Co., 1942), p. 213.

With regard to Veblen's point that the Dynastic State could not get along either with the machine technology or without it, it is worth noting one or two special features of German military history that afford useful perspective. The connection of the military with the State has been most intimate in Germany, so that at times it has even been difficult to make a distinction between the two. But the military has been in some ways rather sharply separated from the population at large and from its workday concerns and preoccupations. Imperial Germany had very effectively instilled in its officers a martial or bellicose attitude, a sense of being distinctively marked off from the rest of the population as a superior group or caste, and a corresponding disposition to look down upon other groups as rather contemptible. "The soldier is the first man in the whole State." [29] In the Prussian army in particular, the nobility played a very large role, one reinforced by the circumstance that from the middle of the seventeenth to the end of the eighteenth century, Prussia manifested a lack both of geographical unity and of genuine national feeling among its subjects. In the absence of national feeling, reliance was placed upon the personal loyalty of aristocratic officers to their lord the king. The feudal tradition of knightly fealty was consequently more in evidence than the type of national-patriotic sentiment vesting in the generality of modern mass armies. Frederick the Great established the exclusively noble character of the Prussian officers' corps, and the reformer Scharnhorst, who tried to limit the nobility's monopoly upon it, was in the end very far from stamping out "the inflexible social composition of the officers' corps." [30] Although the number of commoners in the officers' corps increased rather steadily during the nineteenth century and at the beginning of the twentieth, the infiltration was slow, and such commoners as did "make the grade" tended to come from families with attitudes generally congenial to, or at least not critical of, the tradition and behavior of the aristocratic officer.[31] The rather radical separation of the military from the bulk of the population is quite evident.

Closely associated with this is the separation of aristocracy from

29. *Cf.* Alfred Vagts, *A History of Militarism* (New York: Norton, 1937), p. 487.

30. Fried, *The Guilt of the German Army*, p. 61.

31. *Ibid.*, p. 62.

technology. In Bavaria in 1911, the highest percentage of aristocratic officers was in a cavalry regiment (45%) and the lowest in an engineers' battalion (4%). The Bavarian communication units had no aristocratic officers at all. "This distribution indicates the preference shown by aristocratic officers for the traditionally feudalistic cavalry, and their disinclination toward technical weapons."[32] Even in the peacetime army of Germany after 1918, "the technical branches were still shunned by the nobility, especially if the regiment was not stationed in a desirable garrison."[33]

The military, as an indispensable adjunct of the Dynastic State (or of the Nazi State) also needs the modern technology: it cannot get along without it. Yet the heart of the military, its most "purely" military component, is "opposed" to technology: that is to say, the military nobility represents and carries forward quite different values from those that may be connected with carrying forward technological endeavor. The opposition which Veblen noted between the Dynastic State and the modern technology (which can here be taken simply in the sense of an opposition between the norms of the Dynastic State and those tending to develop for an urban-industrial proletariat, other things constant)—this opposition within the larger social structure is symbolically reproduced inside the army itself, where the most typically military (aristocratic) elements are most aloof from the more technical devices necessary to carry on war. At least, a very considerable part of German political and military history bears this out.[34]

## II. OVERT NORMS: THE CONTRAST OF ENGLAND AND GERMANY

We have stated the contrast between England and Germany marked by Veblen. Is it borne out by modern studies?

Certain Englishman have latterly taken up the task of explaining Germany, in terms of national character, both to their countrymen and to the world. In Lord Robert Vansittart's view, the Germans are

32. *Ibid.*, p. 386, note 5 to ch. iv, Part One. The same general point is remarked by Vagts: *cf. e.g., A History of Militarism*, pp. 449–450.

33. Fried, *ibid.*, p. 140.

34. For a contention that the Nazi army represents no *essential* changes from the army of Imperial Germany see Fried, *ibid.*, pp. 67–68.

eminently characterized by *Schadenfreude*. They are, by and large, megalomanic, constantly asserting superiority over other peoples and claiming that they are intrinsically better and more noble. They are envious. They are unimaginative about the needs and feelings of others, but pathologically imaginative and self-pitying about their own. They are "plodding and hysterical," overweening, violently nationalistic and imperialistic, cruel, servile and humorless.[35] Vansittart thinks it quite meaningful to speak of German character, "for national characters do very definitely exist," and the German character has the three main features of envy, self-pity and cruelty. These three features are reducible to a single origin: "They all three proceed from the average German's callous egotism, his utter indifference to the feelings and interests of others. The world in his eyes falls naturally into two categories, one of Germans, the other of 'the others.' "[36]

To reinforce this view, Vansittart asserts that German self-pity occurs only in time of failure, whereas "in victory the German eye is hard and glittering; repentance is impossible if your neighbor has no rights." There is essential continuity between the attitudes and behavior of the Nazis and the historical features found in German character: in fact, it is "not only illogical but misleading to talk of Nazis instead of Germans."[37] National Socialism is, so to put it, the fruit of the modern German development, a fruit ripened after at least one hundred and fifty years of peculiar training and discipline. Indeed, Vansittart contends that there has been a basic consistency in German character for some two thousand years. In support of this view, there are contained, in a chapter in a recent book, quotations from various classical writers, Tacitus leading, uniformly to the effect that the Germans are ferocious and perfidious, intolerable in victory and abject in defeat.[38]

Vansittart does not afford a comparative analysis of the national character of other peoples, and, in the absence of such an analysis, there tends to appear some implication that the Germans are a "deep

35. See *Lessons of My Life* (New York: Knopf, 1943), esp. pp. 91–114 and 240–281.

36. *Ibid.*, p. 200.

37. *Ibid.*, pp. 203 and 83.

38. Vansittart, *Bones of Contention* (New York: Knopf, 1945), pp. 137–141.

black" and other peoples on the whole quite "white." It is necessary to note this point in the interest of indicating the need for basing a theory of national character on solid foundations.

Professor Hearnshaw, who on the whole definitely upholds Vansittart's thesis as to German character, begins with the Germans of antiquity, who were marked by "bottomless treachery as well as merciless ferocity."[39] The long perspective of some two thousand years makes the historian Hearnshaw refer unhesitatingly to "the predatory passions of the chronically dangerous and easily misguided German nation."[40] The judgment is very much the same at any point in the two-thousand-year line. Even random selection reveals typical Hearnshaw comments. Charlemagne fares no better than Frederick the Great. If the latter's "heart had been seared beyond recovery" and his conscience "permanently atrophied," the former was "a German through and through," which meant that he shared the "general Teutonic lust for conquest" and the "perfidy and ferocity of his race." If the Germans in the Franco-Prussian War exhibited all the "latent barbarity of the race," the generals of the Prussian army two generations earlier, in the ill treatment they accorded their men and in their insulting attitude to civilians, were presumably no better.[41]

If Hearnshaw's indictment is heavy, his diagnosis of the case of Germany is simple. At the time when England, France and Spain were achieving the status of strong national states headed by strong monarchs, in the fifteenth century, Germany was in a relatively chaotic condition. Some three hundred and sixty local rulers, an array of independent dukes, counts and barons, numerous free cities, and some fifteen hundred virtually unrestrained imperial knights divided sovereignty and utterly prevented it from achieving focus. Hearnshaw contends that memberships of rising national states are usually characterized by pugnacity, selfishness and unscrupulousness. Germany simply began to achieve its national development some four centuries later than her main European neighbors, and showed these

39. F. J. C. Hearnshaw, *Germany the Aggressor Throughout the Ages* (London: W. and R. Chambers, Ltd., 1940), p. 26.

40. *Ibid.*, p. 281.

41. *Ibid.*, pp. 50–51, 119–120, 150, 219. A painfully careless use of the word "race" marks Hearnshaw's book.

traits at a time when they had lapsed in her neighbors. To this is added a comparison of the English and Germans. The Anglo-Saxons, the Jutes, the Danes, the Normans, "all of them Germanic in blood," manifested in the Britain of the fifth and subsequent centuries "all the main features of their continental kin." They were, in fact, "warlike, aggressive, cruel, credulous, non-moral." The reason the English came in the course of time to manifest different features of character from those of the Germans is simply that "their struggles were carried out in an island." Those struggles resulted in settling all problems of frontiers, and thereby energies could be devoted to non-military tasks.[42]

The essential explanation afforded the case of Germany is in fact too simple. Repeating an error common among national character theorists, Hearnshaw is too prone to overlook differences in social and economic structure. Obviously, in some very important respects, England, France and Spain of the fifteenth or sixteenth century are not comparable with industrial Germany of the later nineteenth and early twentieth. One of the points we have sought to enforce throughout this study is the intimate relationship between character and social structure. Where social structure is in significant respects different, a strong presumption is raised that there will be correlative differences in character structure. Our previous theme with regard to congruity and interdependence between the level of character structure and the institutional level will be recalled. It is by no means necessary to maintain that there are no constants in social structure or character structure, over time or among countries, but Hearnshaw's specific thesis remains unsubstantiated. Thus, he suggests that "Hitler and his gang of international criminals are the political and ethical contemporaries of Caesar Borgia, Machiavelli, Castruccio Castracani, and Ludovico Sforza."[43] Are they also their psychological contemporaries? Hearnshaw contends that perfidy, selfishness and aggressiveness are characteristic for memberships of rising national states. These terms are meaningful enough for ordinary purposes, but any of the phenomena they point to are psychologically quite complex (and the historian, or anyone else, who ventures into national character theory inevitably comes into psychological

42. *Ibid.*, pp. 78–84 and 272–273.

43. *Cf. ibid.*, pp. 83–84.

territory). "Aggressiveness," for example, may have very variant psychological backgrounds and contexts. Are the audacious Spanish adventurers who discovered and conquered new lands in the fifteenth and sixteenth centuries comparable, in point of character structure, with, say, German "tourists" or fifth columnists of the 1930's and 1940's? Overtly, both adventurers and "tourists" might well appear "aggressive." But this does not take us very far for psychological purposes. Hearnshaw's diagnosis has a strictly limited validity.[44] Insofar as valid, Hearnshaw's thesis resembles Veblen's. The emphasis in both his work and Veblen's is upon a peculiar combination of feudal or quasi-feudal and modern circumstances that serves to set off Germany distinctively.

A third example of recent national character approaches to the case of modern Germany is Rohan Butler's *The Roots of National Socialism*. Butler reviews the lines of philosophy and political theory leading up to the Nazi view of things in German literature of the past one hundred years. His method, too, is rather simple. He starts with the discrepancy that ordinary observation appears to find between the (at least ostensible) traits of individual Germans—"decent, warmhearted men and women, lovers of family and the home"—and the traits observed when these same Germans take leave of the everyday and "eagerly merge their being in a national whole distinguished for its aggressive ferocity and its ruthless disregard of the accepted principles of conduct in civilized society." [45] Butler's method is neither to study the "kindly" German individual nor the supposed transformation of traits that occurs in national organization or mobilization, but to fix attention upon a middle link, namely, the "distinctive outlook on society" which has been in the making in Germany for some hundred and fifty years: "In the case of Germany, this middle link, the distinctive outlook on society, has won much less recognition than the superficial characteristics and the historical action of the German people. This fact is the more remarkable since the dominant German outlook springs from a very bold and imaginative corpus of thought. . . ." [46]

44. The type of national character theory under review will inevitably recall some of Kardiner's views with regard to basic personality in Western society.

45. *The Roots of National Socialism*, pp. 9–10.

46. *Ibid.*, p. 10.

It is not difficult for Butler, in reviewing this bold and imaginative corpus of thought, to demonstrate a strain of rather thoroughgoing amoralism in the history of German political theory.[47] The State is "all," and all it does is beyond question and beyond the restrictive scope of ordinary moral principles. This strain has been remarked, certainly, by others, but Butler's study is noteworthy in that he seeks to infer from his materials some important German psychological characteristics. We note one typical and central line of thought in this attempted inference. After remarking a pronounced "negation of the sanctity of the individual" and a curious separation of the individual from his ideal (to such effect that the ideal does not grow out of the individual's own being but is superimposed) Butler comments that the

> tendency of Germans to overtax themselves follows, indeed, almost necessarily, from the negation of the sanctity of the individual which implies that such worth as he may possess depends not upon what he is, but upon what he achieves. The German can rarely take himself for granted. This leads further in two directions. In the first place the necessity of overcoming this lack of spontaneity, of standing up to the strain of proving oneself to oneself by achievement, may perhaps have been responsible, partially at least, for the development of German will-power in its formidable intensity and concentration; and for its sporadic snapping in suicide or mania. Secondly, if the value of the individual as such is not high his life is naturally held cheap. Hence the German practice of wanton sacrifice of life to a cause, and willingness to be so sacrificed, both

47. This "amoralism" is set in the following perspective by John Dewey: "In the grosser sense of the words, Germany has not held that might makes right. But it has been instructed by a long line of philosophers that it is the business of ideal right to gather might to itself in order that it may cease to be merely ideal. The State represents exactly this incarnation of ideal law and right in effective might." *German Philosophy and Politics* (New York: Putnam, 1942), p. 113. Butler's point would then be that the presumption of genuine "ideality" running through all this is highly questionable. It is worth noting, incidentally, that another of America's premier philosophers is in agreement with Dewey. Thus, for example, Santayana summarizes as follows the sense of Fichte in connection with what it is necessary for Germany to do to fulfill its mission: "If the people are disinclined to obey the Idea, the Government must constrain them to do so." *Egotism in German Philosophy* (London: J. M. Dent, 1939), p. 66. See also, *ibid.*, pp. 151–173 and Filmer S. C. Northrop, *The Meeting of East and West* (New York: Macmillan, 1946), ch. v. It is not necessary to deny a strong element of "ideality" in German philosophy and political practice, but it is necessary to define it carefully and do justice to its peculiar character.

quite natural and admirable for those imbued with a sense of the insignificance of the individual in the face of the magnificence of the impersonal ideal.[48]

This statement is made by a writer who does not pretend to apply the categories and terms of clinical psychology to the analysis of German character structure. Nevertheless, his analysis forcibly suggests some of the clinical symptoms of compulsion-"neurosis," a suggestion scarcely mitigated by Butler's repeated insistence on the features "of oppressive earnestness, of peculiar strain and over-exertion, lacking in spontaneity." [48] Other features of Butler's analysis similarly recall crucial conceptions of clinical psychology.[49]

The views of German life and character that have been put forward by men like Vansittart, Hearnshaw and Butler have not gone unchallenged. In a certain sense, partly because these writers have attempted no serious or systematic comparative analysis of other peoples beside the Germans and partly because they have occasionally yielded to the temptation of being merely eloquent, it is not difficult to find shortcomings in their presentation of their thesis. Thus, Julius Braunthal, rather like Hearnshaw, except that his aim is to refute theses such as the latter's, finds it easy to show that other nations besides the Germans have repeatedly waged long and bloody wars and have had, to put it euphemistically, "unpleasant" rulers. It is easy for him to point out some resemblances between historical figures among, for instance, the French and Germans. Braunthal thus sees in Napoleon III a French Hitler, and in the notorious General Gallifet a French Himmler. (How far the resemblances may be pushed, Braunthal does not inquire any more than Hearnshaw when the latter suggests the similarity of a Hitler and a Borgia.) He also raises some questions not entirely easy to answer, as when he asks whether it was really sixty or seventy million German workers, peasants, shopkeepers, etc., who wanted war in 1914 and in 1939.[50]

48. *Ibid.*, p. 291.

49. *Cf.*, generally, *ibid.*, pp. 276–299. The treatment of the theme of the *Doppelgänger* (*ibid.*, p. 299) recalls both the distinctive normative component discriminated by Adler and R. Dalbiez' phrase, "the less human elements in human nature" (*ibid.*, vol. II, p. 327).

50. *Need Germany Survive?* pp. 29, 71–75, 81.

Is it, however, necessary, in order to see an element of validity in the Vansittart-Hearnshaw-Butler view, to prove that an overwhelming statistical majority of the Germans were supporters of Wilhelm II and the National Socialists? Vansittart himself actually takes some such view. So does Friedrich Wilhelm Foerster, one of the severest critics of modern Germany. Writing in 1940, Foerster repudiates the notion that in 1914 a peaceful people were "dragged to the slaughterhouse by lunatic leaders," but contends rather that "a people which had become bellicose demanded a bellicose policy from its rulers." He avers that a plebiscite held in 1940 would find ninety percent of the voters voting for Hitler (irrespective of coercion).[51] But even Foerster would concede that the "common man" has a much more peaceable disposition than his leaders.[52] How far can we get by pursuing this kind of analysis? It is instructive to observe how, with exactly the same evidence before them on the voting behavior of the German electorate in the early 1930's, Konrad Heiden, on the one hand, contends that the German electorate clearly repudiated Hitler and all his works, and William Ebenstein, on the other hand, that—as he says with emphasis—"Germany is the only country in the world in which Nazism was voted into power." [53] Further analysis might well introduce greater clarity into these issues, but it is not our design to follow this path. Criticisms of the type of Braunthal's do not, in any case, finally dispose of the Vansittart-Hearnshaw-Butler type of thesis.[54]

Since an important part of Veblen's thesis was his contrast between England and Germany, and since one of the shortcomings of some recent analysis of Germany of the national character type is its fail-

51. *Europe and the German Question* (New York: Sheed and Ward, 1940), pp. 177, 317, 407.

52. *Ibid., passim.*

53. Heiden, *Der Fuehrer,* ch. xxii; William Ebenstein, *The German Record: A Political Portrait* (New York: Farrar & Rinehart, 1945), p. 261; italicized by Ebenstein.

54. It is of interest to note Braunthal's itemization of elements in the Nazi credo, ranging from the doctrine of the transcendent nature of the state to the ideology behind Nazi eugenics, and from "the tenet of the charismatic character of the dictator" to "the concept of war as a law of nature." These elements and the others he lists are, according to Braunthal, all "elements of the European tradition" (*ibid.,* p. 59), but, however this may be, he never stops to inquire whether the Nazis may not have made a unique synthesis of them.

ure to adduce comparative terms, we may return to this contrast. The Dynastic State, it will be remembered, was in Veblen's analysis, by comparison with the English, much more coercive and disciplinary of its underlying population. At the same time, Veblen was well aware that the Dynastic State was an institutional phenomenon in the fullest sense, that is, it rested upon a certain consensus or broad base of popular support. In the complex of German society, these features were scarcely incompatible. Simultaneously coercive of recalcitrant elements and resting on a certain consensus, the Dynastic State even further appeared in Veblen's view to be involved in tensions and conflicts that might at a suitable time cause it to intensify both its discipline of the recalcitrant and its support by the acquiescent.

Veblen's contrast of England and Germany is on the whole well borne out. Some modern studies usefully broaden this contrast into an analysis of politically relevant attitudes and traditions of the English on the one hand and the Germans on the other. J. P. Mayer, for instance, in a recent work, contends that "tolerance, fairness, love of freedom, not the *raison d'état* of the power-State are the unconscious traditions of the English," and that since Lord Acton a distinctive theory of the State has been in process of development which is opposed to "the theory of the power-State which ultimately paved the way for Nazism." [55]

Is this type of contrast really secure? We may obtain some answer by closely following Hermann Kantorowicz in his study of *The Spirit of British Policy and the Myth of the Encirclement of Germany*. Kantorowicz supplies to an appreciable extent that vital comparative-analytical element that has been lacking in the Vansittart-Hearnshaw-Butler work. Throughout his book there is always present an implicit or explicit contrast of England and Germany. Ostensibly, the book is mainly devoted to an analysis of the underlying social forces and motives of modern British policy. As major effective factors in that policy, Kantorowicz discriminates chivalry, objectivity, humanitarianism and irrationality.

Chivalry is defined as the will and habit, derived from conscious-

55. *Max Weber and German Politics* (London: Faber and Faber, Ltd., 1944), pp. 34, 45.

ness of power, to enter voluntarily into a fight or enterprise directed to a good cause, while one's antagonist is treated with respect and an attempt is perhaps made to better his position. Kantorowicz claims that nowadays (he writes in 1931) "there is one country only where chivalry survives as a quality of the masses, as a postulate of the public conscience, as a power that forms society and informs institutions . . . England." [56]

The ideal of the gentleman, an ideal of character that is both prominent in England and pervades all classes in appreciable degree, may be said to be the modern form of the chivalric ideal. In England, "practically everyone would like to be a gentleman," while the Prussian ideal of the officer, which in Germany had a prominence and influence comparable to that of the gentleman in England, was always alien and often repugnant to German peasants and workers. In reviewing the English ideal of the gentleman Kantorowicz most pertinently notes that "it is the tendency of modern democracy to ignore the class element of the idea of the Gentleman." [57] This serves to point up a significant weakness in his analysis. He never conscientiously raises the question whether this "class element" may be a factor in the history of what might be called "exceptions"—such as English behavior and procedure in Ireland, India and Egypt [58]—to the generally more or less chivalric and humanitarian "spirit of British policy." Even these "exceptions" do not prompt Kantorowicz to modify his thesis seriously, and he finds even in these phases of the history of English politics and enterprise, while conceding in effect that they are "exceptions," ample evidence of the chivalric and humanitarian elements usually at work. It must be emphasized that his thesis gets its meaning and significance precisely from *contrast.* He does not assert flatly "that English policy is governed by idealistic principles," but is willing to assert that in modern times "the policy of England has contained a greater idealistic element and has been subject to more powerful idealistic inhibitions than that of any other great power" on the continent.[59]

56. *The Spirit of British Policy,* p. 56. 57. *Ibid.,* pp. 72, 59.

58. *Cf.* his treatment of these and other "exceptions," *ibid.,* pp. 266–290.

59. *Ibid.,* p. 139. We are content, for our purposes, to follow Kantorowicz in his analysis of the broad modern trend and contrast (especially plain between

If we return, now, to the concept of chivalry, there is a significant passage in Kantorowicz's work in which he clarifies chivalry by contrasting it with dignity. Since the passage goes to the heart of some of Kantorowicz's socio-psychological argumentation, it may be quoted in full:

Dignity is the opposite of Chivalry, for Chivalry is based on a keen sense of the rights and interests of others. Just as Chivalry constitutes the most important element of the ideal of the Gentleman, so does Dignity constitute the most important element of the ideal of the Warrior. For the warrior who holds himself ready always for the annihilation or the subjection of his opponent would sink in his own eyes to the rank of robber or murderer if he were not filled with the consciousness of a better cause. In this way the mechanism of self-esteem creates the feeling of Dignity and its appropriate conduct. But if Chivalry and Dignity are opposites in this sense they are in no way psychological contradictions, and they can very well be incorporated in the same person: the Germanic Middle Ages, with their ideal of the "Gentle Prince," actually aimed at the maximum of both qualities in the same person. Beyond the maximum, however, there lies perversion, and the perverted forms *will* be found to contradict each other. It is a noteworthy confirmation of our view that the perverted form of either quality represents the minimum of the other. The perversion of Chivalry leads to lack of Dignity, the perversion of Dignity involves lack of Chivalry. On the one hand it is possible to go so far in making concessions to the rights and interests of others that one may end by losing one's former superiority; and such magnanimity may degenerate into a lack of regard for one's own rights and interests which may lead to one's allowing one's rights and interests to be attacked and hurt, so that even insults are suffered passively. On the other hand, it is manifest that an exaggerated regard for one's own Dignity may lead to an unchivalrous and brutal disregard for others.

All of these things are of great practical importance; misunderstanding of them has often enough been fatal for the two parties concerned. The Dignity of the German people has been continually attacked by its opponents, England included; English Chivalry has been continually outraged by German methods of warfare. It would be irrelevant to dwell here upon the first of these two propositions, and it is better not to touch upon the second. It will suffice to note with a view to the future that he who insults German Dignity will bite on granite; and that he who places his trust in English Chivalry will build upon a rock.[60]

---

England and Germany) covering a century or so, without attempting an independent analysis of the past decade and a half.

60. *Ibid.*, pp. 74–75.

In Germany in its Nazi phase there have certainly been enough examples of what Kantorowicz denominates the "perversion" of dignity. Chivalry and dignity as thus expounded should of course be taken as ideal types. Germany is described as a country where "everything relating to national dignity is carried to an extreme," while England, on the other hand, has "a distinct absence of national pride," although it does not lack patriotism.[61]

Objectivity is taken more or less in its common-sense meaning. It therefore refers to the ability to see and think clearly with regard to matters relating to opponents, in a manner not distorted by one's special interests. It is not quite the same as impartiality, but, on the other hand, is closely connected with justice. Here again the indispensable element of contrast appears, and is again reinforced by the contrast of the specific cases of England and Germany.[62] And when turning to the humanitarian element in English policy, Kantorowicz posits a "fundamental antithesis" between this and German policy, the former "never quite without a sentimental element," the latter "always purely egoistic."[63] Humanitarianism is also given a more or less common-sense meaning. Once more, the point is not that the English are either deities or angels, but rather that humanitarianism, or the "ethical element," is a demonstrable factor at work in, and often enough actually effective in, English policy and public life.[64] And once more, the humanitarian ethical element in English policy contrasts with the Prussian case, where the tone is set by the principle of "Treitschkeism," the principle of indefinite increase of State power.[65] There is thus substantial agreement between Kantorowicz and J. P. Mayer on this important point of contrast.

61. *Ibid.*, pp. 179 and 181. For numerous proofs of these propositions, *cf.*, generally, *ibid.*, ch. ii.

62. *Cf. e.g., ibid.*, p. 149.

63. *Ibid.*, p. 196. In dealing with humanitarianism as an element in English policy, incidentally, Kantorowicz does not deny the presence of cant in English policy or in English life in general, but notes, nevertheless, on the one hand, the craving on the part of the English public for an ethical justification for English policy and the factual part that ethical motives frequently do play in English policy in virtue of the power of public opinion, and, on the other hand. the English emphasis on justifying an action by an appeal to *duty* instead of to the presumed superiority of the state to all law. *Ibid.*, pp. 191–193.

64. *Cf.* the proofs afforded, *ibid.*, pp. 185–290.

65. *Ibid.*, p. 295.

By irrationality, Kantorowicz technically understands the intrusion of motives into State-policy other than those that have as their essential aim "the development, the assertion, the enlargement or the preservation of the State's own power." The intention is by no means to stigmatize "irrationality" in politics, but to afford a serviceable definition. This purely definitional aspect is clearly brought out in the statement that "frequently it is chivalry and objectivity that import into policy an irrational element . . . that runs counter to an egoistic striving after power which forms the *ratio* of politics." [66] The *ratio* of politics is "egoistic striving after power." The intrusion of motives or elements into policy that would mitigate or even eliminate such striving after power is, specifically, irrational. It will be noted, incidentally, how this confirms our own view of irrationality or rationality. The *relational* character of either is inevitably implied. Humanitarianism in policy, for example, is definable as irrational only in virtue of its conflict with the *ratio* of striving after power. If humanitarianism were defined as the specific *ratio* of policy, striving after power would appear as irrational.

Precisely in virtue of the previous elements discriminated in the "spirit of British policy"—chivalry, objectivity and humanitarianism—that policy will appear as "irrational." Loosely, however, Kantorowicz includes in his discussion of irrationality much that is, strictly, not irrationality at all, such as English political ignorance, political shortsightedness and political error. From the point of view, however, of establishing one of his major theses, to the effect that England never pursued a conscious policy of "encirclement of Germany," it is pertinent to adduce English political ignorance and error. Kantorowicz's method is to show the improbability, on psychological and sociological grounds, that a country like England, given the peculiar elements of chivalry and humanitarianism in its political tradition and given its "empirical" step-by-step and occasionally even uninformed and shortsighted political procedures, would ever conceive and act through so unsentimental and so large-scale and deeply conceived a policy as that of the encirclement of Germany. Having shown this improbability his method then is to prove from German documentary evidence that the encirclement of Germany by Eng-

66. *Ibid.*, pp. 293, 303.

land is a myth, largely begun and propagated by German naval interests.[67]

The contrasts previously emphasized come to the fore again in the treatment of the myth of the encirclement of Germany. Thus, the contrast between the ideal of the gentleman and that of the warrior receives renewed emphasis in the further comparison of England and Germany. There emerges with great clarity a

> contrast between the atmosphere of London, which irresistibly envelopes even the German representatives, and that of Potsdam; on the one hand we have the true English spirit of quiet and peaceful business, of living and letting live; on the other the blundering neo-Prussian imitation of an imaginary bullying England, which does not know the meaning of trust and confidence.[68]

Aside from the renewal of these contrasts, there are only two pertinent points in the treatment of the myth of the encirclement of Germany. It is clear, in the first place, that not all the personalities in one way and another involved in the origin and propagation of the myth were necessarily either unscrupulous liars or pathological cases. Many of the statesmen who knew official allegations of encirclement by England to be false simply acquiesced in the convention that quite different standards must be applied to lying in private and lying in the "service of the State." Given this acquiescence, the dominant personalities in the active propagation of the myth could be, and in fact were, surprisingly few. A *combination* of acquiescence and pathological circumstances[69] was therefore sufficient to give the

67. *Cf. ibid.*, p. 365 and the whole of ch. v.

68. *Ibid.*, p. 429. It has been suggested, in effect, that the contrast between the typical behaviors found in English and in German policy might be stated as a contrast between behavior rooted in the type-form of economic transactions, involving an exchange, and behavior rooted in the type-form of the assertion of superior power, involving no exchange. *Cf.* I. Thorner, "German Words, German Personality and Protestantism," in *Psychiatry* VIII (1945), 403–417. The contrast is not inept, and it is particularly useful in serving to remind us precisely of Kantorowicz's repeated point that England appears as it does *by contrast* with Germany. There are, notoriously, many imperfections in economic "exchange" from a "human" point of view. (Veblen would have been the first to point them out, just as he would never have underestimated the "class element" in the ideal of the gentleman.)

69. For evidence showing the unquestionably pathological character of one of the persons most important in the invention of the myth of encirclement, *cf.* Kantorowicz, *ibid.*, pp. 451–452. *Cf.* also the scattered comments on the personality of Wilhelm II, *ibid.*, ch. v.

myth initial support. This is an extremely important reinforcing point in connection with our previous treatment of the theme of psychoanalysis and the leisure class. In order for certain dominant leisure class norms to prevail, it is quite unnecessary for the whole membership of the community to be "neurotic." However, this does not preclude the need for a broad support in the character traits of a mass of the population.

The second point of importance to us in the treatment of the myth of the encirclement of Germany is Kantorowicz's indication that he must use psychological interpretation in making order out of the wealth of historical data he summons:

Mental epidemics have played an important part at all periods, and this period of our own, with all its numerous "isms" is absolutely full of them. There are mental epidemics of every kind; and the Encirclement mania is a case of "persecution mania." Naturally, we have not to deal here with a mania in the strictly pathological sense, as meaning hallucinations; but "fixed ideas," "idiosyncracies" and "inferiority complexes" play no small part, with this restriction, that these terms, normally applied to the individual, must be translated into social psychology. If ever psychoanalysis casts off the domination of sex and begins to throw light on national psychology and psychopathology, the myth of an Encircled Germany will be completely explained; but it will be a long time before this comes about and therefore we cannot wait for the pathological analysis of the myth. The problem is too urgent for that.[70]

To some extent, psychoanalysis has "cast off the domination of sex," but it is precisely because its work on "national psychology and psychopathology" is only in its incipient phases that it is necessary to rely so heavily on contributions like that of Kantorowicz.

Kantorowicz is as far as possible from being a rabid anti-German. It is of interest to observe that he includes Friedrich Wilhelm Foerster among Germans whose love for an ideal Germany has blinded them and made them unjust "to the Germany of reality." [71] Kantorowicz's approach is that of the professional historian and sociologist. Foerster's is that of an impassioned Catholic who wishes to recall Germany to the sense of a mission of taking moral and political leadership in the peaceful union of the peoples of central Europe. It is therefore all the more impressive that on certain vital points

70. *Ibid.*, p. 366.

71. *Ibid.*, p. 174.

there is little disagreement between Foerster and Kantorowicz. One of Foerster's main theses is the radical amoralism of German policy. "Characteristic," he says, "of all those Prussian war-gods is the refusal, nowhere else so complete and so cold, to believe that international life and the destinies of states are subject to moral government." The point of contrast, so frequently brought up by Kantorowicz, is found also in Foerster, as in the statement that, around the turn of the century, "in America, as also in England, traditional religious pacifism was incomparably stronger than in German Protestantism. . . ." [72] Numerous additional statements to the same general effect, all exhibiting the amoralism of German policy, are made.[73]

With regard to points vital to the contrast of England and Germany, J. P. Mayer, Kantorowicz and Foerster are at one. Furthermore, there is a good deal of agreement between the analysis of these three men and that of Vansittart, Hearnshaw and Butler. Mayer and Kantorowicz, more especially, might not go so far as, say, Lord Vansittart in his descriptions of German character, but the implications of their analysis do not leave them holding to a thesis radically different from Vansittart's. Kantorowicz's analysis (which, incidentally, was written before the Nazis came to power) is partly psychological and partly sociological. He works partly on the level of the "spirit of policy," that is to say on the level of the norms or standards that influence and inform policy, and partly on the level of the analysis of important personalities who have sustained the norms exhibited in policy. The difference of these two levels is more clearly realized by Kantorowicz than by some of the recent English writers on the subject of modern Germany, but Kantorowicz does not fail to see connections between the two levels. The norms and traditions that influence policy by the same token also influence personality, and the point we have ourselves so often emphasized that there is congruity or interdependence between institutional and individual levels is, implicitly, entirely clear in Kantorowicz's work. Certain types of personalities will sustain and reinforce policy on the German line, and other types of personalities will not, and exactly the same statement will hold of policy on the English line. Accordingly, the

72. *Europe and the German Question*, pp. 69, 164.
73. See, *e.g.*, *ibid.*, pp. 217, 221, 230, 318, 320, 423.

norms of German policy, in their unmitigated German form, did not and could not find lodgment in England.[74]

The strains of thought reviewed have, on the whole, quite different sources: recent English national character theory originating in an understandable attempt by Englishmen to explain some of the characteristics of their enemy in the recent war (Vansittart, Hearnshaw, Butler); the work of a political scientist dispassionately comparing English and German political institutions through the medium of an analysis of Max Weber's political theory (J. P. Mayer); the work of a historian, sociologist and student of law with considerable practical political experience and first-hand knowledge of both England and Germany (Kantorowicz); the analysis of a German reformer taking a frankly Christian point of view (Foerster). Mayer and Kantorowicz stand perhaps the closest to one another, but even if they are taken as one, there are three distinct strands or traditions of thought. And yet, there is a good deal of significant agreement in the three strands. In all three would be found substantial support of the thesis of German amoralism in politics, of the existence of a moral contrast between English and German policy, and, by implication, of significant differences in English and German personality. With regard to the last point, the *degree* of agreement is not altogether clear. This comes partly from the circumstance that a writer like Kantorowicz would not go so far as one like Vansittart in a description of German personality, and partly from the fact that the various writers mentioned have not addressed themselves to exactly the same questions, so that, to compare Kantorowicz with Vansittart once more, the latter is explicit in his description of German personality while in the case of the former one must proceed inferentially to arrive at something of a picture of German personality.

In a manner subject to limitations already indicated in this study, but none the less really, the existence of distinctive types of institutions will carry implications with regard to the character of the personalities sustaining them. Consequently, if certain crucial German institutions have been correctly described—institutions such as that

74. For a relevant implicit comparison of personalities, *cf.* Kantorowicz, *ibid.*, pp. 343–345 on Viscount Grey and ch. v at large on Wilhelm II. The latter is described as "obsessed by the myth of Encirclement," *ibid.*, p. 470.

of a predominant military imposing its ideals of life, conduct and organization upon an entire nation, and even molding that nation in its own shape and forms,[75] or institutions such as those involved in German foreign policy—the question must inevitably be asked: What traits of character must be present to sustain these institutions? If we ask what character traits would be *theoretically* necessary to uphold the German type of militarism, the German type of foreign policy or recent Nazi policy of extermination of alien peoples, one avenue of approach is opened. This avenue would consist simply in making a *fit* between institutions and character traits. Thus, for example, if we follow Foerster's analysis of German political and social behavior at large, we are able to abstract certain features on the following lines: the elimination of moral considerations from political affairs (combined with a curious kind of ascetic devotion to this principle of elimination itself); incapability of respect for foreign traditions; self-exaltation.[76] Vansittart's finding of envy, cruelty and self-pity as German character traits will be recalled. Not to attempt to give a comprehensive analysis, since we are here only exemplifying, certainly the feature of "cruelty" would seem to give a good *primary fit*[77] especially with the first of the patterns that precipitate out of the analysis of Foerster (or, for that matter, out of the analysis of many another writer).

There are at least two limitations upon this sort of analysis by effecting primary fit. Firstly, it does not make room for a distinction between *acquiescence* in certain patterns (or lukewarm acceptance) and *vital support* of them. It may be true that only "cruelty" could give support to and sustain a certain specific pattern of behavior, but this does not necessarily mean that there will be "cruelty" on the part of everyone who, in one way or another, actively or passively, helps to sustain the pattern. Secondly, the analysis by primary fit is not genuinely psychodynamic. Cruelty is a trait of character; so is self-pity; so is envy; or, at any rate, they all may be traits of character. But to adduce these traits is not to afford an analysis of character, which, when clinically described, appears as a psychological unity informed by a dynamic that, when grasped, makes *understand-*

75. *Cf.* especially Fried, *ibid., passim.* 76. Foerster, *ibid.,* chs. iv–viii.

77. This means neither that *only* this trait would "fit" nor that institutions are to be explained in terms of this or other traits.

*able* traits of cruelty, envy, self-pity or others. "Cruelty" may be an adventitious trait in that it may appear in a variety of significantly different character types. Vansittart's combination of the three traits he mentions is no doubt "suggestive," but it is still very far from constituting a clinical picture, which, it must be said, he does not attempt to give.[78] It has been observed in passing that some of Rohan Butler's descriptions suggest the clinical picture of compulsion-"neurosis," but we are still left far from anything like a reasonably secure or systematic clinical, or clinically grounded, presentation.

We have used the term "acquiescence" above in a somewhat technical sense, to point to the fact that in order for any normative structure to receive support and be sustained, it is unnecessary for all personalities connected with it to possess traits that specifically reinforce it. In another sense, "acquiescence" has been frequently remarked as a trait of the German population, as when Veblen noted "the servility" of the underlying population of Germany. Much the same phenomenon is sometimes referred to as "political docility." J. P. Mayer summarizes conveniently a frequently encountered historical explanation of the influence of German Protestantism upon this docility:

> While Luther directed the German individual soul to its mystical depth, he accepted "order" and "authority" with regard to the worldly state. Personal religiosity and State were thus fundamentally separated. Once the religious soul was assured of its intimate mystical union with God, the individual could submit to State obedience, being convinced that the sphere of the State could never interfere with his "real" depth. So the "free Christian" easily became the slave of the State. The Prussian State was predominantly Protestant. Church and Army concluded an alliance which explains, at least historically, what has been termed here political docility.[79]

Acquiescence in this sense, or political docility, is not to be under-

78. He nevertheless quotes without misgivings the following utterly confused statement by the psychologist William Brown: "Germany appears to be a definitely paranoid nation, on account of her native aggressiveness. . . . It is not surprising that she has accepted a paranoid individual as her leader. . . ." Quoted in *Bones of Contention,* p. 22.

79. Mayer, *ibid.,* p. 60. *Cf.* also Ernst Troeltsch, *The Social Teaching of the Christian Churches* (tr. O. Wyon, London: Allen & Unwin, 1931), vol. II, p. 540 *sqq.;* R. H. Tawney, *Religion and the Rise of Capitalism* (London: J. Murray, 1936), pp. 79–102; Howard Becker, *German Youth: Bond or Free* (London: Oxford University, 1946), pp. 158–160, 225.

stood as necessarily implying the absence of traits specifically reinforcing a normative structure. In fact, it may be suggested that the peculiar disjunction between the "private" and the "public" sphere [80] which has the general effect of implying the insignificance of the individual's "private" being for all "public" purposes, generates tensions and discomforts that, on the whole, tend toward a "sadistic" outlet.

We may now turn to the place of a psychiatric interpretation of modern Germany.

### III. THE PLACE OF A PSYCHIATRIC INTERPRETATION

Modern England constitutes an effective term of contrast with modern Germany. The machine technology in Germany has been subservient to the uses of groups committed to policy that, by comparison with the English, may be said to be in the direction of ruthlessly maximizing State power and, if necessary, rather unhesitatingly suppressing all manifestations by an "underlying population" of disinclination to obey the behests of the supreme State. In both these directions, modern English practice has been considerably "milder." We have broadened Veblen's contrast of England and Germany, but there still remains some question about the basic dilemma of the Dynastic State which he posed. That State, it may be repeated, was, in Veblen's analysis, incapable of getting along with the machine technology and also incapable of getting along without it. That it should be unable to get along without it is entirely clear since in the modern world no state aspiring to supreme power over others could dispense with an up-to-date technology. But Veblen insisted that the Dynastic State could not get along with the

80. This disjunction recalls Rohan Butler's comments on the superimposed character of the ideal. If "public necessity" or "reason of State" suggests norms out of conformity with private conscience or private dictates or thought, that does not matter very much, since "public" and "private" have nothing to do with one another. To introduce "private" norms into "public" affairs would constitute an impertinence and an irrelevance. It is significant that Butler contends (*ibid., passim*) that modern German political theory has, by contrast with Western political theory at large, preoccupied itself with the relation of the individual to himself, rather than with his relation to others.

machine technology because that bred an urban proletariat whose point of view was unsympathetic to the Dynastic State. If, in substance, this analysis is correct, it would be expected that the Dynastic State or any similar organization, formally dynastic or not, would attempt to resolve the dilemma. Since the modern technology is absolutely indispensable, and since the groups interested in the maintenance or resurrection of a Dynastic State or an equivalent thereof would not desist, only one road has remained open: to "harmonize" or "co-ordinate" all recalcitrant elements. The details of the "co-ordination" practiced by National Socialism have of course been most various, ranging from simple elimination of "undesirables" to vast propaganda efforts.

To resolve the dilemma by the technique of "co-ordinating" or influencing recalcitrant elements was not altogether easy. In a sense, National Socialism itself had to be raised up and nourished in order to accomplish this resolution. This is well brought out in Fried's *The Guilt of the German Army*. In Fried's view, the German army is primarily responsible for the second World War. The officers and the military in general after the last war were interested in further, large-scale military enterprise as an ultimate goal. They could not simply impose militarism on the German masses, given certain democratic elements and impulses in German life. The technique of again engaging the German people in a large-scale war had to be circuitous. How to capture the masses? National Socialism provided the answer. It was precisely a technique for handing over the masses of the nation to the uses of the army. German militarism, Fried goes so far as to claim, and National Socialism have, essentially, been both *one* and *at one*. The latter copied many of its crucial features from the former, it was supported and nourished by the former, it might well have perished without the former.[81]

*Mein Kampf* contains ample evidence that "capturing the masses" was a major aim, and that "Marxism" was considered the greatest obstacle to its realization. "Marxism" stands in the way of a unified, solidary community. Time and again it is stated that the masses must be wooed from Marxism and won for Hitler's type of nationalism.

81. For the considerable evidence favoring this thesis, *cf.* Fried, *ibid., passim.*

The "nationalization of the deliberately anti-national masses" must be effected.[82] Nationalization itself involves the reconstruction of the community: both "employers" and "employees" are emphatically stated to be "guardians of the entire national community."[83] The past is to be redeemed by a "new view of life." The German "collapse" that occurred after the World War was either caused by, or marked by, the phenomena of reduction of the peasantry while the urban proletariat increased, the "economization" or involvement in mere material values of the German people,[84] the flourishing of the "Jewish" press, the "mammonization" of love, the looseness of the individual's human ties in the city, the lack of important community symbols, the loss of uniform and effective religious convictions and political aimlessness. Throughout Hitler's presentation of the "causes of the collapse" there is a very marked stress on the decline of primary relations, of community and solidarity, of the integrating power of commonly accepted moral codes.[85]

From almost every page of *Mein Kampf* it is clear that the National Socialists were willing to use any technique to gain an end: force, argument, cajolery, specious and even partly correct sociological analysis, moral appeal and exaltation of specific German institutions or practices such as those giving the German army its distinctive character. But one of the major ends was to create and intensify sentiment for a nationally unified Germany, ostensibly without class distinctions, precisely the kind of Germany that could be "handed over to the army" and go to war relatively undisturbed internally, with a minimum number of "traitors" within and a maximum feeling against such "traitors" on the part of the population at large. This is the National Socialist answer to the dilemma Veblen posed. It is scarcely a new answer, but it was made with unprecedented singlemindedness and devotion—and it was remarkably successful.

82. *Mein Kampf* (New York: Reynal and Hitchcock ed., 1941), p. 461. *Cf.* also *ibid.*, pp. 458, 463–465, 788, 987 and *passim*.

83. *Ibid.*, p. 875.

84. *Cf.* Hitler's contrast of a "material Republic" with an "ideal Reich," *ibid.*, p. 651.

85. *Cf. ibid.*, vol. I, ch. x. Of course Hitler does not rest his case with his presentation of the "causes of the collapse." Underlying everything else is the factor of "race": *cf. ibid.*, vol. I, ch. xi.

It is certain that Nazi ideology fell on soil that was to an appreciable extent fertile. Is a psychiatric interpretation of the success of this ideology or of National Socialism in general in any way cogent or relevant? In answering this question two issues must be kept clearly separate. The first is an issue with regard to most feasible applied procedures. Undoubtedly, it would scarcely be practicable to psychoanalyze a large mass of the German population, and for the purpose of making significant changes in German policy and behavior, manipulation of the German institutional framework is more promising.[86] Theodore Abel contends that "treating Germany for paranoia" will not change her essentially and that the psychoanalyst cannot afford help "in a situation where only a drastic change of the basic conditions of living can tip the balance in favor of a social reconstruction of Germany." [87] But to give this conclusion unqualifiedly is to neglect a second issue, which is precisely an issue of interpretation. The question, "Is a psychiatric interpretation of the German enigma necessary?" easily misleads. Is a psychiatric interpretation of the Alorese "enigma" necessary? Yet Kardiner has afforded one. Logically, it makes no difference that Germany is involved in one case and Alor in the other. An interpretation or explanation is obviously necessary or not, depending upon what it is desired to interpret or explain. No one has yet shown that Nazism does not have psychological roots *among others,* and, while, for certain gross yet vital changes in Germany that other nations may be interested in seeing, certain rough institutional manipulations may be quite adequate, two qualifications must be noted: (1) this does not exhaust the task of a theoretical explanation, in which it is perfectly legitimate to attempt to exhibit psychological among other sources of "the German enigma"; (2) for countless concrete practical purposes, it may be useful to have a psychological knowledge of the Germans which, unfortunately, has not yet developed very far, and even certain gross institutional manipulations may be helped out by specific psychological knowledge: in practice, institutional and psychological phenomena shade intimately into one another.

86. *Cf.* Talcott Parsons, "The Problem of Controlled Institutional Change," *Psychiatry* VIII (1945), 79–101.

87. See "Is a Psychiatric Interpretation of the German Enigma Necessary?" *American Sociological Review* X (1945), 457–464.

If the psychiatric or psychoanalytical interpretations that have thus far been offered were radically out of line with the presentations of well informed historians, sociologists and others, there would be reason for claiming not, indeed, that psychiatric explanation was out of place—for every society has psychological foundations and it is entirely legitimate to pose the problem of how its psychological mesh with its social foundations—but that there should be nothing but skepticism for the offerings that psychiatrists or psychoanalysts have thus far made. However, when properly criticized, a residue remains in the offerings thus far made which is quite compatible with the results found by professional students of institutions. In fact, there is sometimes rather remarkable convergence. We may give an instance of this, relating to a rather central matter.

Talcott Parsons expresses implicit agreement with the members of a recent conference on Germany after the war on "the existence of a typical German character structure which predisposes people to define all human relations in terms of dominance, submission and romantic revolt." [88] Along with members of the conference, Parsons defines two types of components in modern German character structure: the first, " 'an emotional, idealistic, active romantic component which may be constructive or destructive and anti-social' "; and the second, " 'an orderly, hard-working hierarchy pre-occupied, methodical, submissive, gregarious, materialistic' component." Parsons further states:

> The peculiarity of the Nazi movement is that it has harnessed [the] romantic dynamism to an aggressive, expansionist, nationalistic political goal—and an internal revolution—and has utilized and subordinated all the motives behind the [second] component.
>
> [It is desirable] to eliminate the specific Nazi synthesis of the two major components of German character, or to divert it from its recent distinctive channels of expression if this is possible.[89]

This view of the matter bears a rather remarkable resemblance to that set forth by F. W. Foerster. Foerster, as has been noted,

88. "The Problem of Controlled Institutional Change," 79.

89. *Ibid.*, pp. 85, 87. It is of interest, incidentally, to note that whatever might be his opinion of Abel's view that "treating Germany for paranoia" will not change her, Parsons in any case does not hesitate to speak of "the German type of mentality . . . with its paranoid characteristics." *Ibid.*, p. 93.

approaches Germany and the phenomenon of Nazism from a frankly Christian point of view. His thought certainly does not have a psychiatric orientation. He refers repeatedly to the absence of moral elements (in the sense that they have been seen to prevail in the English political tradition) in Prussian and German policy. But this Prussian amoralism, in Foerster's analysis, is peculiarly interwoven with a spirit of asceticism and religiously inspired self-sacrifice that leads back, historically, to the Order of the Teutonic Knights. "A host of critics have failed to perceive the important positive aspect of Prussian militarism, indeed the presence in it of Christian asceticism and self-sacrifice. . . ."[90] Foerster's view is, in effect, that splendid resources of order, organization, ability to work hard and methodically and selflessly, in fact, "religiously," are harnessed in the service of goals that the consensus of Western nations would hardly regard as "splendid." This sectors out a most important strain in the complex component previously referred to: "an orderly, hard-working hierarchy preoccupied, methodical, submissive, gregarious, materialistic" component. It sectors out, precisely, the strain of the "orderly" and "hard-working" and "methodical," and suggests a religious background for it. On the analysis that Parsons sets forth, Nazi strength came rather particularly from the harnessing to Nazi goals (an outgrowth of the first component Parsons mentions) of elements like "orderliness," "hard work" and "methodicalness" (plus the other elements specified in the second component).

On Foerster's analysis, there occurs a peculiar mixture of hard-working, even religiously grounded, asceticism, and an utter lack of what, from the point of view of Western nations, would be "ideality": a combination, in other words, of idealism and absence of idealism: a rare devotion to goals exhibiting utter "moral confusion." It is true that an "idealistic" element has, in Parsons' summary, been placed within the first component, but whatever may be the utility or convenience of making the particular separation Parsons has made, his dichotomy neither necessarily implies the absence of all "idealistic" strains in the "orderly," "hard-working" "methodical" elements of his second component nor obscures an essential similarity with Foerster's analysis. What, in fact, Foerster does, is to

90. *Cf.* Foerster, *ibid.*, pp. 59–60 and ch. iv.

examine the "romantic anti-social" strain in the first of Parsons' components, in its combination with the "orderly, hard-working, methodical" strain in the second of Parsons' components. *This* specific synthesis is for Foerster the quintessence of Prussianism: " 'Prussianism' " in the widest sense can be most accurately defined as *a highly developed morality in the service of pure immorality: an admirable order in the service of the most appalling disorder, namely the disintegration of Europe; organization in the service of disorganization. . . .*"[91]

Foerster's language is scarcely the usual language of psychiatrists, but the psychiatrists who agreed on the two components Parsons has summarized are in substantial agreement with Foerster on some very important points.

Convergences of the sort thus instanced demonstrate that the suggestions that psychiatrists have made, so far from being radically out of line with the results of other students, sometimes rather show remarkable agreement with those results. Nevertheless, it remains to inquire what *specifically psychiatric* or psychoanalytical interpretations have been like, and we shall consequently review briefly two relevant recent contributions, with an eye both to exhibiting their points of strength and points of weakness and to noting agreement or disagreement between psychological and non-psychological literature.[92]

Brickner presents the thesis that there has been in Germany a pronounced tendency for a hundred years toward paranoid trends on the part both of the country's leaders and of a considerable portion of the population. German "paranoid symptoms" are dealt with under the caption of megalomania, the need to dominate, persecution complex, projection and retrospective falsification. Brickner has no difficulty in adducing from German history, from the testimony of first-hand observers and from statements by German philosophers and politicians material that seemingly bears out the contention that

91. Foerster, *ibid.*, p. 449.

92. In the interest of limiting our treatment, it has been decided to consider only Richard Brickner's *Is Germany Incurable?* (Boston: Lippincott, 1943) and Fromm's *Escape From Freedom.* Brickner's book is of particular interest because of its espousal of the now widely held thesis of German paranoia; Fromm's because it is one of the more cogent psychoanalytical interpretations of Nazism.

there is a lush existence of paranoid trends. It is Germany, in German conceptions, that is always beset and "encircled" by jealous and implacable enemies. Germany is the greatest and best of nations, and the moral character developed within its borders should serve to reform the rest of the world. Other peoples are possessed of lesser light and it is only proper that they should be dominated. The hierarchization of peoples is duplicated within Germany itself, where the sense of rank and status is extremely vivid, especially on the part of the military, subservience to which has been faithfully observed by the population at large.

Aside from Brickner's insistence on the presence of certain clinical phenomena (*e.g.*, "persecution complex") and mechanisms (*e.g.*, "projection") the thesis he presents is much like that, say, of Vansittart. But its value as a contribution by a psychiatrist has to be assessed on the basis of its success in establishing the existence, scope and manner of operation of the clinical complexes and mechanisms which Brickner claims to see at work. Brickner may be right in the contention that paranoid trends are especially pronounced in Germany, but to attempt to prove it by *identifying* institutions with psychological trends and forces is fruitless. Paranoid trends, Brickner avers, have permeated and now permeate Germany to such an extent that it is justified to speak of German culture as a "paranoid culture." He might well have been warned of the dangers of employing a clinically originated term to designate an institutional system by Kardiner, whom he mentions.[93] "Paranoid society" and "group-paranoia" are phrases occurring in a single sentence. Again, paranoia is referred to as "the predominant German culture-trait."[94] This could perhaps be only pardonably loose language, and might be brushed aside as such were it not that much of Brickner's thesis depends on the implicit argument that analogies are identities. If a certain line of behavior has some *resemblance* to paranoid behavior, that does not prove it to be paranoid. Thus, Brickner states:

While insisting that Germany had to have more room or die, the Nazis were simultaneously scolding the German people for having allowed the birthrate to fall during the Republic and, when they reached power, instituting elaborate programs of prestige and subsidy to produce more chil-

93. *Is Germany Incurable?* p. 22.

94. *Ibid.*, pp. 42, 118.

dren to produce the population pressures that they were already using as a pretext for demanding Lebensraum. . . . Again the apparent inconsistency can be resolved only on the hypothesis that we are dealing with paranoid group-behavior.[95]

The "apparent inconsistency" is easily resolved without recourse to the hypothesis that we are dealing with "paranoid group-behavior." Thus, Hitler indicates in *Mein Kampf* four "ways out" for the German people, given their high fertility.[96] It is sufficient for the present purpose to adduce two of these. One is for the Germans to lower their birth rate artificially. This, Hitler rejects. It is an expedient not in conformity with his view of a nation as a naturally expanding biological or quasi-biological entity inevitably struggling with other similar entities. The other "way out" of interest here is to engage in large-scale continuous expansion of the German land-mass in Europe, at the expense of Russia. This expedient Hitler regards as the best of all. Nazi policy was to have a high birth rate and expand the German land mass. The situation involves no inconsistencies. Brickner misses the whole Nazi point of view. On Nazi premises, *Lebensraum* is needed. Should the birth rate therefore be low, as it was under the Republic? It should be encouraged. More need (or the presumption of more need) for space is to be created, and then the space is to be obtained. Whatever else this may be, there is not the slightest reason for calling it paranoid. It might still be contended that the whole policy ultimately roots in paranoia, but this would have to be proved. Brickner might observe groups of businessmen in many nations outside of Germany setting forth the complaint that labor constantly goes on strike, while nevertheless doing everything possible to lower wages. It would be unwise to take this "apparent inconsistency" as evidence of paranoia. In fact, many "apparent inconsistencies" found in Germany are also found elsewhere, and may be explained without recourse to the concept of a "paranoid culture." Simply to adduce such inconsistencies as proof of the existence of a "paranoid culture" is, substantially, to assume what has to be proved. A systematic comparative analysis, taking, say, England and Germany again as the comparative terms, might have been of considerable aid to Brickner's analysis. In the absence of an informed

95. *Ibid.*, p. 284.

96. *Cf. Mein Kampf*, vol. I, ch. iv.

comparative analysis providing concrete terms allowing geniune differentiations it becomes easy to claim in a good many instances that "the same thing" happens elsewhere than in Germany.

With regard to the psychological mechanisms that Brickner adduces, the loose method of his approach must leave a good deal of uncertainty as to the scope or extent of their operation. It may be observed that the Nazis have claimed that the Jews have been engaged in a conspiracy against the Christian world, whereas, in point of fact, it is much nearer the mark to say that the Nazis have been so engaged. The German claim, often to the fore in modern German history, to the effect that other nations plot to "ençircle" Germany, may be set beside the facts of German aggression against, or "encirclement" of, other nations. The proposition that other nations are envious of Germany may be set beside concrete evidences of German envy of other nations. In each of these cases, and in many others that might be adduced, it certainly seems as if there is present the mechanism of "projection." *Of whom,* however, may it be said that projection is at work? Tradition, education and propaganda obviously may inculcate the views that the Jews conspire against the Christian world, that Germany is in constant danger of "encirclement" and that other nations envy Germany. Theoretically, in the absence of other evidence it may be said that in the case of many of those who absorb these views by these means, projection in the clinical sense may not be present at all. The conclusion is inescapable that the phenomena Brickner treats are too complex to be fitted neatly or unambiguously into his categories. He occasionally points a line of possible investigation that might prove more fruitful. Thus, there is unquestionably a sounder methodological approach, potentially at least, in the following passage than in many others of his work: "The observable fact remains that every child born into German society for at least five generations has stood more chance than children elsewhere of coming into contact with attitudes—and institutions that foster attitudes—corresponding exactly to those found in individual paranoids in the doctor's office." [97]

This passage plainly distinguishes "attitudes" and "institutions that foster attitudes." Moreover, it points clearly to the need of a

97. Brickner, *ibid.*, pp. 139–140.

sound and thorough comparative analysis in its juxtaposition of the "child born into German society" and "children elsewhere."

The method Brickner adopts is too loose and ambiguous to allow of much more than some unco-ordinated insights, although these may be individually excellent. Despite his qualifications as a psychiatrist, Brickner substantially remains at the level attained by Vansittart in his observation of the traits of envy, self-pity and cruelty in German character. The presentation of a definite psychodynamic theory of German character is still lacking in Brickner's work. Presumptions, even if they have a clinical flavor, are no substitute for such a theory.

Erich Fromm's *Escape From Freedom* formulates a basic contrast between "freedom from" and "freedom to." The individual has not achieved "freedom from" while he is very strongly attached to organizations such as the family and clan in primitive society or church in medieval society, *i.e.,* while he remains a highly conformist type undifferentiated from his fellows and participant with them in a thorough traditionalism. Self-realization and the development of rational and critical faculties are blocked by the primary ties of individual to group in a traditionalistic society, but at the same time the individual's integration with the group affords security and the sense of having an unquestionable place in life. "Freedom from," the breaking of the ties of traditionalism, is consequently frightening and difficult despite or because of the opportunities of self-development it holds forth. In the Western world (which has inevitably witnessed considerable "freedom from") the individual unready to take full advantage of his "freedom to" is potentially dangerous: he may easily fall prey to the suasions of fascist groups which invite him to a new "slavery" seeming attractive because of the fear of isolation and loneliness that "freedom to" may stimulate.

The relevance of this analysis to the development of Nazism is demonstrated particularly for the members of the German lower middle class. For this class, the authority of the monarchy, of religion, traditional morality and the family remained strong until the 1918 "revolution," despite the peculiar insecurity of the class within the social structure and in terms of economic status. But the postwar years culminating in the depression of 1923 put in doubt the solidity of the rocks of monarchy and family, and the brief economic improvement of the next few years again terminated in a depression in which the middle class was the most defenceless and hardest hit group.[98] The members of the lower middle class therefore had to bear, simultaneously, economic hardship and the psychological insecurity attendant upon the collapse or weakening of cherished institutions. The typical membership, consisting of small shopkeepers, artisans and white collar workers, manifested a character structure which, by and large, made for stress upon thrift, frugality, caution, asceticism. But precisely these virtues became liabilities in an economic order that paid largest dividends to qualities like initiative, willingness to take risks and aggressiveness. Or else, thrift and the like had small opportunity to operate as the possibilities for small shopkeeping and cognate activities became increasingly restricted by economic conditions.

There emerges therefore the picture of a class whose membership possesses traits of character that were once, if within limits, genuinely adaptive and successful, but have become liabilities. When such frustration, simultaneously a psychological and a practical economic frustration, occurs, we have a situation, according to Fromm, in which psychological forces are no longer cementing the social structure. But the psychic needs of the members of the middle class continued to exist and had to find some sort of satisfaction. For being frustrated at accustomed loci, they only sought others, and, in Fromm's view, there occurred a shift of "narrow egotistical striving for one's own advantage, as it had characterized the lower middle class," from the individual to the national plane, at the same time as the sadistic impulses that had been manifest in private competition were "partly shifted to the social and political scene, and partly intensified by frustration." [99]

Thus character structure reacts on the social process that had created it. The rudiments of a theory of social change emerge, and a most essential part of it is the indication of the relevance to the general institutional framework of the psychological elements adduced in the argument.

It is indicated how the Nazi ideology gave satisfaction to the sado-

98. *Escape From Freedom*, p. 214.

99. *Ibid.*, pp. 214, 285.

masochistic trends embodied in the middle class authoritarian character structure. The disappointments and disillusionments of the middle class had powerfully stimulated such trends in persons who had been frustrated in respect of essential needs, had lost prestige, were "caught" between two other classes, and felt themselves strengthless, abandoned, and lost in a social organization that gave them no particular regard and let them shift for themselves as best they could under conditions where their specific "virtues" were useless or even handicapping. They could not "rise" in the social scale, most definitely not after 1929, and they had a heritage and traditions that made extremely uncongenial the notion of "sinking" to the proletarian level. In effect, they were "trapped," and the consequence of the hatreds and resentments generated and continually thrust back for want of opportunity of expression was the emergence of strong feelings of anxiety, helplessness, and isolation. They could therefore hardly value their "freedom from," and the Nazis, with the hope they held forth of a new prestige and "self-respect" and a new removal from the individual of the responsibility for his self-direction and self-development under conditions where such responsibility was decidedly painful—the Nazis made potent appeal.

The Nazis also were prepared to satisfy some of the specific cravings of the authoritarian character structure: "It was not only the Nazi ideology that satisfied the lower middle class; the political practice realized what the ideology promised. A hierarchy was created in which everyone has somebody above him to submit to and somebody beneath him to feel power over. . . ." [100]

In view of Fromm's recognition of other than psychological elements in his analysis of the forces that made for the Nazi rise to power, it is not surprising that he says: "Those psychological conditions were not the 'cause' of Nazism." [101] His intention, in other words, was to give specific attention to psychological factors, especially as they were operative among the members of the lower middle class, but not to claim that herein alone would be found the full explanation of the emergence of Nazism.

Fromm has made at least a beginning in genuine psychodynamic analysis. His reliance is not exclusively upon isolated character traits,

100. *Ibid.*, p. 236. 101. *Ibid.*, pp. 217–218.

but rests to some extent upon an exposition of character structure. This specifically differentiates his work from that of a writer like Vansittart; and, at the same time, Fromm escapes most of the strictures that must be made on the work of a writer like Brickner. His analysis is, however, quite limited. Logically, the problem of explaining the interplay between character and social process partially involves a demonstration of the compatibility of the features of character structure described with institutional forms. These two facets of the total socio-psychological phenomenon must have analytical accordance. Thus, for example, it obviously would not do to attempt to explain the psychological underpinnings of German institutions under Nazism in terms of the traits or features of an exceptionally "secure" character structure. But this is an elementary requirement. A more advanced requirement is that an explanation in terms of character structure shall have organizing power. That is to say, it should make intelligible the simultaneous occurrence of many superficially unrelated traits and, when used for sociological analysis, it should, ideally, explain a good deal of the psychological underpinning or sustainment of any going institutional scheme. If there are either numerous "exceptions" to the propositions of the theory of character structure or if there are large ranges of data left outside its scope which it might be expected to explain or illumine, the theory is inevitably limited. This is only a familiar general methodological point. The scientific value of a theory lessens as its organizing power diminishes. In this sense, Fromm's theory is a somewhat narrow or limited one. Ideally, a theory of character structure in modern Germany would exhibit the character structures of memberships of all important class groupings and demonstrate how the complicated interplay of institutions, classes (and perhaps other groups) and of the psychological forces associated with class structures operated to rear the system of fascism. Present psychological resources and present prospects for the integration of sociological and psychological theory and data would indicate that this is an extremely difficult task.

Fromm's virtually exclusive attention to the lower middle class, while it constitutes a limitation, nevertheless in a certain sense constitutes a point of strength. Virtually all non-psychiatric students of Nazism are agreed that the lower middle class was a crucially important group in its development. This is a by no means insignificant convergence. On this same line, Fromm's appeal to the significance of authoritarian features of social structure and of character, and to "sado-masochistic" character patterns, shows an important general agreement with the repeated emphasis of students of modern Germany on institutional manifestations and psychological aspects of power relations and rank or status relations. Psychological emphasis on strivings for power and tendencies toward subordination would appear to be especially cogent for a social structure exhibiting the general features proper to modern Germany.

A final limitation on Fromm's work in *Escape From Freedom,* previously remarked in connection with other work we have reviewed, may be mentioned. If we grant that many members of the lower middle class were in the social and psychological condition Fromm describes, it should be noted that what he succeeds in explaining is simply a coincidence of individual feelings and behaviors. It is as if he were saying: "These people are ripe for certain changes." But just how the transition is made from the emotions of a large number of people, who experience these emotions as individual human beings, to the sphere of social change, which requires leadership, organization, etc., is not made clear. In other words, Fromm goes from social structure to individuals' emotions, and then back from the latter to social structure. His theoretical implementation of the last transition is weak. If people in large numbers are "frustrated," precisely *how* does this frustration translate itself on to the *institutional* level? After all, they might be "frustrated" and nurse their grievances in private. How the frustration builds back into and affects the social structure is left unexplained.

Some major points may be summarized:

1) Germany "borrowed" the modern technology from England. But in the borrowing process two sets of factors differentiating Germany from England were operative:

a) Germany did not have the peculiar English traditions with regard to "doing business," and took over the modern technology into a framework in which many important technologically inhibitive business practices were absent, and where, moreover, the interference of a strong state in business enterprise guaranteed that there would not take place a considerable industrial waste incident to English ways of doing business.

b) At the time of borrowing, Germany was comparatively a poor country, with large numbers of industrious but frugal workmen and numbers of skilled and talented persons willing to work for relatively low compensation. Also, certain leisure class practices reducing economic substance had not yet taken hold in Germany.

The combined effect of these two sets of factors was to allow Germany to spurt ahead industrially and to achieve in a few decades what, substantially, in the English case, it had taken a century and a half to achieve.

2) But the modern technology, in Germany, fell into a political and social system generally quite different from that of England. Modern social classes ("bourgeoisie" and "proletariat") had scarcely developed in Germany up to 1848. The class system was nevertheless extremely rigid. The tradition of making war was more deeply ingrained and had more potent general appeal than in England. The influence of the institutions of the powerful German army tended to permeate the social system at large. The Dynastic State, geared to the achievement of power without the intrusion of "sentimental" or humanitarian elements, was willing to go far in disciplining to its ends the underlying German population. This state was confronted with a dilemma when the modern technology came to Germany. With the growth of that technology there grew also an urban proletariat which was regarded as dangerous to the foundations of the state, but which was an unavoidable concomitant of the technology, itself in turn indispensable to the uses of the achievement of power among modern nations and to the conduct of modern war. The aliency of the Dynastic State to the machine technology, the former in essence very old and the latter very modern, was symbolized in that most important of German social groups, the army, whose most aristocratic or noble elements tended characteristically to dissociate themselves most from the technological aspects of warfare.

3) The contrast between England and Germany has been broadened by modern writers into a wider contrast couched in the terms

of national character. Recent English writers on the subject of German character have tended to leave the contrast in implicit form. An indispensable explicit contrast is afforded in works like those of Kantorowicz, which show the operation in the field of public policy of marked contrasts between England and Germany. Other writers, like J. P. Mayer, substantially agree that the tradition of the power-state, operating unhampered by "sentiment" or humanitarianism, and in a violently subjective spirit, has been much more deeply ingrained in Germany than in England.

4) This tradition revived under National Socialism, which, rearing a new state form carrying on where the Dynastic state had left off, faced again the dilemma that the latter had faced, and sought to resolve it by a more determined all-out attack on "Marxism" than had ever been witnessed in Germany before. Undoubtedly, some important business groups sustained National Socialist efforts along this line. The success met with was very appreciable.

5) A question arises whether a psychiatric or psychoanalytical investigation of this success is in any way cogent. Our review of the work of the neo-Freudians and our inquiry into "psychoanalysis and the leisure class" have reinforced the view that relations of connection, and, further, of congruity and interdependence, obtain between phenomena of the psychological and of the institutional order. The real strength of a psychiatric interpretation of the modern German situation lies, in a certain sense, in the success that has already been achieved in the psychiatric interpretation of other social systems or specific institutional aspects thereof. Many conceptual changes or changes in the structure of the theory of psychoanalytical sociology, and many modifications, may be necessary before any considerable concrete success is met in grappling with the problems of psychological explanation of complex phenomena like "modern Germany." A psychiatric interpretation of the "German enigma" is "necessary" insofar as there is interest in explaining aspects of that "enigma" which cannot be explained otherwise than by appeal to psychiatric theory.[102] Institutional studies like those of Kantorowicz, Mayer and

102. This reference to "certain aspects" may already be sufficiently clear from our foregoing treatment. However, in order to clarify our meaning further, illustrative reference may be made to a prominent popular-Darwinian strain in *Mein Kampf*. The book makes survival and victory the test of "fitness" or

Foerster, the first quite explicitly, as we have seen, *point* to the need for carrying on psychiatric studies if certain obtrusive phenomena are to be explained. If these institutional studies point to the need for exploring "deeper levels," essayistic endeavors like those of Vansittart, claiming that German character structure is marked by envy, self-pity and cruelty, virtually demand a deeper psychological check, whether to vindicate the existence or prominence and indicate the incidence (*e.g.*, by class groupings) of these traits or to explain these and other traits psychodynamically, *i.e.*, as outgrowths of a concretely described character structure. Finally, it is pertinent to note here again that every institutional system, that of modern Germany included, inevitably has psychological foundations, and inquiry into these is entirely legitimate.

Three rudimentary cautions with respect to psychiatric interpretation of the case of modern Germany may be rehearsed.

Firstly, it is plain that a psychiatric interpretation must find its proper place. It is useless to psychologize institutional phenomena. Modern Germany has both a history and a present and recently past institutional system that give the terms for indispensable historical, economic and sociological approaches to the study of it. Any psychological threads pointed to must be interwoven with the historical and social threads. This is in fact precisely what makes the whole problem difficult. If indiscriminate psychologizing is practiced, the problem becomes "simple" only by the technique of enchanting away some of its most important elements.

Secondly, the comparative terms afforded by the contrast of Eng-

excellence. Since the Germans lost in 1918, by the criterion of reality they were "unfit," and, according to Hitlerian doctrine, if it were perfectly consistent and contained no other elements, they only "deserved" defeat. But of course they had been betrayed: the heroic soldiers at the front were defeated by the "Marxists" at home. Thus, 1918 may be explained. A possible future Nazi movement would have to explain 1945 also, possibly in more recondite terms than those used for 1918. As the terms become more recondite, the Darwinian "realistic" criteria are more and more left behind, and there can only be left a very "metaphysical" presumption of a reality higher than that given by the Darwinian criteria: it stands written in the books of the cosmos that Germany *must* rule the world. Hans Ernest Fried captures the essence of this type of "thinking" in his reference to "the secret knowledge that the real world was not real at all" (Fried, *ibid.*, p. 242), which "knowledge" was widespread in postwar Germany. In this "thinking" and this "knowledge," it is safe to say, there is an ineluctable element that will interest the psychological clinician.

land and Germany serve to eliminate naïve conceptions that the Germans are utterly "black" and all other peoples a pure "white." The Germans appear as they do precisely in virtue of contrast. It is not that the comparison between them and the English shows them in a favorable light, from the point of view of dominant Western values: quite the contrary. But it does serve to remove any implication except the one that the record of other peoples, such as the English, is better, in the light of those values. By "democratic" criteria, the "gentleman" is not faultless, and the contrast is not between angelic virtue and diabolical vice. (At the same time, however, depending on what our emphasis is, we may be interested in pointing out that there is quite a difference between the "gentleman," even given the "class element," and the thoroughgoing National Socialist.)

Finally, it has been indicated that it is not necessary for everyone to be "neurotic" in order for certain distinctive leisure class norms to be sustained. Similarly, it has been seen from Kantorowicz's analysis that it was not necessary for all the figures connected with the origin and propagation of the myth of the encirclement of Germany to be pathological cases. There is no reason to think that all Germans are paranoiacs—not even Brickner holds to this view—nor is there reason to think that all Germans are characterized by envy, self-pity and cruelty.

6) The specifically psychiatric endeavors to explain German character structure made by Brickner and Fromm have certain obvious limitations. Brickner's analysis, especially, is of restricted value. Fromm, however, has made a start in genuinely psychodynamic analysis, and his endeavor on this line, although of limited scope, makes central the role of the lower middle class and the influence of dominance-subordination patterns and sado-masochistic features of character structure. This emphasis converges with general emphasis made by non-psychiatric literature on Germany.

7) Although the literature reviewed in our analysis is relatively quite limited, it shows a rather impressive *general* convergence, whatever the starting-points of the writers studied, whether essayistic, historical, sociological or psychiatric.

It has been repeatedly suggested that it would be desirable to have a systematic comparative-analytical study addressed to the contrast of English and German personalities, carrying Kantorowicz's study of overt norms to the covert level, and perhaps adding a considerable analysis of class structures. In the interim, in the absence of such a systematic study, it may be well to ponder the deeper meaning of some words mockingly growled by the Cockneys in the first World War, in imitation of a German model:

"We 'ave but one enemy, England." [103]

103. This chapter is allowed to stand as written early in 1946.

# *Index*

# *Vita*

Louis Schneider was born March 22, 1915, in Vienna, Austria. He attended DeWitt Clinton High School in New York City and the College of the City of New York, receiving the B.A. degree from the latter institution in June, 1935. He took his M.A. at Columbia in 1938 and his Ph.D., also at Columbia, in 1947. He has previously published "Toward An Institutional Psychology" in the *Journal of Social Philosophy,* VII (July, 1942), 334–57.

Bei Fragen zur Produktsicherheit wenden Sie sich bitte an:
If you have any questions regarding product safety,
please contact:

Walter de Gruyter GmbH
Genthiner Straße 13
10785 Berlin
productsafety@degruyterbrill.com